Research Skills for Management Studies

The recent growth of interest in the systematic study of management has transformed a once neglected area of research into one that now attracts a huge number of postgraduate students. But despite this, there has been a distinct lack of research guides tailored specifically for management studies. *Research Skills for Management Studies* fills that void.

Designed as a comprehensive introduction to the main phases of a research project, this textbook leads students from the very first stage of initiation right through to final publication. It considers the nature of research skills and the fundamental elements of the research process, while also exploring the institutional context in which management research is carried out.

Tackling current debates and the philosophical and strategic issues at hand, *Research Skills for Management Studies* combines the key theories with the best practical advice to offer a completely rounded introduction to the topic. It includes guidance and specific reference to real management research projects, as well as case examples, activities and further reading lists.

Essential reading for anyone undertaking or thinking of undertaking a management studies research project.

Dr Alan Thomas is Visiting Senior Fellow in Sociology and Organizational Behaviour at Manchester Business School, University of Manchester. He has written extensively in the field of organizational behaviour and management and has taught research methods to doctoral level. Previous books include *Controversies in Management*, Second Edition, Routledge, 2003.

Research Skills for Management Studies

Alan Berkeley Thomas

Routledge
Taylor & Francis Group

LONDON AND NEW YORK

First published 2004
by Routledge
11 New Fetter Lane, London EC4P 4EE

Simultaneously published in the USA and Canada
by Routledge
29 West 35th Street, New York, NY 10001

Routledge is an imprint of the Taylor & Francis Group

© 2004 Alan Berkeley Thomas

Typeset in 10/12pt Times NR by Graphicraft Limited, Hong Kong
Printed and bound in Great Britain by The Cromwell Press, Trowbridge, Wiltshire

British Library Cataloguing in Publication Data
A catalogue record for this book is available from the British Library

Library of Congress Cataloging in Publication Data
Thomas, Alan (Alan Berkeley)
    Research skills for management studies/Alan Berkeley Thomas. – 1st ed.
        p.   cm.
      'Simultaneously published in the USA and Canada.'
      Includes bibliographical references and index.
      ISBN 0-415-26898-2 (cloth) – ISBN 0-415-26899-0 (pbk.)
      1. Management – Study and teaching.   I. Title.
    HD30.4.T428 2004
    658'.007'2–dc21   2003010827

ISBN 0-415-26898-2 (hbk)
ISBN 0-415-26899-0 (pbk)

To Mary G. with love: *amor vincit omnia*

Contents

Illustrations

Figures

Tables

Boxes

Activities

Preface

Over the past few decades there has been an enormous growth of interest in the systematic study of management among scholars if not among professional managers. As a result, a much-neglected area of research has been transformed into one to which increasing numbers of postgraduate students are attracted. At the same time, the range of research approaches and techniques available to management students has widened considerably. While providing more choice about what kind of studies to undertake and how to carry them out, this has also made the tasks of teaching and learning in management research more demanding. Instead of being introduced to a well-defined research tradition, students of management today are likely to encounter a rather bewildering set of methodological orientations, perspectives and techniques, and widely differing opinions as to which are more or less appropriate for the study of management, however defined.

This diversity is a reflection of three broad trends. First, the epistemological and methodological pluralism which emerged in the social sciences in the 1970s has continued to develop. Methodological exclusivity, centred upon positivistic conceptions of scientific method, has been challenged by a range of alternatives including phenomenology, realism and post-structuralism among others. Similarly, the dominance of quantitative methods, the experiment and the survey has been reduced with the rapid development of qualitative research strategies and methods. Although management research has sometimes been slow to incorporate these wider developments, they have nonetheless begun to have a significant impact within management studies.

Second, although there have been some attempts to identify management as a distinct area of inquiry, the field remains diverse. The term 'management research' implies some commonality of content and/or method, but this is misleading. Those who teach and research in management departments and business schools are a heterogeneous population who as yet possess little in the way of a common research outlook and tradition. Scholars committed to quantitative, positivistic conceptions of research can be found alongside those who favour qualitative, constructionist approaches, typically within the same department or school and often within the same management discipline. In part, of course, this reflects the diversity of subjects that now figure in business school curricula.

Third, the emergence of 'critical' approaches to the study of management has added a new twist to an old debate: should management research be geared to attaining some specific group's ends, be that managers, shareholders, women, workers or whoever, or should it aim to produce knowledge 'for its own sake', as some other disciplines claim to do? On this, as on narrower methodological issues, there are few signs of consensus.

From the teacher's point of view this situation can also be seen as problematic. Where, as in Britain, more emphasis is being placed on the systematic inculcation of research skills through coursework, rather than through the sometimes haphazard and arguably inefficient processes associated with the traditional research apprenticeship, management teachers are likely to face student groups from varied disciplinary backgrounds, often with research interests in fields other than their own. In an ideal world, perhaps, a polymath might be able to meet these diverse needs in depth, but I must say that I, at least, have never met such a person. I certainly make no claim to be one myself. The organization and teaching of research methods courses to management students can thus pose a significant challenge.

The approach that I have used when teaching research methods and that I have adopted in this book is to focus on issues of generic interest. My assumption has been that all management researchers, irrespective of their field or topic, need to acquire at the start of their studies a broad understanding of the basic issues that face anyone setting out to research the social world. For research students this includes some acquaintance with philosophical issues as well as with the social context in which research is carried out. In addition, they need a general knowledge of frequently used research strategies and techniques that they may decide to use subsequently during their degree projects. They will undoubtedly need deep immersion in whatever research strategy and methods they do eventually adopt, but that comes later and requires specialist support from the tutor or supervisor.

Until recently, newcomers to management research have largely had to make do with research textbooks that have been written for students in older, better-established social science disciplines – psychology, sociology, education, and so on – rather than for management researchers themselves. Although some of those texts have been excellent, a few having acquired the status of classics, they have not been written with the management researcher in mind. The question of whether management research possesses any distinctive methods that might justify its separate treatment is an unresolved issue. But even if it is the case that management research has no unique methods and shares its methodology with other social sciences, the application of those methods to management gives the field its own flavour and has created its own body of published work. In this book, therefore, illustrative examples are largely drawn from management research – largely but not exclusively so, for students of management can only benefit from exposure to the experience of the wider social science community to which they as management researchers belong.

Acknowledgements

The inspiration for this book arose from my experiences of teaching social research methods to the members of the Doctoral Programme at Manchester Business School. Many of these former students have subsequently become well-established management researchers and in some cases now occupy chairs in universities around the world. I certainly learned a great deal from working with these talented individuals and I have tried to inject something of both the style and substance of the teaching that they helped to create into these pages. Although they no longer need it, the book is in part for them.

Much of the text was written in challenging circumstances and I would like to thank the following for their support: Pamela Burt, Kevin Gaston, Paula Hyde, Ali Nasralla, Heather Spiro, Peter Swann and, above all, Mary Gorman. Once again, the help of Kathy Kirby and the staff of the Library and Information Service at Manchester Business School has been indispensable. Thanks also to my editor, Francesca Poynter, and to Rachel Crookes and Karen Goodwin at Routledge for managing the smooth production of the book and for being a pleasure to work with.

Dr Alan Thomas
Manchester Business School

1 Research skills and how to acquire them

There are only two kinds of researchers: those who have got problems and those who are going to have problems.

Researchers are sometimes thought of as rather special and perhaps even peculiar people. The cartoon image of the research worker as a 'mad scientist' or an inspired genius still has some credence with the public. Yet it was the prolific inventor Thomas Edison who, when asked how he accounted for his success, replied, 'Genius is one per cent inspiration, ninety-nine per cent perspiration.' Research is very largely a problem-solving activity, and while inspiration is certainly needed in order to make progress, it is rarely sufficient. Successful researchers are those who possess the knowledge and skill that enable them to overcome the problems inherent to the process of research. They may appear to proceed purely by means of flashes of insight and serendipitous hunches but in fact they are specialists in complex problem-solving.

This book is intended as a guide to these problem-solving skills for those who are preparing to undertake research projects in management. Although written mainly for research students who are studying for degrees at master's or doctoral level, undergraduates are also likely to find much of the material presented here to be of value to them. The fundamental ideas and outlooks that underpin research are common whatever the level or scale of the project undertaken. Similarly, managers engaged in research investigations for professional purposes, or who need to use the products of management research, may also find this book a helpful source of insight into what goes on behind the scenes in academia. It may also provide them with guidance on how their own research may be carried out more effectively.

Management is a field of study with indistinct boundaries and it includes a wide range of specialisms such as marketing, organizational behaviour, strategy, human resource management (HRM), accounting, finance and operations as well as multidisciplinary studies which cross these boundaries. You may already have an undergraduate degree in business studies or one of the social sciences and possibly an MBA, but research students in management tend to be drawn from a wide range of disciplinary backgrounds. Whatever your previous experience

---

Box 1.1 The value of research skills

Whilst a key element of the ESRC mission is to train postgraduates for careers in academic research it is recognized that not all research post-graduates wish, or will be able, to pursue a career in academic research. Nor might they be able, whatever their career patterns, to pursue research solely related to the specialized topic of a thesis. Of those who do follow academic careers, many will be required to supervise or teach research students using or assessing the applicability of a wide range of meth-odologies and methods. . . . Whatever career paths PhD graduates may follow, there are clear advantages to students if they have acquired general research skills and transferable employment-related skills.

(Economic and Social Research Council, 2001, Section D1)

---

and irrespective of your current field, this book should prove helpful in develop-ing your research skills.

Some basic assumptions

This book makes a number of assumptions about the nature of research and ways of developing expertise in it. They are briefly outlined below although several of these points will be taken up in more detail later.

Assumptions about research

Among the most important assumptions I have made about research are the following:

The world of management research is a messy world

The management scientist Russell Ackoff has argued that managers do not solve well-specified problems in well-specified ways. Rather, they grapple with 'messes': whole collections of complex and interrelated problems (Ackoff, 1979, 1993). The domain of management is messy. Not surprisingly, then, doing research in management studies is a bit like that. This is because the world of research methodology is also a messy world.

Sometimes research methodology is portrayed as if it were simply a set of tools and techniques used to solve research problems. The tools and techniques are not themselves seen to be problematic, and learning about them seems likely to be a rather dull and dreary business. Methods are thus seen as peripheral to the substantive issues facing a discipline.

But this is far from being the case. As May (1997, p. 1) says, 'Research methods are a central part of the social sciences', and methodology in social research has been an area of great controversy and debate. Many fundamental questions about our capacity to know the social world are raised when we set out to do research and to help others learn how to do it. Such questions are as relevant to management research as they are to other social research fields. Encountering them at first hand in the course of designing a research project can be far from dull!

There is no one best way to do research

Once upon a time something called 'the scientific method' dominated understanding of the proper way to do research. This advocated the use of carefully controlled experiments and quantitative measurements in order to test hypotheses about causal relationships between phenomena. Implicit in this view was the idea that there was 'one best way' to do scientific research; good research was taken to follow this method.

One alternative to this 'monistic' view is methodological nihilism (Feyerabend, 1975; Phillips, 1973). This denies that science proceeds according to any specific method at all; there is no need to discuss research methods because 'anything goes'. Methodological 'pluralism' (Bell and Newby, 1977), on the other hand, is a point of view that holds that there are many approaches to doing scientific research and many ways of producing knowledge rather than one or none. This is now a widely accepted view and it is the one adopted here.

In keeping with this pluralist view, research is not to be equated with hypothesis-testing. This is too narrow a definition to encompass the range of possibilities in management research. A broader conception is likely to be more helpful, so here we define research as the process of obtaining and analysing data in order to answer questions, solve problems or test hypotheses and so contribute to our understanding and knowledge of the world.

There are common elements in all research

Although there are many different ways to do research, and although different fields have their preferred research styles, all research does share certain features:

- Research is empirical; it involves studying the world outside ourselves.
- Research adopts systematic and explicit methods; it is essentially a public endeavour in which it is possible, in principle, for others to repeat investigations and check on their accuracy.

Research is a complex craft

There is a tendency to associate research with the idea of precise results obtained by means of controlled experimentation using sophisticated techniques and technologies. This image significantly underplays the messiness and uncertainty that accompany researching. Reports by researchers of how they have actually conducted their studies give a very different impression from the one given by the formal, prescriptive accounts found in methodology textbooks (see, for example, Bell and Newby, 1977; Bryman, 1988; Hammond, 1964). In practice, research projects have to be adapted to local circumstances, and adapting them may involve considerable ingenuity and methodological improvisation. There are few, if any, research procedures that can be applied with completely predictable results; much depends on the context in which they are used. There is much uncertainty surrounding research methods and many judgements have to be made.

Box 1.2 The craft of research

Research involves basic attitudes and ways of thinking. Research is a craft. Like other crafts activities are not analyzable. . . . Cause–effect relationships are not clear. Unexpected problems appear. Procedures are not available to describe each aspect of research activity. The learning of craft skills may take years of trial and error. Through practice one learns how to ask research questions, how to conduct research projects, and what to strive for when writing a research paper. Significant research, then, is the outcome of a way of thinking that can be called craftsmanship.

(Daft, 1983, p. 539)

Furthermore, every research study is unique. Research projects are not standardized products but custom-built enterprises that require considerable skill and judgement in their design and execution. The research process can thus be thought of as akin to making a sculpture: the artist starts with a formless mass of stone and then, after much careful chipping and shaping, the finished product emerges. The final form partly reflects the sculptor's initial vision but is also a result of the insights and ideas that have developed during the sculpting process. Doing research is literally a creative activity.

Assumptions about learning to do research

Experiential learning pays

Research is a skilled craft and, like any craft, learning about it from books can only take one so far. There is no substitute for hands-on practice. Professional musicians, for example, have to learn music theory as part of their musical education, but it is unlikely to be of much help when it comes to playing an instrument and performing in front of an audience. A good deal of any craft must be learned by experience, both directly, through practice, and indirectly through learning from accomplished practitioners. In research, in order to develop skill in interviewing it is necessary to interview people; to become a competent questionnaire designer you need to design questionnaires; to become an expert in case-study method you need to conduct case studies; and so on.

Box 1.3 Acquiring research skills: more than learning the rules

Acquisition of researchers' basic skills is no different from acquisition of other skills. Researchers do not need to be able to formulate rules for their skills in order to practice them with success. On the contrary, studies show that rules can obstruct the continuous exercise of high-level skills. There is nothing which indicates that researchers at expert level – those who have achieved genuine mastery in their field – use mainly context-independent rules or traditional rationality in their best scientific performances, even though they might depict it as such when they get around to writing their scholarly articles or memoirs.

(Flyvbjerg, 2001, p. 34)

Because research is a craft, it is not surprising that the traditional way of acquiring research skills is by apprenticeship. The research student is apprenticed to a master craftsman or craftswoman who supervises their work and leads them towards achieving the standards of excellence established within the craft. Students learn partly through their own direct experience and partly from the experience of the master. Today, however, this traditional system is being increasingly supplemented by formal courses of training in research methods. Indeed, you may well be reading this book as part of such a course. While there is much to be learned from reading, experiential learning is also needed. The exercises and activities in this book can help to provide some of the practical experience that is required.

Prior experience can be misleading

Previous experience can often be helpful when setting out to develop new skills. But prior experience can sometimes be misleading when it encourages us to overestimate the similarity between what we already know and what we are about to learn.

Many students embarking on research degrees already have some acquaintance with research methods from projects they have carried out as part of their earlier education. In management studies, research students have often taken an MBA before starting a research degree and this will often have included a dissertation. However, it is essential to understand that working for a research degree is a very different enterprise from studying for an MBA. The differences include:

LARGER SCALE

In comparison with an MPhil dissertation or a PhD thesis, most of the assessed work that is produced at undergraduate or MBA level is relatively small-scale. A PhD thesis is expected to be anything from 80,000 to 100,000 words long (requirements differ from university to university). It is sobering to realize that many fully fledged academics never again write anything as long as their PhD thesis. The sheer scale of even writing 100,000 words, let alone carrying out the research that underlies them, is daunting, although there are ways of making the writing task more manageable, as we shall see in Chapter 13.

LONGER DURATION

An undergraduate project might require ten or twelve weeks' work, an MBA dissertation six to nine months', a PhD thesis two to three years' – some students may take even longer to complete, much to the annoyance of funding bodies! Part-time students inevitably face an even lengthier haul. A significant mental adjustment is needed in order to cope. It's a bit like a sprinter or middle-distance runner moving up to the marathon. That is why 'endurance' is one of the qualities required of the successful research student.

Box 1.4 An MBA student's view of doctoral research

DOCTORAL STUDENT: You MBAs have got it easy. Doing a PhD is an *immense* task.

MBA STUDENT: Who are you kidding? A doctoral thesis is a two-week project stretched out to two years!

HIGHER STANDARDS

Research students are expected to bring high standards of rigour to their research. They have to demonstrate that the factual claims they make, the arguments they deploy and the conclusions they reach can withstand demanding critical scrutiny.

PRODUCER ORIENTATION

As undergraduates or even MBA students, we are mostly consumers of know-ledge produced by others. We read the textbooks and perhaps articles published in scholarly journals and are then asked to show the examiners what we have learned from these and other sources. As researchers, however, our primary role is different. We now take on the responsibility for producing knowledge.

This requires that we switch our mind-set from consumer to producer and take responsibility for our own knowledge claims.

It's easier to learn when there's a need to know

Real learning, the kind that sticks, tends to be driven by the need to know. It helps if you have clear aims in mind, are under pressure to achieve them and can see how the learning will help you do so. Doing research is hard work and requires high levels of motivation. It's important to be honest with yourself about why you are studying for a research degree and to be clear about why research matters to you.

The researcher's skills

If research is a complex craft that utilizes many skills, what precisely are they? Before you read on, complete Activity 1.1.

Activity 1.1 The skills of the effective researcher

What skills do you think you need in order to be an effective researcher? What sorts of things do you need to *know*? What sorts of things should you be able to *do*? And what sorts of *attitudes* will be helpful? Make a list of your ideas. Then rate yourself according to how proficient you think you are in each attribute from 1 = 'hardly at all' to 5 = 'highly proficient'.

Knowledge, skills, attitudes   *Self-rating*

_____

_____

_____

_____

_____

_____

_____

_____

_____

Box 1.5 What effective researchers need to know and be capable of doing

- Knowledge of their special subject area/discipline
- Knowledge of related subject areas/disciplines
- Awareness of philosophical issues (epistemology)
- Literature searching skills
- Knowledge of research strategies and designs and the capacity to apply them
- Knowledge of methods for obtaining qualitative data
- Knowledge of methods for obtaining quantitative data
- Skill in obtaining qualitative data
- Skill in obtaining quantitative data
- Ability to understand and apply qualitative analysis techniques
- Ability to understand and apply quantitative analysis techniques
- Textual skills: writing, summarization, text management, etc.
- Rhetorical skills: how to create a persuasive, logical argument
- Oral presentation skills
- Computer skills
- Planning and time management skills
- Knowledge of how to work effectively with a supervisor
- Knowledge of how to gain cooperation and support from colleagues, research subjects and others
- Ability to participate in networks and develop contacts
- Awareness of standards: what counts as good- or poor-quality research
- Being self-critical; but without self-paralysis
- Awareness of own strengths and weaknesses
- Creative ability, originality, innovativeness
- Emotional resilience: the ability to cope with emotional highs and lows
- Endurance: the ability to keep going over long periods
- Ability to improvise, to find ingenious ways of overcoming obstacles

Source: Adapted with additions from Easterby-Smith *et al.*, 2002, figure 2.1

As you can see from Box 1.5, the competent researcher needs to possess a wide range of knowledge and skills and a few important attitudes. You will almost certainly be proficient in some of these areas already but some are likely to be new to you.

It is obviously important to know your own special subject well, but familiarity with related fields is often necessary too. This is especially important in a multidisciplinary field such as management studies. Some understanding of philosophical issues in research, such as the problematic nature of 'knowledge' and 'science', is also needed. You must be able to find and process research literature from a variety of sources effectively and efficiently. You need to be aware of the range of research strategies that are available and be able to apply them, together with appropriate methods for obtaining data. Proficiency in both quantitative and qualitative analysis techniques is desirable. You must be able to present your work professionally, both in writing and orally, and organize it around a clear, logical argument.

You need a wide range of computer skills for literature searching, data analysis and text preparation. You must be able to plan and organize your work within time and financial constraints. You must be socially skilled so that you can develop a productive working relationship with your tutor or supervisor, gain the support of others who can help with your research, and participate in academic and other networks. Social skills are also important if you are using such methods as interviews or participant observation to obtain data directly from people.

You must develop an understanding of the standards of excellence that apply in research, be self-critical but without undermining your self-confidence, and know what you are good at and what you are less good at. You must have a creative spark. You must be able to cope with the emotional ups and downs that you are bound to experience, and have a capacity for endurance so that you can keep going when the going gets tough. Finally, that uniquely human capacity for improvisation is almost certain to be needed: as in management itself, the one thing you can expect in research is the unexpected!

It is not simply a matter of needing many skills, but of needing many different *kinds* of skill. The competent researcher has somehow to combine *contradictory* skills and this can be difficult. For example, it is important to be open-minded and creative in order to generate original ideas, but the ability to carry out and complete a host of routine, mundane tasks – making lists, entering data into computer files, recording references, proof-reading manuscripts, and so on – is also necessary. Both originality and at least a tolerance of the routine are important if a research project is to be completed successfully or even at all. Similarly, even the most quantitatively inclined researcher has also to be a capable wordsmith; he or she must have a capacity for planning but also a flexible outlook permitting improvisation as required; and for degree studies he or she must have the ability to work alone but also with a supervisor. This ability to be 'ambidextrous' does not come easily to most of us but it can be developed with practice.

Research can be risky

However experienced you are in research, it always involves substantial uncertainties and risks. Results may not turn out as expected and, if they did, we might wonder whether there was any need to carry out research in the first place. If we already know the answers, what is the point of doing the research?

Of course, we do not know the answers to many pressing questions, and setting out to explore the unknown is the researcher's lot. This can be exhilarating

---

Box 1.6 Research can be risky

Research involves an element of risk: exploring the unknown, opening up new areas of knowledge and going boldly where no one has gone before. At least, that is part of its heroic image. It is perhaps as well to remember, then, that during the Age of Exploration, when adventurers set out in fragile ships to search for strange lands:

- Some explorers found what they expected to find and returned home safely to a hero's welcome.
- Some explorers didn't find what they were expecting to find but found something else instead.
- Some explorers came back empty-handed.
- Some explorers never came back!

---

but it does entail some risk. Fortunately, you do not have to set out alone and you are strongly advised not to do so. In most fields someone has been there before – if not to the exact location for which you are bound, at least to somewhere similar. There is plenty of knowledge and experience to go on and you should expect to make full use of it. In particular, your supervisor or tutor is a key source of information and guidance, so developing a good working relationship with that person is vital.

Supervision is important

It is worth investing some time in thinking about what sort of supervision you need and discussing these needs with your supervisor at an early stage. Experience suggests that students and supervisors may differ in their preferred styles of supervision (Jeffcutt and Thomas, 1991). Some supervisors lean towards close supervision and strong direction, but some favour a largely non-directive approach, giving students the freedom to learn from their mistakes. Students also differ accordingly, some wanting to be given close guidance while others prefer to be left alone to follow their own path. Most of us find that at some times we want one emphasis and at others another, but much confusion can occur unless both the student and the supervisor display a good deal of interpersonal sensitivity and awareness. That is not easy for either party but, despite any appearances to the contrary, it seems to reasonable to assume that supervisors really are human and can be approached accordingly.

Methodology matters, but . . .

There is a lot that is technically complex in research and a large literature has developed that deals with methodological procedures and techniques. It will certainly be necessary at some point for you to immerse yourself in some of this material. But a word of caution is in order: it is possible to become so enamoured with technicalities that the purpose of doing research gets lost. This obsession with methods has been dubbed 'methodolatry' (Gouldner, 1967), a worship of methods akin to idolatry. It amounts to 'a preoccupation with selecting and defending methods to the exclusion of the actual substance of the story being told' (Janesick, 1994, p. 215). Sufferers can be identified as follows: when asked what their research is about, they will respond in terms of methods rather than topics: 'I'm doing time series analysis . . . multiple regression . . . a Solomon's two control group experiment . . . a factor analytic study . . .' Technical proficiency is a legitimate goal of research training but is a means to an end rather than an end in itself.

The structure of the book

In the next chapter I introduce some basic research concepts and present a model of the research process as a series of stages through which any project is likely to pass. The book is organized largely in terms of this model, with the intention of taking you systematically through all the main phases you are likely to encounter in your research.

Chapter 3 deals with some difficult but important philosophical questions that attend research: what is knowledge, how can it be acquired and what are the distinguishing features of science? In Chapter 4 we focus on problem fields and examine the ways in which knowledge is organized in management studies. In Chapter 5 we deal with a crucial issue for researchers: how to identify and select topics and problems that are both worthwhile and feasible – the two key criteria for selecting research problems. Chapter 6 discusses the ethical aspects of management research, while Chapters 7 and 8 provide an overview of some of the main types of research strategy applied to management: the experiment, the survey, the case study, ethnography and action research. The next three chapters explore some frequently used ways of obtaining and constructing data: by asking questions through questionnaires and interviews, by observation, and by reference to documents and records. Some basic strategies and techniques for analysing and interpreting both quantitative and qualitative data are presented in Chapter 12. The final chapter examines the important tasks of research writing and publication.

Finally, why do research?

In this chapter I have argued that research is a highly skilled and complex craft which cannot be successfully carried out simply by following rules and procedures, which entails significant risks, and which takes considerable time and effort to learn to do well. The financial rewards are modest and the likelihood of fame remote. Tayeb (1991) has written of the 'sufferings and joys' of doctoral research while Mitchell (1992) has compared the process of producing

---

Box 1.7 The skills of the fully professional researcher

First, . . . it means that you have something to say that your peers want to listen to.

Second, in order to do this, you must have a command of what is happening in your subject . . .

Third, you must have the astuteness to discover where you can make a useful contribution.

Fourth, you must be aware of the ethics of your profession and work within them.

Fifth, you must have mastery of appropriate techniques that are currently being used, and also be aware of their limitations.

Sixth, you must be able to communicate your results effectively in the professional arena.

Seventh, . . . You must be aware of what is being discovered, argued about, written and published by your academic community across the world.

(Phillips and Pugh, 2000, p. 21)

---

a doctorate to that of bearing and giving birth to a child! You may well wonder, then, why anyone commits themself to becoming a fully professional researcher.

Apart from the obvious reasons – to get a degree, to contribute to knowledge and to develop oneself and one's career – there is, I think, a further compelling motivation. Doing research, for all its difficulties, can be an exciting, even thrilling, experience. Although it is true, as Lupton (1985a, p. xii) has said, that 'we never speak of the wonders of social science', there is still something uniquely satisfying about carrying through a research project to a successful conclusion and in seeing one's name at the head of a published paper or on the cover of a book. No one as yet has been awarded the Nobel Prize for management studies. Even so, it's worth bearing in mind – it could be you!

Activity 1.2 Familiarize yourself with the end product

One way of developing your understanding of what is required of a research degree is by reading some successful dissertations or theses. Visit your library and find two or three theses in your field. You don't need to read them from start to finish, but skim through them to get a feel for the way they are organized and the style of writing. Make a note of what you notice.

Key points

1   Research is a complex craft requiring many different, often contradictory, skills.
2   Successful researchers have to be able to combine a creative outlook with the capacity to deal with the repetitive and the routine.
3   Careful planning of your project is vital, but you must be flexible and willing to adapt initial plans to changing circumstances.
4   Research is inherently risky but can also be personally satisfying.
5   Establishing a good working relationship with your tutor or supervisor is essential.

Key reading

Cryer, P. (1996) *The Research Student's Guide to Success*, Buckingham, UK: Open University Press.

Further reading

Daft, R.L. (1983) 'Learning the Craft of Organizational Research', *Academy of Management Review*, 8, pp. 539–46.

Jeffcutt, P. and Thomas, A.B. (1991) 'Understanding Supervisory Relationships', in N.C. Smith and P. Dainty (eds) *The Management Research Handbook*, London: Routledge, pp. 237–44.

Mitchell, V.W. (1992) 'The Gravid Male: An Essay on Delivering a PhD', *Management Research News*, 15 (8), pp. 18–23.

Phillips, E. and Pugh, D.S. (2000) *How to Get a PhD*, Buckingham, UK: Open University Press.

Tayeb, M. (1991) 'Inside Story: The Sufferings and Joys of Doctoral Research', *Organization Studies*, 12, pp. 301–4.

Watson, T.J. (1994) 'Managing, Crafting and Researching: Words, Skill and Imagination in Shaping Management Research', *British Journal of Management*, Special Issue, 5, pp. 77–87.

2   What is research?

If you ask people what 'research' is about, they will often say that it is concerned with 'finding things out'. If you ask experienced researchers the same question, they will probably say much the same thing but in a rather more complicated way.

A good deal of mystique surrounds research work, but in essence its aims and techniques are rooted in everyday practices. In general, researchers aim to find out what is happening and why it is happening, to describe, to explain and to understand. That is no different from what everyone does at some time, especially when faced with a personal problem or puzzle. But researchers usually deal with problems and puzzles that are defined within academic disciplines or by interest groups, such as managers, and do so using more explicit and more technical methods than in everyday life.

In this chapter I introduce some basic terms and distinctions. This is especially necessary because there is no complete consensus on how many research terms are to be understood. I therefore need to say how they are being used here.

The basic tasks of research: describing and explaining

The two fundamental processes of research are those of describing and explaining phenomena. The specialized techniques and processes adopted by researchers are very largely focused on achieving these ends in a systematic and rigorous fashion.

Describing

The formulation of descriptions is the bedrock of research. If our task is to explain 'how the world works', a prerequisite for this is an accurate description of what it looks like. We have therefore to engage in what Phillips and Pugh (2000) call 'intelligence gathering', the process of obtaining data in order to answer 'what' questions. For example, if we want to understand why some firms survive and grow while others shrink and die, we will need to observe firms and the environments in which they operate, and record our observations. The resulting descriptions do not explain anything by themselves but they do play a significant part in the explanatory process: without them there is nothing to explain.

When we think of descriptions, we probably think of someone using words as we might do when describing someone we know: 'She is tall and slim.' But we can also treat measurements as descriptions, as numerical descriptions rather than verbal ones. So we could have described our acquaintance by saying, 'Female, 1.60 m, 60.5 kg.' In fact, this might be regarded as a more precise and unambiguous description than the one given wholly in words. But in both cases the statements are aiming to tell us something about the characteristics of our associate. The processes of describing, by means of words, and measuring, using numerals, can therefore both be seen as ways of producing descriptions.

Descriptions are often of entities, but the relationship between entities can also be described. Suppose we found that 'the larger an organization is, the slower it is to respond to change'. This describes a particular state of affairs, in this case a relationship between an organization's size and its speed of response to change. Statements of relationships can therefore also be considered as descriptions.

Description may seem easy, but it is not. For research purposes high-quality descriptions are required. This means that they must be objective, reliable and valid. Carefully crafted techniques for obtaining data are applied in order to increase the chances that they will be. Explicit theoretical frameworks are also needed: in research we should be able to justify why we describe what we observe in the way that we do (Bechhofer and Paterson, 2000).

Researchers are much concerned with formulating descriptions. There is not much point in trying to explain the phenomenon we have described unless those descriptions are of high quality. The quality of descriptions is, however, frequently taken for granted more often than is warranted.

Explaining

Research may be carried out with the sole purpose of providing an accurate description of some phenomenon. Employee attitude surveys or political opinion polls, for example, provide a snapshot of people's views but they do not explain why those views are held, or why different groups display different attitudes or hold different opinions. More usually in academic research the intention is not simply to describe but to explain. Explanation is concerned with asking 'why' questions: Why are some firms profitable while others are not? Why do some people work harder than others? Why do managers receive higher salaries than shop-floor workers? Why are there so few women in top management? and so on.

What exactly is to count as an explanation is a matter of considerable philosophical debate. Different styles of research are associated with different conceptions of explanation. Some quantitative approaches treat explanation largely in statistical terms: a phenomenon is explained when it can be shown to be related statistically to other phenomena that are assumed to be its cause. In other, more qualitative approaches, patterns of human behaviour are considered to be explained when meaningful accounts of those patterns have been provided. Irrespective of precisely how explanation is understood, researchers aim to produce high-quality explanations, ones that can be considered valid, that can explain past behaviour and events, and that can perhaps predict future behaviour and events accurately.

The distinction between describing and explaining should not be taken too literally. It can be argued, for example, that to describe adequately what someone is doing involves referring to the purposes of their actions. By describing their motives for acting as they do, we are at the same time explaining their behaviour. As with many key terms in social research, exactly how 'describing' and 'explaining' should be understood is a question that is answered in somewhat different ways in different research traditions.

Theorizing

The idea of explaining something is related to the notion of theorizing. Theory is an important word in the researcher's lexicon. Broadly speaking, a theory is any systematic body of reasoning that attempts to explain phenomena. Scientific explanations are derived from systematically constructed theories, and in order to explain what they observe, researchers engage in theorizing. Theorizing is not, however, an activity that is restricted to the explanation of research findings. For example, some philosophers are concerned with developing theories of knowledge, or 'epistemologies'. These are attempts to give reasoned and coherent accounts of the nature of knowledge and the conditions that have to be met for knowledge to be acquired.

One way of thinking about theories of empirical phenomena is to treat them as causal maps. A geographical map represents a physical terrain and indicates what is there (hills, roads, rivers) and where they are located in relation to each other ('the river is north of the road'). A scientific theory is like a map, but instead of representing a physical terrain it depicts a conceptual domain. That is, it depicts variables and their causal relations. Such a theory, at its simplest, shows the way in which two variables are causally related, for example by stating that 'X causes Y'.

Kerlinger and Lee (2000, p. 11) define theory in this fashion. For them, 'a theory is a set of interrelated constructs (concepts), definitions, and propositions that present a systematic view of phenomena by specifying relations among variables, with the purpose of explaining and predicting the phenomena'. On this view, a theory explains phenomena by showing how variables are related to each other, so enabling predictions to be made about the behaviour of some variables on the basis of knowledge of others. In other styles of research, however, explanation is not tied to reference to variables. Historical explanation, for example, can be understood as the process of reconstructing the practical reasoning that led an actor to implement a particular course of action in particular circumstances (Polkinghorne, 1983, p. 184).

Researchers engage with theory in two ways: by theory-building and theory-testing. The aim of theory-building is to create an explanatory structure that can account for existing observations. This can be done by:

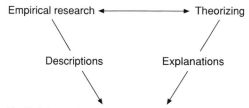

Figure 2.1 Basic research processes.

• *A priori reasoning.* Also known by the more homely phrase 'armchair theorizing', this approach to theory-building works from general principles that are known, or are assumed, to be true in order to construct a plausible explanation of the phenomena of interest.
• *Empirical observation.* By using the grounded theory approach (Glaser and Strauss, 1967), theory is generated during fieldwork so that it is closely related to the phenomena that are to be explained. The approach is a style of research in itself. Its use in management research has been discussed by Locke (2001) and Partington (2000). Goulding (1998) discusses its role in marketing research while Turner (1983) and Martin and Turner (1986) examine its application to organizational studies.

Theory-testing involves deducing how the world should look if the theory's propositions are valid and then setting out to obtain data to see if reality matches expectations. A theory that is untested remains speculative: it is 'just a theory'. It may have explanatory value or it may not. If it is tested and fails, the theory may be modified, scrapped or be retained to face further tests. If it is well supported by evidence, it may achieve the status of 'the best available explanation'. Few researchers today would be likely to claim that even the best-established theory is absolutely true and beyond subsequent revision or replacement.

Describing and explaining go hand in hand, as do the processes of conducting empirical research and of theorizing. Concern only with describing produces accumulations of facts, an approach to research that Mills (1959) dubbed 'abstracted empiricism'. Exclusive focus on thinking up explanations results in 'mere theories', which may or may not explain the phenomena of interest. By combining descriptions with explanations, empirical research with theorizing, the intention is to produce theories that have been tested by research and research findings that are intelligible in terms of theory.

Types of research

Research comes in many forms and can be put to many uses. In Chapter 3 we will be looking at the organization of knowledge into fields, but here we introduce some broad types of research.

Social (science) research and natural (science) research

The term 'social research' is sometimes used as an alternative to 'social science' in the belief that the word 'science' has misleading connotations when applied to the study of the social. But that is not the most significant reason for introducing the term. The important implication is that to study the social is to study a qualitatively distinct subject matter that is unlike that studied by natural scientists such as physicists and chemists.

A basic contrast can be drawn between the study of the social world, comprising humans, their social relationships and institutions, and the study of the natural, physical world consisting of atoms, molecules and chemical and biological processes. In the German intellectual tradition this distinction was enshrined in the notions of *Geisteswissenschaften* and *Naturwissenschaften*, two distinct forms of knowledge based on different methods of inquiry. On this view, the methods of social science are specific to the study of the social world and those of the natural sciences to the study of the physical world, although both may be claimed to share the same logic inquiry and the goal of producing reliable knowledge based on empirical observation.

Management research deals with human behaviour, such as leadership, decision-making, and so on, and social institutions, such as firms, organizations and cultures, and can therefore be considered as one field of social research.

Theoretical and pure research

Some research is concerned purely with solving the theoretical puzzles scholars have identified or created within their discipline. These puzzles may well be unrelated to everyday practical problems and may be unintelligible to those outside the discipline. Research aims to extend knowledge 'for-its-own-sake'. A good example is the field of pure mathematics: these mathematicians often seem rather proud of the fact that their work has no conceivable applications at all!

Applied and policy research

Governments and many large commercial organizations are able to fund substantial research activity. The results of these researches are intended to help policy-makers, whether government ministers, senior managers or administrators, to make informed policy decisions. Government surveys in Britain cover such matters as housing, health needs, education and transport. Commercial companies engage extensively in market research and may also undertake internal studies, such as employee attitude surveys.

Pure and applied research are often thought of as rather different fields, the former highly theoretical and 'blue sky' but the latter somehow pragmatic and a-theoretical. In fact, there is far more continuity between these activities than is sometimes thought. Differences are more to do with the cultures of research in these areas than with basic differences of method.

Evaluation research

Some research focuses on issues of evaluation, typically of action programmes whether in education, health or business. Such studies are closely tied to concerns with accountability and are used to discover whether programmes and expenditures intended to bring about certain changes or to reach specified policy objectives have in fact achieved their goals. Since this type of research is intended to underpin significant judgements of effectiveness and success, it tends to be highly politicized and controversial.

Action research

Action research is intended to improve understanding of and prospects for change in organizations by involving organizational members in collaborative relationships with specialist researchers who jointly design and carry out research studies. Although this may not be a suitable type of research for degree studies, partly because of the high risks involved, it is an important species of research in business and management. Some of its proponents argue that it is perhaps the only way of advancing knowledge of organizational behaviour and of integrating the social sciences with management practice. We look more closely at action research in Chapter 8.

Critical and feminist research

Business and management have been increasingly exposed to radical critiques from a variety of standpoints. Critical researchers question many of the basic assumptions that more conventional research approaches take for granted. Some are concerned with the oppressive nature of contemporary capitalism and see the goal of research as being to contribute to the emancipation of humans from the effects of the capitalist system of society. A useful source on critical social research is Harvey (1990). Critical management research is described in detail by Alvesson and Deetz (2000).

Feminists have also argued for research which contributes to the advancement of women and the ending of women's oppression, and some have argued for a distinct form of feminist research (Brunskell, 1998; Reinharz, 1992; P. Usher, 1997). Other disadvantaged groups, such as gay people, have also called for research in their name. However, it is unclear whether these approaches entail distinct methodological claims.

Quantitative and qualitative research

A distinction is frequently made between research which relies on quantitative measurement and numerical data, and that which deals mainly with meaningful accounts or narratives and verbal data. Whether this is a helpful distinction between types of research is debatable (see, for example, Bryman, 1988a; King *et al.*, 1994). Personally I think not, particularly in a multidisciplinary field such as management. Here at least a basic competence in both quantitative and qualitative methods is desirable for all researchers. Self-identification as either a qualitative or a quantitative researcher seems unlikely to foster methodological broad-mindedness or to facilitate collaborative work across the boundaries between different management subjects.

Strategies, methods and designs

Designing a research project is all about making decisions. These range from broad, general decisions about what approach to adopt in order to tackle a particular topic, to narrow, more specific decisions about what specific data to obtain, from where and how.

The most general decisions are those concerning research strategy. Research strategies are rather like literary genres, indicating very broadly the style of the work, perhaps a survey, an experiment or a case study. Decisions about research methods involve choices of techniques of data construction and analysis: interviews or observation, this statistical procedure or that. Research design involves deciding how the strategy and methods will be implemented in the context of a specific inquiry, indicating more precisely where, when and how data will be obtained and the method to be used to analyse and interpret those data.

The outcome of the research design process is an operational plan detailing each activity and its expected duration. Although the extent of the detail to be included in a research plan depends on the nature of the topic and the type of strategy adopted, clear and careful planning is important, especially for research degree projects. The preparation of research proposals is discussed in Chapter 5.

Fortunately, perhaps, it is rare for research to be carried out from scratch with no prior history of work on the same or a similar problem. Particularly in degree research, students tend to be recruited to existing subject areas or disciplinary groups, and in these it is likely that more or less well-established research styles and traditions will be in evidence.

Research strategies

In this subsection I briefly introduce the main research strategies of social research. Each is examined in more detail in later chapters, together with its applications in management research.

The experimental strategy

The experimental strategy aims to identify causal connections between variables. At its simplest it is used to investigate the relationship between two variables. Ideally, one of these (the causal or independent variable) is under the control of the investigator whilst the other (the effect or dependent variable) is not. The experimental strategy aims to isolate the dependent variable from all likely influencing factors except the independent variable, and measure the extent to which changes in the value of the independent variable are associated with changes in the values of the dependent variable. The favoured research methods have included psychological tests, non-participant observation and quantitative analyses.

This strategy has been particularly associated with the disciplines of individual and social psychology. This is partly because this branch of social research grew out of an initial concern with the biological aspects of human behaviour where the experiment was the favoured research approach.

The survey strategy

The survey strategy aims to produce generalizations about populations by collecting information from samples. Surveys may aim to describe the characteristics of the population or they may seek to test explanatory theories by using correlational analyses that follow the same logic as the experiment. Survey research methods include various sampling designs and techniques, the use of interviews and self-completion questionnaires, and mainly quantitative analyses.

Historically, surveys have been closely associated with sociology, partly because of the discipline's commitment to studying large-scale phenomena such as entire societies and the groups within them

The case-study strategy

In archetypal form, the case-study strategy seeks to examine a single instance of some broader class of phenomena in order to generate a rich and complex understanding of it. Cases may be defined at any level of analysis from the individual and group to the organization, industry, economy, society, and so on. By virtue of its aims, using this strategy often means engaging in a wide range of research methods such as interviews, questionnaires, observation and the analysis of documentary records. Both quantitative and qualitative analytical methods are likely to be required.

The case-study strategy has been used in a number of disciplines including psychology, sociology, political science and anthropology. Almost every discipline has had occasion to study one or a few units of interest in depth, be they clinical cases, social or political organizations, or societies.

The ethnography strategy

The ethnography strategy aims to illuminate social behaviour by generating accounts of the actors' world as seen 'from the inside'. Explanations are generated in terms of the categories and motives given by the actors themselves, although the investigator may also introduce 'second-order' conceptual schemes in order to facilitate comparative analysis.

Ethnography aims to achieve an understanding of human behaviour and social institutions by direct observation of the members of social groups in natural settings. Its favoured research methods are therefore long-term participant observation, informal interviewing and qualitative analyses.

These methods are a legacy of ethnography's origination in classical anthropology, which was concerned with the study of 'strange' societies and cultures. In the absence of any understanding even of the language used by the members of these societies, total immersion in field settings was necessary (Bechhofer and Paterson, 2000).

The action research strategy

The aim of the action research strategy is simultaneously to promote changes in organized social practices and to develop knowledge of these change processes and practices. It therefore requires specialist researchers and non-specialist social practitioners (such as managers, teachers, hospital workers, public servants) to collaborate in research projects that are jointly directed, managed and executed. These projects are undertaken on immediate, live problems in a series of steps that involve diagnosing problems, implementing solutions, and assessing their effects.

The strategy is open to a wide range of research methods. Its eclectic stance is partly due to its policy-oriented applications and to its concern to engage directly with practitioners. Because the boundaries of organizational problems rarely coincide with those of any single discipline, collaboration encourages a multidisciplinary, multi-method approach.

Table 2.1 shows the main research strategies and associated research methods that have been favoured in some of the basic social science disciplines and in

Table 2.1 Rough sketch of the association between disciplines, research strategies and research methods.

	Research strategy				
	Experiment	*Survey*	*Case study*	*Ethnography*	*Action research*
Discipline/field					
Anthropology			x	x	
Psychology	x				
Sociology		x	x	x	
Management	x	x	x	x	x
Research method					
Sampling		x			
Interview		x	x	x	x
Questionnaire		x	x		x
Tests	x				
Non-participant observation	x		x	x	x
Participant observation			x	x	x
Documents, records			x		x
Quantitative analysis	x	x	x		x
Qualitative analysis			x	x	x

management research. Although there is much variety among and even within disciplines, there is a tendency for the substantive focus of a discipline, its favoured research strategies and its dominant research methods to cluster together. It can be seen that research in management studies embraces a wide range of strategies and methods.

The table presents at best a rough sketch of these patterns. Although it does capture some of the methodological differences between these fields, it should not be taken to imply that other combinations do not occur or are impossible (see Activity 2.1). Nor should it be assumed that actual research projects must necessarily closely fit one of the main research strategies. As was mentioned in Chapter 1, each research study is a unique, custom-built project and novel research designs are always a possibility.

Activity 2.1 Explore your own subject area's research strategies

What research strategies have been adopted in your subject area? Using the matrix given in Table 2.1, search the literature in your subject area for examples of studies using each type of research strategy.

Is there a predominant pattern? Are some strategies missing? Could any of the missing strategies be implemented? For example, experimental research seems unlikely in the field of economics. Yet Ball (1998) has reviewed research, teaching and practice in experimental economics (see also Davis and Holt, 1993; Mestelman, 1998). So the unlikely may still be possible.

Multiple approaches and triangulation

In the case of specific studies, multiple methods are often adopted, and even multiple strategies. The well-known Hawthorne studies adopted both (see Box 2.1). The use of multiple approaches has increasingly been justified in terms of the likelihood of improving confidence in the validity of data and findings. Triangulation, as it is called, is 'the combination of methodologies in the study of the same phenomenon' (Denzin, 1978, p. 291). Originally conceived in terms of using different methods of obtaining data (Webb *et al.*, 1966), the idea has been extended to cover many kinds of multiple usage. Denzin (1978) refers to the use of different methods of obtaining data (methodological triangulation), sampling data at different times, in different places, from different people (data triangulation), using multiple observers or investigators (investigator triangulation) and using different theories (theory triangulation). The work of Hassard (1991) is an example of a multi-perspective study in management studies.

**Box 2.1 Multi-methods in management research:
          the Hawthorne studies**

The Hawthorne studies are probably the most famous series of investigations ever conducted in the field of management research. Undertaken at the Hawthorne Works of the Western Electric Company in Chicago between 1927 and 1932, they have been at one and the same time highly influential in management theory and practice as well as the focus of extensive criticism. These studies utilized not only multiple research methods but also multiple research strategies.

Research strategies

The Hawthorne research can be seen as a piece of *action research*. It provided Western Electric's management with practical information and contributed to the development of theory in the field of industrial behaviour. The research took place at one site over an extensive period of time and so might be considered to have been a *case study*. It has also been described as an *ethnographic field study*. Often known as the 'Hawthorne experiments', the studies began with the famous illumination *experiments* in which various environmental factors, such as lighting levels, were systematically varied to assess their effects on output. These were followed by the Relay Assembly Test Room and Mica Splitting Test Room experiments. The researchers also deployed an extensive *interview survey* involving more than 20,000 employees. The Hawthorne studies therefore adopted in full or in part all the strategies discussed in this book: the experiment, the survey, the case study, ethnography and action research.

Research methods

The studies made extensive use of *non-participant observation* during the illumination experiments and the bank wiring room study. The programme used both *structured interviews* and non-directive, *conversational interviews*. The studies utilized both *quantitative analysis* (e.g. of output patterns) and *qualitative analysis* (of interview materials).

As Schwartzman (1993, p. 15) suggests, from a methodological point of view 'the most significant contribution of this project is its demonstration of the value of allowing both research questions and methods to evolve and change during the course of an investigation'.

For further information on the Hawthorne studies see Carey (1967), Madge (1963), Roethlisberger and Dickson (1939) and Schwartzman (1993).

The research process

We can obtain an overview of what is involved in research by examining some models of the research process. These models attempt to depict key research activities and their interrelationships in a general, abstract way. Real research projects can, however, vary substantially in the degree to which they conform to these models.

The elements of research

Figure 2.2 portrays research according to the hypothetico-deductive model. This model depicts the research process as being driven by the testing of hypotheses. A hypothesis is defined by Kerlinger and Lee (2000, p. 26) as 'a conjectural statement of the relation between two or more variables'. For example, 'larger firms are more efficient than smaller firms' and 'the management styles of men and women are different' are hypotheses. Research aims to test hypotheses by comparing observations of the world with hypothetical expectations.

In this model, the research process begins with theory. By a process of deduction, hypotheses are created. Data collection 'instruments', such as questionnaires or interview schedules, are designed and a sample of units is selected. Observations of these units are made and summarized in the form of generalizations. These empirical generalizations are compared with the hypotheses, which are consequently accepted, affirming the theory, or rejected, disconfirming it. The empirical generalizations may also yield new concepts and propositions which are incorporated into the theory.

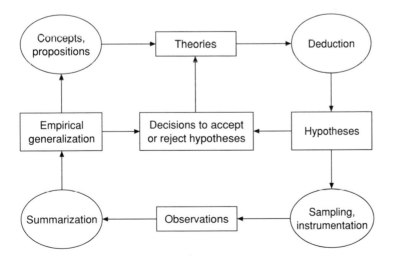

Figure 2.2 Elements in the research process.
Source: Adapted from Wallace (1979, figure 1.1).

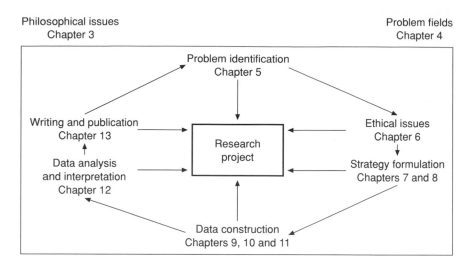

Figure 2.3 The stages of a research project.

The research cycle

Figure 2.3 represents the research process as a series of stages through which a project passes in sequence. Unlike the previous model, which depicted the core processes involved in hypothesis-testing research, this model depicts the main activities associated with any research project.

The process begins and ends with the research problem. At the start of the project it is an unsolved problem or a question awaiting an answer. At the end of the project it is, hopefully, a solved problem or a question answered. Although real projects are unlikely to be implemented in such a linear fashion, it is usually necessary to consider each of the items shown when designing a study.

The cycle begins with *problem identification*. During this stage a problem must be identified as a candidate for research and evaluated to assess its suitability before resources are allocated to pursuing it. The problem or question is identified and formulated by reference to a problem field.

Problem fields are the metaphorical pastures in which problems roam. They contain a potentially infinite number of problems that might be researchable. Management studies is a complex problem field containing many different kinds of problems, some of which are drawn from the management disciplines and subject areas and some from the world of management practice. Familiarity with the contents of the problem field is a prerequisite for problem identification.

It is also important that the researcher be aware of the *philosophical issues* surrounding social research. Many of the problems that are identified in the problem field are themselves likely to have been defined within certain theoretical and philosophical traditions. More generally, an understanding of some of the debates surrounding science and social science is necessary in order to make reasoned decisions about strategies and methods.

At an early stage of a project, the researcher will need to consider the likely *ethical implications* of the study. Some problems may be either prioritized or eliminated from consideration on ethical grounds. Awareness of ethical issues will also help in the choice of research strategy and research methods.

During *strategy formulation* the researcher must decide what general strategy will be adopted in order to tackle the research problem. This decision will largely determine the overall style and the general direction of the project.

The *data construction* stage is crucial, for if the wrong data are obtained or the data are invalid, then no amount of subsequent analysis can rescue the project. Important decisions must be made at this point concerning what data to obtain, by what means and from what sources.

Many research methods texts refer to 'data collection' rather than 'data construction'. No terminology is entirely innocent of presuppositions. The implication of the 'data collection' usage is that data are like pebbles on a beach, simply there waiting to be picked up or, as Bateson (1984, p. 5) puts it, are ' "givens", waiting to be picked like flowers in a hedgerow'. But this supposition diminishes the significance of the role that the researcher plays in generating research data. So many decisions about data have to be made by the researcher that it seems preferable to think in terms of data construction.

Data analysis and interpretation involves reducing the 'raw' data by means of statistical and/or linguistic summarization to a more concise form, relating the results to the research questions. A wide range of analytical techniques may be deployed for the analysis of both quantitative and qualitative data.

At the final *writing and publication* stage the study comes full circle to complete the cycle. The entire study must be 'written up' in final form, showing how far it has gone towards solving the problem identified at the start of the project. Ideally the study's results will be published, perhaps as a series of articles in academic and practitioner journals or even as a monograph or book.

This model is a good way of approaching research planning because it provides a comprehensive guide to the various activities that will need to be undertaken to conduct a research project. However, it must not be assumed that implementing the plan will necessarily follow these stages in a step-by-step sequence. In reality, any research project is likely to take a less straightforward path. For example, when planning a project it may be necessary to cycle through the stages several times before a satisfactory plan is produced. During the implementation of the plan, various aspects of the work may have to be redesigned according to eventualities that were not evident at the initial planning stage but have emerged during early attempts at implementation. It is for this reason that most research requires a pilot study or trial run in which a provisional plan is implemented on a small scale in order to see what works and what doesn't.

Nor should it be expected that all projects will require the same amount of attention to be given to all of the stages. For example, in some fields there are well-established research agendas with well-known research procedures so that identifying researchable problems is relatively unproblematic. If, however, you are working in a new field in which there is little by way of established research tradition, problem identification and formulation can be a major problem. Similarly, some fields depend for their data on existing databases, so that data construction is not a major issue. In others, data have to be created specifically for the project so that data construction may be one of the most time-consuming stages of all. Work in finance on the analysis of stock-market behaviour typifies the former situation whereas most behavioural research, such as that dealing with managerial patterns of work or consumer behaviour, exemplifies the latter.

Influences on the research process

You can expect your research project to progress through these research stages. What actually happens during a research project is, however, the outcome of a series of influences such as those depicted in Figure 2.4. This diagram indicates that a project will be influenced by the nature of the substantive problem that is being investigated; by the assumptions that the investigator makes about how to create knowledge; by the dominant style of investigation that prevails within the researcher's discipline; by the researcher's abilities, preferences and attitudes to whatever is being studied; and by the practical constraints that surround the project. To make matters more complicated, these influences tend to be interlinked. Disciplines, for example, tend to deal with specific species of problems and may also be closely associated with particular assumptions about knowledge or 'epistemologies'. We will look at some of these interrelations later. For now, let us examine each influence in a little more detail.

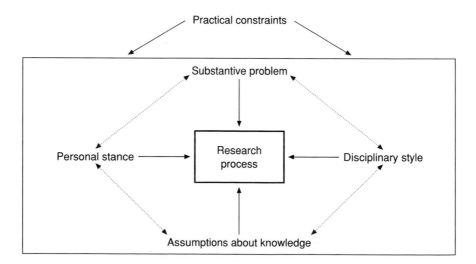

Figure 2.4 Influences on the research process.

The nature of the problem

The problem being investigated has a strong influence on the methods used to investigate it. Some problems may be approached in a variety of ways, but for some there may be only a few ways or even only one way of researching it. Mathematical modelling looks appropriate for the analysis of scheduling problems or stock-price valuations but less so for the study of the influence of unconscious psychological processes on leader behaviour. Laboratory experimentation may be possible when studying behaviour in small groups, but not if you are interested in studying industries or economies. Interview surveys may be ideal for studying consumer attitudes and behaviour but may not be applicable to research in business history.

Assumptions about knowledge

Assumptions about knowledge – what it is and how it can be obtained – are philosophical concerns. Methodological and epistemological pluralism indicate that there are several ways of knowing. Assumptions about the appropriateness and legitimacy of alternative methods of seeking knowledge underlie all research, although these may not be made explicit by the researchers. Indeed, sometimes they may not be particularly aware of them; they simply use what appear to be common-sense procedures. Sophisticated researchers are aware of their assumptions although this does not mean that they have to become full-time philosophers in order to be so.

Disciplinary style

Management disciplines vary greatly in their preferred ways of doing research. This is partly a result of their links with traditional social science disciplines and partly due to the traditions that have been established within management research and the fashions that are current there. The types of problems the discipline chooses to research are also an important influence. Researchers in finance and operations research, for example, tend to have a very different style from those in organizational behaviour or HRM.

Personal stance

The knowledge, skills and attitudes that an investigator brings to bear on a research project will have a major influence on how it is carried out and with what outcome. For example, in the field of consumer research Hirschman (1985) has argued that the personal characteristics of researchers will influence their research choices and preferred scientific styles.

A project may be thought worth researching and require a particular approach, but that does not necessarily mean that you are the person to do it. You may not be interested in the topic. You may lack the necessary skills and be unable or unwilling to acquire them. Fortunately, styles of research in management vary widely so that there is plenty of room both for those with an affinity for quantitative methods and for those who are adept at qualitative work.

Practical constraints

Research does not take place in a vacuum. It is carried out in an institutional context that both sustains and constrains it. Research students, for example, are located in an academic department that provides research facilities and supervision. But their work is also subject to various university regulations and supervisory requirements. Even professional researchers have to work within the constraints of budgets, competing demands on their time and the policies and procedures of their employer. Factors outside work can also have a crucial effect: family relationships, financial circumstances, health problems, and so on. Usually no mention of these constraints is made in research publications, though they are often revealed in researchers' inside stories. But it is important to be aware of them. The way they are managed can make or break a project.

Evaluating research: five key questions

There are many different kinds of research, but perhaps the most important distinction, and one that is likely to be uppermost in the minds of research students, is between good and poor research. Because of the enormous variety of research approaches and topics, each project must be judged on its merits. But there are five key questions that can be asked of all research. The first refers to the research topic, what the research is about. The remaining four, suggested by Shipman (1988, pp. ix–x), refer to the research methods, results and presentation. Researchers should ask themselves these key questions again and again as they design and execute their projects and as they read the research reports of other investigators' studies:

1   *Is the topic of the investigation important?* This question draws attention to the significance of the matter being researched. Is it worthwhile, important, valuable? A topic can be important for different reasons, for different people and in different ways and it can be so to varying degrees. But unless the project possesses at least a minimum of significance, the other questions are unlikely to be worth asking.

2   *If the investigation were to be repeated by different researchers, using the same methods, would the same results be obtained?* This question concerns the investigator's research methods. Two considerations apply, namely the *objectivity* of the methods and their *reliability*. If the methods used to produce data are objective, then they will reflect the world as it is rather than be biased by the observer's beliefs, preferences or perceptual idiosyncrasies. If different observers agree on the descriptions of what they observe, then we assume that those observations have captured reality. If the methods are reliable, then if

they are applied again and again to the same phenomenon the same description will result. An elastic tape measure, for example, is unreliable since on repeated application to the same object it is likely to yield different measurements. Good research adopts objective and reliable methods of investigation.

3 *Does the evidence reflect the reality under investigation?* This question refers to the validity of research results. Sometimes it is referred to as 'internal validity'. In commonsense terms, we ask whether the research evidence is true or valid. If, for example, we have obtained evidence by means of asking questions, how likely is it that the answers are true? Might those questioned have had poor memories, or have been careless in giving answers, or even have had something to hide? A related concern is whether the evidence is adequate. Is a paper-and-pencil test adequate as a way of describing someone's knowledge, ability or personality? Are published accounts adequate as a basis for assessing the financial state of a company? Even if research evidence is objective and reliable, it may still be of questionable validity. Good research produces valid findings.

4 *Do the results apply beyond the specific situation investigated?* Here we are concerned with whether the research results can be generalized. The generalizability of results is sometimes called their 'external validity'. Research is often undertaken using samples but with a view to saying something about the larger group, or 'population', from which they are drawn. If general claims are made on the basis of limited research evidence, how can those claims be justified? Good research provides clear justification for any claims about the generality of its findings.

5 *Has sufficient detail been provided on the way the evidence was produced for the credibility of the research to be assessed?* This question refers to the way research is reported. It is possible to answer the first three questions only if the details of the research methods used have been made explicit. Vagueness over methods and failure to provide crucial methodological information may indicate lack of rigour or even an attempt to disguise a poor piece of research. At best, a study lacking those details should be regarded as incapable of being judged and therefore as suspect. Good research is reported in such a way that its quality, in terms of its objectivity, reliability, validity and generalizability, can be assessed by its readers.

It is important to appreciate that most of these criteria are continua in that they are usually met in various degrees but never completely. They are ideals that researchers strive to achieve but in the knowledge that they can never be attained in full. In practice, a research project is likely to be 'fairly' important, its findings are likely to be 'more or less' objective, 'reasonably' reliable, 'considerably' valid and 'probably' of general applicability. In short, there is seldom much room for dogmatism about the outcomes of social research but usually plenty of room for caveats and qualifications, for 'ifs' and 'buts' and 'maybes'.

During the rest of this book we travel through the research process following the map provided in Figure 2.4. This journey should give you a good overall appreciation of the sorts of problems and opportunities you will encounter as you design your own research and of the way they have been dealt with by management researchers.

Activity 2.2 Start a research glossary

Every specialist field has its own vocabulary, and research is no exception. It may be jargon to outsiders but it's technical terminology to us! Learning this vocabulary is an important part of the task of becoming an effective researcher.

Whenever you come across an unfamiliar research term in your reading, note it down in your research glossary and record a definition for it and the source. Watch out for the term's occurrence in other places, perhaps with different meanings or even, in some cases, completely opposite ones – the term 'naturalistic' is a case in point.

Key points

1   There are many types of research but the fundamental research processes are those of describing and explaining.
2   Research strategies and methods tend to be linked in distinct combinations but this does not mean that all research must fall into these established patterns.
3   Different research projects tend to pass through the same stages but not necessarily with the same intensity at each stage, or in the same sequence.
4   Researchers should always keep in mind the Five Key Questions (pp. 30–1) when designing and evaluating research projects.

Key reading

Punch, K.F. (1998) *Introduction to Social Research: Quantitative and Qualitative Approaches*, London: Sage.
Van de Ven, A.H. (1989) 'Nothing Is Quite So Practical as a Good Theory', *Academy of Management Review*, 14, pp. 486–9.

Further reading

Bailey, K.D. (1994) *Methods of Social Research*, New York: Free Press.
Hakim, C. (1992) *Research Design: Strategies and Choices in the Design of Social Research*, London: Routledge.

Kerlinger, F.N. and Lee, H.B. (2000) *Foundations of Behavioral Research*, Fort Worth, TX: Harcourt College Publishers.

Shipman, M.D. (1997) *The Limitations of Social Research*, London: Longman.

Wallace, W. (1979) 'An Overview of Elements in the Scientific Process', in J. Bynner and K. Stribley (eds) *Social Research: Principles and Procedures*, Harlow, UK: Longman, pp. 4–10.

3 Ways of knowing

This chapter explores different approaches to creating knowledge. Research aims to add to knowledge by applying various strategies and methods, but these entail assumptions about what is being investigated and how it can be known. Can we attempt to understand everything by using the same methods of inquiry, or must different kinds of reality be approached in different ways? Is there only one 'way of knowing' or are there several alternative ways? Can any of them guarantee certain knowledge or absolute truth? Is science such a way and, if so, what is science?

These fundamental questions are the province of the branches of philosophy known as ontology, epistemology and the philosophy of science. It is important for research students to have some understanding of the philosophical debates that have surrounded the quest for knowledge. This is not because they need to choose an epistemological position before embarking on a research project. Researchers, as we shall see in the next chapter, tend to be acculturated to the research tradition associated with their discipline or field. They do not so much choose their epistemological position as discover it after the event. But the

---

Box 3.1 Welcome to the philosophical maze!

Research students and fledgling researchers – and, yes, even more seasoned campaigners – often express bewilderment at the array of methodologies and methods laid out before their gaze. These methodologies and methods are not usually laid out in a highly organised fashion and may appear more as a maze than as pathways to orderly research. There is much talk of their philosophical underpinnings, but how the methodologies and methods relate to more theoretical elements is often left unclear. To add to the confusion, the terminology is far from consistent in research literature and social science texts. One frequently finds the same terms used in a number of different, sometimes even contradictory, ways.

(Crotty, 1998, p. 1)

---

main benefit of philosophical awareness is that it helps you avoid making over-ambitious claims for your research. Even a casual reading of what the philosophers have to say should lead you to be cautious about claiming to have achieved 'the truth', 'the final answer' or 'absolute proof'. Conclusive answers of this kind are not to be expected in management research.

Unfortunately, a good deal of philosophical writing on these matters has done more to confuse the issues than illuminate them for any but professional philosophers. If researchers often display an ambivalent attitude towards such writings, this is understandable, particularly because the methodological implications of different epistemologies are often unclear. However, a broad appreciation of the debates surrounding these difficult problems is vital, even at the risk of becoming bogged down in philosophical quagmires. At the very least, this can help us to get our research work into perspective and ensure that we avoid making unsustainable claims for it, overestimating what research can achieve by way of truth, certainty and universality.

How do you know?

Scientists say more and more about less and less: philosophers say less and less about more and more.

Whatever the specific focus of our research, the general aim is to add to what is known. A successful PhD thesis is, indeed, very likely to be judged according to whether it 'makes a contribution to knowledge'. If we claim to know something, then we must be prepared to answer the question of how we know it. It seems reasonable, then, to be concerned with the basic issues of how knowledge can be created and of how we can distinguish knowledge from opinion, belief or falsehood. These are philosophical questions.

Philosophy is one of the oldest academic disciplines, perhaps the oldest. The word was invented by the ancient Greeks and comes from the word *philosophia* = love of wisdom. For the Greeks, philosophy was a general term equated with all systematic knowledge, and only much later in Western thought did it become separated and specialized as a branch of the humanities. Philosophy concerns itself with the most basic questions about knowledge, reality and existence. So, for example, the branches of philosophy include ethics (concerned with problems of what is good, right or moral), metaphysics (concerned with problems of existence) and, especially important from our point of view, epistemology or the philosophy of knowledge (concerned with ways of knowing).

Ontology is a central element of metaphysics. The word is derived from the Greek *on* = being. Ontologists are philosophers whose central interest is in what exists. Ontological claims attempt to specify the sorts of entities which exist and which can therefore be known. Some ontologists, for example, have claimed that an ultimate reality exists which we can never fully know because of the limitations of our perceptual equipment. This reality exists but we can have no complete knowledge of it. Others have argued that some things we commonly believe to exist, such as mental states, do not. On this view, only publicly observable phenomena are to be considered real, and mental states are held not to qualify. Still others have attempted to prove or to disprove the existence of God, without, it must be said, too much success.

Epistemology is the branch of philosophy that asks such questions as How can we know anything with certainty? How is knowledge to be distinguished from belief or opinion? and What methods can yield reliable knowledge? Epistemological theories are philosophers' attempts to provide systematic, rational and coherent answers to such questions. For example, empiricists argue that the only certain knowledge we can have of the world is that based on our sensory observations of it. Rationalists, on the other hand, believe that our senses are unreliable and that true knowledge is acquired through philosophical reasoning.

The chain of being

Ontological and epistemological assumptions are often closely intertwined and for most practical purposes it is difficult to think of them otherwise. But I can illustrate the interrelation between assumptions about being and knowing by reference to a very ancient scheme of thought, the chain of being (Schumacher, 1995).

This ontological scheme proposes that the world contains four distinct but overlapping levels of being: the material, the vegetable, the animal and the human. The material level consists of all inanimate objects: stones, sand, water, and so on. This level of being is dead and is marked out by its lack of the mysterious quality we recognize as life. The vegetable level contains all plants, such as trees and flowers. These entities differ significantly from the material in that they live, grow and die. The animal level consists of entities that are alive but that also possess consciousness, being able to respond to their environments and move within them. The highest level is that of the human. Human beings are material objects comprising atoms and molecules, are alive, and possess consciousness in that they respond to their environment. But humans also possess a further attribute: self-awareness. Humans, uniquely in the world, are aware of their existence and know both that they are alive and that they will die. Humans can reason about their existence and exchange meanings with others through the medium of language whereas animals cannot. Humans can produce art, literature and music; animals, at best, can only grunt and squawk.

These levels are arranged in a hierarchy so that the higher levels of being contain those below. Beings at each higher level possess a greater number of attributes – material existence, life, consciousness, self-awareness – than those below. The levels are thus linked together as a chain. A human has a material body composed of the same sorts of atoms as a stone; is alive just as a tree is; possesses consciousness as a cat or an ape does; but is uniquely distinguished from all other classes of entity by his or her capacity for self-awareness.

Box 3.2 An ontological scheme: the chain of being

Four levels of being:

m = Material = atoms and molecules = existence = m

x = Vegetable = plants = existence + life = m + x

y = Animal = dogs, cats, etc. = existence + life + consciousness = m + x + y

z = Human = people = existence + life + consciousness + self-awareness = m + x + y + z

---

This ontological scheme has several important epistemological implications. Each level of being can be known but only by methods that are appropriate to that level. Most obviously, the ways of knowing the material level cannot be adequate for an understanding of the human level. Indeed, each level of being requires its own way of knowing. We cannot know the inner life of stones or plants because, so far as we know, they do not have any; they lack consciousness and self-awareness. They can be known through observation but not, of course, through questioning. We may, perhaps, glimpse the inner world of animals, for they are closer to us ontologically than plants or stones. But the consciousness of humans is accessible to us by virtue of our shared humanity. We can know others – but only if we know ourselves.

According to this scheme, the methods of the natural sciences, although appropriate to the study of entities at the three lower levels of being, are wholly inappropriate for the study of humans. Inanimate objects lack the capacity for self-determination and are governed by purely external forces. Humans, on the other hand, are self-aware, so their behaviour can never be understood simply as a product of external stimuli.

This does not imply, however, that humans cannot be studied as natural objects. On the contrary, one of the distinguishing ontological features of humans is that they are at one and the same time natural objects and socio-psychological persons. So, for example, if someone jumps off a ladder, their rate of fall will be analysable according to the laws of physics in the same way as that of the fall of a stone. Similarly, the anatomy and physiology of the human body can be investigated in much the same way as those of a fish. The point is that humans possess attributes in addition to those of the stone or the animal: they are simultaneously material entities, composed of atoms and molecules; living entities, capable of growth and of reproducing; conscious entities, able to respond to their circumstances; and self-aware entities who are able to reflect on and theorize about their own existence and actions. Humans can thus be known in more ways than a stone or a fish can. For this reason, knowledge of human beings is one of the most complex forms of knowledge to which we can aspire.

The chain of being is not, of course, the only ontological scheme possible. For example, in much contemporary popular thought it has become fashionable to treat humans as if they are 'naked apes', simply a 'higher' form of animal. This way of thinking is evident in fields such as sociobiology and evolutionary psychology as well as in the approach to knowledge called behaviourism. In the terms of the chain of being, this denies or diminishes the significance of the difference between humans and animals, treating them as if they occupied the same level of being rather than two distinct levels. It also implies that humans and animals can and should be studied from the same methodological frame of reference. Alternative schemes thus propose different pathways to knowledge.

Royce (1964), for example, identifies four 'paths to knowledge' or 'ways of knowing': rationalism, empiricism, intuitionism and authoritarianism. Each of these ways entails a procedure for attaining knowledge and specifies the criteria by which its attainment can be judged:

• *Rationalism* is the way of knowing by means of thinking and reasoning. It assumes that nothing can be true if it is illogical. This way of knowing figures prominently in mathematics and philosophy.
• *Empiricism* is the way of knowing reliant upon sensory perception. It assumes that if something is accurately perceived, it is true. Empiricism plays a key role in science, where observing the world is a central task.
• *Intuitionism* is the way of knowing based on immediate or obvious 'awareness' that perhaps arises from unconscious processes. It assumes that if this awareness yields insight, then it is true. Artistic knowledge is based heavily on intuitionism, as is the personal knowledge gained from contemplation or meditation.
• *Authoritarianism* is the way of knowing based on authority. Something is true because an authority says it is true. In some religions, for example, revealed truth is derived from divine authority.

In general, Royce argues, our efforts to know involve all four of these ways, but specialized areas tend to draw heavily on one or two of them. For example, philosophical inquiry usually adopts the rationalist way of knowing, and attempts to establish its truths through the deployment of arguments and counter-arguments. Physical scientists, on the other hand, base their knowledge claims on carefully controlled and recorded empirical observations that are logically linked to explanatory theories. Each of the paths to knowledge is valid but limited to the particular aspects of the world to which it is suited. Meditation, for example, is a valid way of knowing our inner selves but a poor way of knowing the outside world. If you want to know about that, it is probably best to go and observe it. As with the chain of being, for practical purposes it is important to follow the appropriate path.

Problems arise when the proponents of an epistemology claim that it is the *only* epistemology. The effect is to ignore those phenomena that cannot be known by following that path. 'We are embroiled', says Royce, 'in the following paradox: if we insist on developing a reality image which is made up of only certain knowledge, we emerge with a very restricted and dehumanised world-view' (1964, p. 4). To understand the world in all its manifestations it is necessary to adopt several ways of knowing. Even so, the dominant approach to knowing in many fields remains that of science.

The epistemology of science

Human beings have been in the business of knowing ever since *Homo sapiens*, the wise or reasoning human, first emerged from the swamps some one and a half million years ago. Yet it was not until a few hundred years BC that the quest for knowledge became established as a distinct activity by the ancient Greeks. Even then, this quest for truth was for the most part dependent on reasoning and argument, exemplified by the Socratic dialogue. Reasoning alone, it was believed, could lead to genuine knowledge.

In Europe it was not until the sixteenth century that this rationalist approach to knowledge was supplanted by empiricism. This approach required investigators to study the world around them and not simply speculate about it. From the pioneering work of people such as Galileo, with his experiments on the motion of falling bodies, reputedly carried out from the Leaning Tower of Pisa, something known as the scientific method emerged, an event which has been heralded as one of the greatest achievements of humankind.

The development of scientific method was, however, more than simply the creation of a new set of procedures for creating sound knowledge. Scientific method entailed reasoning but allied with systematic empirical observation and experimentation. It also entailed a significant shift of attitude. While scientific method ruled some things in, it also ruled some things out. The Aristotelian conception of knowledge based on speculation and authority was rejected in favour of the idea that knowledge should be based on the facts of experience.

Scientific method arose in the context of investigation of the physical world. Some of its earliest achievements were in the realm of astronomy. It was only much later, in the nineteenth century, that the possibility of the scientific study of human beings was seriously advocated. So successful had the natural sciences been that it seemed possible that equally spectacular successes could be achieved by the application of scientific method to the human realm. The work of Charles Darwin (1809–82) on evolution had a decisive impact. Human beings were henceforth to be understood not as unique inhabitants of the planet Earth made in the image of a supernatural god, but as a species of animal sharing a common ancestry with the apes. Humans, it was proposed, should be studied in much the same way as the other entities in nature. From these beginnings emerged what we now know as the social sciences.

Scientific methods

Closely related to broad questions of epistemology are those associated with the philosophy of science. The aim of this branch of philosophy has been to provide a rational account of how science works and, sometimes, to provide prescriptions indicating how it ought to work. Much attention has been given to the workings of the natural or physical sciences, such as physics, chemistry and biology. Another important theme has been the vexed question of whether the social sciences can or could work in the same way. This issue remains very much a matter of controversy.

Scientific knowledge is held to be 'real' knowledge because of the methods used to generate it. According to Behling (1991), the natural science model has the following characteristics:

1   It prescribes publicly specified procedures – which rules out, for example, revelation in dreams as a source of knowledge.
2   It prescribes precise definitions of terms and concepts – so that there is no ambiguity over what is being asserted.
3   It prescribes objective methods of data collection – data must be observable by anyone and not distorted by the personal beliefs, attitudes or values of the observer.
4   The research must be replicable – it must be possible for the research to be repeated by other investigators.
5   Research must be systematic and cumulative – the aim is to produce generalizable knowledge.
6   The purpose is to yield explanations, understanding and predictions – rather than simply descriptions of particulars.

Also closely associated with this model are the ideas that research should be quantitative, based on careful and precise measurements; that experimental methods are the ideal form of investigation; and that all sciences share the same fundamental method.

Whatever the merits of this view, it does have one serious limitation if it is taken to define all high-quality knowledge: some accepted forms of knowledge do not conform to these specifications. Mathematics, for example, seems problematic, for it is difficult to say what counts as 'data' to a mathematician. Mathematics does not appear to be an empirical science, for the ontological status of numbers has proved highly problematic. But that surely does not mean that there is no such thing as mathematical knowledge. Similarly, historians clearly cannot carry out experiments to test their explanations of historical events. Does this mean that there can be no historical knowledge? Historians themselves have been much troubled by the nature of historical knowledge, but that does not stop them from writing history. In short, the idea that there is 'one best way' to create knowledge that is applicable to all fields of inquiry seems questionable. An alternative way of thinking about what we can know is shown in Figure 3.1. On this view, not every way of knowing is necessarily scientific, and 'unscientific' ways of knowing are not necessarily nonsense.

Science: not so much a method, more a state of mind?

The defining characteristics of science as a set of techniques or methods have proved hard to identify with any certainty. As Sayer (1992, p. 7) says, 'There is

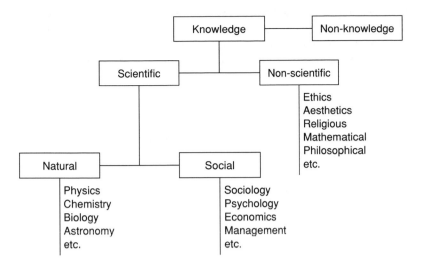

Figure 3.1 A typology of knowledge.

little agreement on what kinds of methods characterize science beyond the rather bland point that it is empirical, systematic, rigorous and self-critical, and that disciplines such as physics and chemistry are exemplars of it.' Perhaps what scientists have in common, then, is not a method for carrying out research but an outlook or, as Merton (1973) called it, an ethos. The scientific ethos is a set of attitudes and values that underpin scientific inquiry and that inform scientists' attitudes to the investigative process. It defines what it is permissible and right for scientists to do as well as what is forbidden and wrong, and it forms a key part of the institutional environment of the scientific community.

Merton identified four 'institutional imperatives' as comprising the ethos of science. They have become known by the acronym CUDOS:

- *Communism.* Science is a collective and collaborative enterprise and the findings of science are public property. They are not the private possession of the scientist and they must be communicated openly to all.
- *Universalism.* Scientific findings are impersonal and are accepted on the basis of observational evidence and their consistency with existing knowledge rather than because of the status or other personal attributes of the scientist making them.
- *Disinterestedness.* Science is concerned with advancing knowledge irrespective of the gains or losses that might accrue to scientists.
- *Organized scepticism.* Everything is open to questioning, investigation and critical scrutiny and there are no sacred or untouchable subjects that are to be excluded in principle from study.

To the extent that management researchers subscribe to this ethos they may, on this view, be considered to be members of the scientific community. But even that still leaves a lot of room for differences of outlook and belief about proper ways of producing knowledge. Science may be informed by a common ethos but that still leaves room for many different ways of doing science. Even self-professed scientists may differ greatly in their epistemological orientations.

Epistemological orientations

Two major epistemological orientations have dominated debate in the social sciences: positivism and constructionism. Although there are several variants within each orientation, we will outline the main ideas associated with each position. The precise nature of these orientations and the extent to which they overlap or are quite distinct are questions that continue to be much discussed.

The key difference in these views arises from their different conceptions of human beings and how their behaviour can be understood. These conceptions reflect different ontological assumptions about the nature of the world. Positivists argue that people and things are sufficiently similar for them both to be studied in the same way. They argue for the unity of science, claiming that there is but one path to a scientific understanding of the world. Constructionists, in contrast, argue that while positivism may be an appropriate epistemology for the natural world, it is inadequate for the understanding of the human world. For the study of humans as social beings it is necessary to adopt a non-positivist orientation to investigation.

Positivism

The term 'positivism' was coined by the nineteenth-century French philosopher and sociologist Auguste Comte (1798–1857). To English readers the word might seem to denote an attitude, of being positive or affirmative rather than negative and sceptical. But in French, *positif/positive* means 'real' or 'actual'. Comte intended positivism to refer to an approach to knowledge which restricts itself

---

Box 3.3　What is positivism?

An approach in the philosophy of science, positivism is characterized mainly by an insistence that science can deal only with observable entities known directly to experience and is opposed to metaphysical speculation without concrete evidence. The positivist aims to construct general laws or theories which express relationships between phenomena. Observation and experiment will then show that the phenomena are or are not related in the predicted way; explanation of phenomena consists in showing that they are instances of the general laws or regularities.

(Abercrombie *et al.*, 2000, p. 269)

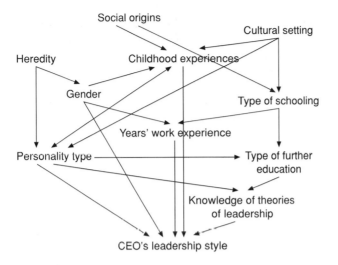

Figure 3.2 Hypothetical variable net.

to observable facts and their relationships and which excludes reference to non-observable entities such as 'gods', 'essences', 'first causes' or 'ultimate ends'. Hence positivism is to be equated with knowledge of the observable.

Positivism assumes that humans are natural objects, like stones or fishes. As such, they have an existence and possess properties that exist independently of any observer. Knowledge of objects can be obtained by observations that are expressed as descriptions. Descriptions are valid to the extent that they depict the properties the object actually has and exclude any elements that cannot be verified by multiple observers. Objective description is therefore an essential requirement of any genuine science: the world must be depicted as it is. Moreover, causal relationships between objects are to be identified in the same way, by careful observation of the conjunction of events over time.

The world assumed by positivism can be thought of as a set of interacting variables. A variable is anything that can be considered as varying. The underlying image is of the universe as a great machine whose workings are to be unravelled by careful measurement of the variables which comprise it and the identification of relations between the variables. The whole world is thus to be thought of as a gigantic variable net of the kind depicted in Figure 3.2.

Identifying relationships between variables is achieved by experimental research designs, which enable some variables to be isolated and their interactions observed, and/or by correlational methods that permit statistical associations to be uncovered. In this way the behaviour of the net, or those parts of it which have been selected for study, can be explained, predicted and perhaps understood. Positivist inquiry thus proceeds by means of variable analysis.

In the social sciences, positivism is closely associated with a theoretical orientation known as behaviourism. In its extreme form, behaviourism refuses to acknowledge the existence of mental states, which are held to be non-observable. Behaviourism therefore limits itself to observations of behaviour and seeks to identify regularities, which are to be explained largely in relation to the impact of external stimuli. In effect, human beings are treated as objects akin to chemicals or animals that react in various ways according to the stimuli to which they are exposed. Behaviourism has been an important influence on the discipline of psychology, although its former dominance has now been challenged by cognitive psychology, which does admit mental or cognitive states to its onto-logical ground. However, it has a much broader application. Any epistemology that seeks to explain human behaviour purely in terms of reactions to external forces can be considered behaviourist in spirit.

Constructionism

Unlike positivism, constructionism (or constructivism) assumes that humans are different in kind from other entities in the universe. Most specifically, humans are self-aware and endow the world they live in with meanings. In itself this world is meaningless (Spinelli, 1989). People *construct* meaning and social reality (Berger and Luckmann, 1967). Their behaviour cannot be understood unless the observer understands those meanings, and such meanings have to be interpreted according to the contexts in which they occur. Furthermore, researchers themselves are engaged in processes of construction: they do not passively record and describe what they observe but interpret the world in the act of observing it.

Box 3.4 What is constructionism?

Constructivist, constructivism, interpretivist, and *interpretivism* are terms that routinely appear in the lexicon of social science methodo-logists and philosophers. . . . The world of lived reality and situation-specific meanings that constitute the general object of investigation is thought to be constructed by social actors. That is, particular actors, in particular places, at particular times, fashion meaning out of events and phenomena through prolonged, complex, processes of social interaction involving history, language and action.

(Schwandt, 1994, p. 118)

Human beings live in a meaningful world and they share this meaningfulness with their fellows as members of a culture. What constructionism requires for the understanding of human behaviour is cultural analysis, the investigation of human meanings. This cannot be achieved by the same methods as are used to study non-humans; distinctive methods are required and are indeed made pos-sible because of specifically human attributes. In particular, because of the uniquely human capacity to communicate meanings, observation of behaviour is insufficient for understanding and predicting it. Participation in social life in different social settings, the acquisition of the language used there, the questioning of social actors, and the interpretation of documents written by them are among the key ways in which human behaviour can be better understood.

Constructionism is associated with a number of related epistemological frameworks including phenomenology, interpretivism and philosophical hermeneutics. It also has its counterpart to behaviourism in the theoretical orientation called symbolic interactionism. Developed from the work of G.H. Mead (1863–1931), symbolic interactionism depicts human social life as a complex of interactions mediated by symbolic exchanges. Through the medium of language, humans are able to represent the world to themselves and others, to imaginatively reconstruct the past and to preconstruct the future. Human behaviour is purposeful: people direct their own behaviour according to the meanings it has for them and the intentions and plans they create. To try to understand and predict their behaviour as if they were billiard balls driven by external forces is therefore completely mistaken.

Although positivism and constructionism are not the only epistemologies that underpin social research, they do represent the two dominant approaches. Table 3.1 gives a summary of the main differences between them in simplified form. Despite these differences, in practice there can be a degree of crossover. For example, variable analysts do sometimes take account of the actor's perspective and cultural analysts do sometimes use quantitative methods. Similarly, a piece of research inspired by positivism may use participant observation, and some constructionist research may aim to generalize. In short, it is by no means clear that these approaches are mutually exclusive. Rickman (1990), for example, has attempted to reconcile these epistemologies. He argues that, given the duality of humans as both physical entities and socio-psychological persons, both positivistic and interpretative, constructionist approaches are necessary for the study of the human world.

Nonetheless, this major division in research thinking has given rise to some passionate debates and controversies between those who identify strongly, even dogmatically, with their chosen view. Positivists have sometimes seen cultural analysis as:

- unscientific or pre-scientific;
- a prelude to the development of quantified hypotheses, which are the basis for 'real' research;
- subjective and unreliable;
- unable to cope with macro-phenomena such as social structures, economies, markets and organizations;
- failing to produce substantial knowledge.

Constructionists, on the other hand, have sometimes seen variable analysis as:

- unscientific or scientistic, inappropriately borrowing the methods of the natural sciences;

Table 3.1 Positivism and constructionism: the great divide in social research.

Epistemology/theory of knowledge	Positivism	Constructionism
Preferred conceptions of:		
The human world	Set of natural objects	Set of human meanings
Analytical approach	Variable analysis	Cultural analysis
Theory of human behaviour/action	Behaviourism	Symbolic interactionism
Relation between structure and action	Explain actions in terms of structures	Explain structures in terms of actions
Knowledge	General, nomothetic, universal	Particular, ideographic, contextual
Data	Given, found	Constructed
Method of securing data	Data collection via observation	Data construction via interpretation
Description	Quantitative measurements	Qualitative descriptions
Explanation	Statistical relations	Narrative accounts
Causal emphasis	External to internal	Internal to external
Prediction	Based on statistical forecasts	Based on understanding of typical behaviour in typical situations
Preferred research approach:		
Research strategies	Experiment, quasi-experiment, survey	Case study, ethnography, action research
Research methods	Self-completion questionnaire, structured interview, structured observation, psychological tests	Unstructured interview, participant observation, personal documents (diaries, letters, etc.)
Analytical method	Multivariate statistical analysis	Hermeneutics
Methodological problems	Internal validity, contextualization	Generalization, replication
Symbol/image	Hard, science, physics, variable net	Soft, humanities, anthropology, cultures

- divorced from the real world;
- unable to cope with the ambiguity and complexity of human behaviour;
- reifying phenomena by treating 'macro-phenomena' as if they were things rather than meanings;
- failing to produce substantial knowledge.

Both positions have themselves been attacked from other epistemological perspectives. As Remenyi *et al.* (1998, p. 35) say, once researchers have taken up an epistemological position, 'it is not uncommon for there to be a fervent adherence to the approach chosen, often leading to acrimonious debate'.

Before moving on, we will briefly consider two further epistemological orientations, realism and post-structuralism. Both are relative newcomers to the field of management and neither has so far been as influential – as guides to research practice – as positivism and constructionism, though for different reasons. In the case of realism this is partly because its most significant implications impinge on the structure of theorizing rather than on the nature of research methods. For post-structuralism it is because it radically undercuts conventional conceptions of research so as to make the whole enterprise seem either impossible, absurd or both!

Realism

The philosophical perspective known as realism is associated with the work of the philosopher Bhaskar (1989) and has been given prominence within social science by Sayer (1992, 2000). Like positivism, realism assumes that there is an outside world that exists independent of our knowledge of it. However, unlike positivism, it does not assume that this world can be known directly without any interpretation on the knower's part. In that, it shares with constructionism the idea that the world is not inherently meaningful but is made meaningful by our interpretations of it. Where realism parts company with both positivism and constructionism is over the matter of causes and explanations. Whereas positivism assumes that explanations must be based on observable regularities, realists seek to explain what can be observed in terms of underlying structural mechanisms. 'On this view then, a causal claim is not about a regularity between separate things or events but about what an object is like and what it can do and only derivatively what it *will* do in any particular situation' (Sayer, 1992, p. 105). What is observed is an outcome of the interaction of the 'causal powers' of the object, which it possesses necessarily in the light of what it is, with the conditions in which the object is situated.

Realism is seen by some as a bridge which links alternative philosophical schemes. For example, social entities, such as organizations, are seen as meanings but also as structures of meaning that cannot be wished away. Social reality thus has a recalcitrant quality similar to that of the natural world even though it is created through the meaningful actions of individuals.

The implications of realism for an understanding of management have been discussed by Tsoukas (2000). He presents a 'metatheory' of management which is derived from the application of realist epistemology. Using this framework he is able to integrate previous perspectives on management, so illustrating the claim that realism can bring together important aspects of epistemologies that are seemingly mutually exclusive.

One difficulty with the contemporary state of realism in management studies is that relatively little guidance is given on the implications of this epistemology for the conduct of research. Does realism imply distinctive research methods and, if so, what are they? But this may not matter too much in practice, for some of its leading exponents believe that much management research has been tacitly informed by philosophical realism whether researchers are aware of it or not. They also claim that in some areas it has already become the orthodox approach (Ackroyd and Fleetwood, 2000).

Post-structuralism

Post-structuralism originated as a movement within literary criticism but has since been influential in the broader realm of cultural and social studies. It is closely associated with the work of Derrida (1976). It draws attention to the importance of language in the production of knowledge and questions the assumption that words can represent things in any stable or fixed fashion. Texts, which include not only written documents but any form of symbolic representation, including social life itself, have no definite nor immutable meanings. Indeed, some post-structuralists have claimed that 'there is nothing outside the text': all texts are ultimately self-referring, just as a dictionary defines the meaning of a word solely by reference to other words in the same dictionary.

On this view, structures, the orderly configurations of experience, are not fixed and awaiting discovery, as positivism assumes. Rather, they are a product of language: organizations, for example, are considered as texts and accordingly can be read or interpreted in many ways:

> From the poststructuralist point of view, what readings reveal are potentially infinite, and potentially infinitely varied, orderings, sense-makings, of the experienced world of organization. Readings may be utterly different, may contradict each other, but none has a right to be considered more correct than any other and none may be considered, *a priori*, inappropriate – a manager, for example, does not have an intrinsically 'better' view of the organization than a worker. For Poststructuralists, it is the explanation itself that creates order, gives structure to experience. Structure is the meaning given to experience. Structure is immanent in the subject not in the object, in the observer not in the observed.
>
> (Jackson and Carter, 2000, pp. 42–3)

Since order is seen to be not 'out there' independent of the observer, the idea of research as discovering or revealing order is replaced by that of research as a means of creating it. Similarly, data are to be thought of not as simply existing and awaiting collection but as being manufactured by the researcher (Farran, 1990). In general, taken-for-granted terms such as 'empirical', 'facts', 'data' and 'reality' are seen to be meaningful only in relation to particular epistemologies, and their meanings are contestable (Scheurich, 1997). In short, post-structuralism throws into doubt the very existence of a stable and knowable world that is amenable to investigation by conventional means.

Epistemological orientations in management research

Management research has been strongly influenced by positivist assumptions. In part this is a historical legacy because the systematic study of management and organizations has developed in a context in which positivism dominated the social sciences. But it is also because of the vocational nature of the field. Positivism holds out the prospect of knowledge that can be used to control human affairs and so appeals to practical managers and those who teach them. Its association with science and quantification also gives positivism the smack of no-nonsense utilitarianism. In short, positivism has seemed rather businesslike.

This positivist consensus has, however, been fragmented in recent years as the field has been opened up to the influence of alternative epistemologies. This reflects both philosophical and methodological developments in the social sciences and the expansion of management education. Growth in the number of courses and of institutions providing them has brought an increasing number of scholars trained in the basic social science disciplines into the arena of management studies. Epistemological variety has increased, perhaps as part of a general 'crisis' in management knowledge (Thomas, 2003a).

Box 3.5 The epistemological paradox of management research

Probably the most striking feature on which there is consensus within the discipline is that management research operates no single agreed ontological or epistemological paradigm.

(Tranfield and Starkey, 1998, p. 345)

Today, although the influence of positivism is still strongly felt, no one theory of knowledge is dominant in management research. While the finance subject area, for example, continues to be strongly wedded to positivism, research in organizational behaviour is being undertaken by researchers of many different epistemological persuasions.

Keeping philosophy in its place

On the face of it, the relevance of epistemology to researchers seems clear. All claims to knowledge are based on assumptions about what the world is like and how knowledge about it can be acquired. As there is no one universally accepted scientific method, it is necessary to choose methods of investigation from those that are available. Faced with the necessity of choice, we need to be able to justify these methodological decisions both to ourselves and to the critic who challenges us with the question: How do you know?

How far it is possible to do this by reference to philosophy is unclear. One difficulty, already mentioned at the start of this chapter, is that the epistemological arguments are themselves often confused and inconclusive. This is not necessarily the fault of philosophers, for the issues are complex and arguments deployed to deal with them can be abstruse. A further problem is that epistemologies are not self-contained and distinct but tend to overlap and interpenetrate. As Sayer (1992, p. 5) points out, particular philosophies 'involve loose bundles of arguments weaving tortuously across wider fields of philosophical discourse'.

These difficulties place limits upon the extent to which it is possible to provide coherent and convincing philosophical justifications for methodological decisions. Empirical research, it would seem, floats on a sea of epistemological uncertainty. This does not appear to trouble too many natural scientists, for they pursue their research successfully without much if any reference to philosophy. This is perhaps not surprising because, according to at least one epistemologist, 'philosophy or methodology of science is of no help to scientists' (Chalmers, 1982, p. 169).

Social scientists have been much more self-conscious than natural scientists about their knowledge claims and methods, perhaps rightly so. But there is a risk of becoming overly sensitive to epistemological issues. I once heard of a student whose philosophical investigations led him to believe that he did not exist! Worries about epistemological respectability can seriously undermine confidence in the possibility of undertaking worthwhile empirical research, particularly on the part of novice researchers. Most epistemological issues are open to further debate. Such inconclusiveness can induce an uncomfortable sense of exposure because one's research seems to be standing on insecure foundations. It may well be that it is, but if so, it will be no different from anyone else's.

Box 3.6 Can you afford to be philosophical?

I once suggested to my PhD supervisor that life for researchers would be much simpler if we had a Phone-a-Philosopher service. Instead of having to wade through reams of heavy philosophical writings, many of them contradictory, we would simply call Phone-a-Philosopher and ask for the latest answer to such questions as 'Is it possible to derive "ought" from "is"?', 'Is the existence of other minds amenable to proof?' and 'What is the meaning of life?' It seemed like a good idea but my supervisor pointed out a snag: the phone bills would be astronomical!

It is tempting to believe that because no research method can guarantee the production of sound knowledge we must stop doing research and wait until the philosophers have discovered the Road to Truth. Unfortunately, that may mean waiting a very long time indeed (see Box 3.6). Some aspiring researchers may even be tempted to give up the idea of conducting empirical research altogether – and become full-time epistemologists!

In general it would seem that although, from a philosophical point of view, the unexamined life is not worth living, research, like life itself, stubbornly goes on regardless.

Activity 3.1 The plane in the jungle

Once upon a time, a team of Western anthropologists set out to visit a tribe in a remote jungle. They travelled by plane but unfortunately it ran out of fuel en route and they all bailed out. The plane flew on and eventually landed more or less intact in the jungle. Before long, members of the local tribe discovered the plane in the undergrowth. Never having seen such an object before, they reasoned that it was a bird god and set about worshipping it.

How would (a) a positivist, and (b) a constructionist set about 1) describing, and 2) explaining, the behaviour of the tribe?

Key points

1 All research proceeds on the basis of fundamental assumptions about the nature of its subject matter and the ways in which it can be known.
2 These assumptions have been grouped together by philosophers into epistemologies or theories of knowledge.
3 Two of the most influential epistemologies are positivism and constructionism, and these can be linked broadly to different styles of research.
4 Different epistemologies are not necessarily exclusively related to distinct research methodologies.
5 Over-concern with epistemological issues can lead to withdrawal from empirical research in favour of philosophy.

Key reading

Easterby-Smith, M., Thorpe, R. and Lowe, A. (2002) 'The Philosophy of Research Design', in *Management Research: An Introduction*, London: Sage, pp. 27–57.

Filmer, P., Jenks, C., Seale, C. and Walsh, D. (1998) 'Developments in Social Theory', in C. Seale (ed.) *Researching Society and Culture*, London: Sage, pp. 23–36.

Gill, J. and Johnson, P. (2002) 'Making Methodological Choices: The Philosophical Basis', in *Research Methods for Managers*, London: Sage, pp. 161–92.

Lazar, D. (1998) 'Selected Issues in the Philosophy of Social Science', in C. Seale (ed.) *Researching Society and Culture*, London: Sage, pp. 7–22.

Further reading

Chalmers, A.F. (1982, 1999) *What Is This Thing Called Science?*, Buckingham, UK: Open University Press.

Crotty, M. (1998) *The Foundations of Social Research: Meaning and Perspective in the Research Process*, London: Sage.

Gellner, E. (1987) 'The Scientific Status of the Social Sciences', *International Social Science Journal*, 114, pp. 567–86.

Pepper, S.C. (1948) *World Hypotheses: A Study in Evidence*, Berkeley, CA: University of California Press.

Polkinghorne, D. (1983) *Methodology for the Human Sciences: Systems of Inquiry*, Albany, NY: State University of New York Press.

Rickman, H.P. (1990) 'Science and Hermeneutics', *Philosophy of the Social Sciences*, 20, pp. 295–316.

Sayer, A. (1992) *Method in Social Science: A Realist Approach*, London: Routledge.

Scheurich, J.J. (1997) *Research Method in the Postmodern*, London: Falmer Press.

Schumacher, E.F. (1995) *A Guide for the Perplexed*, London: Vintage.

Thomas, A.B. (2003) 'The Coming Crisis of Western Management Education', in P. Jeffcutt (ed.) *The Foundations of Management Knowledge*, London: Routledge.

Tsoukas, H. (2000) 'What Is Management? An Outline of a Metatheory', in S. Ackroyd and S. Fleetwood (eds) *Realist Perspectives on Management and Organisations*, London: Routledge, pp. 26–43.

4 Problem fields

Research projects generally originate in what I have called 'problem fields'. Problem fields contain the accumulated record of whatever has been discovered, theorized, postulated or proposed about the problems or topics that have become associated with a distinct area of inquiry. Getting to know the content of the field is therefore a prerequisite for identifying potential research problems. Researchers usually expend a great deal of effort familiarizing themselves with previous work by means of a literature search (see Chapter 5) and with 'keeping up with the literature' thereafter.

The purpose of this chapter is to explore the contents of the field known as management studies. What currently is defined as the content of this field? Where do the boundaries of this field lie and what is contained within them?

We will approach these questions in three ways. First, we consider the subject matter of management research and the research strategies associated with different subjects. What topics and subject areas are taken to fall within the scope of management studies? What general research approaches are found there? The field is certainly broad and embraces very different research traditions. It is important to be aware of and appreciate these differences since collaboration between members of different disciplines is often needed in management research.

Second, we consider the social organization and cultures of management research. The knowledge located in a field does not exist in a vacuum. It is created, developed and recorded by the people who inhabit that field. Depending on its nature, a field's inhabitants may include both academics and other groups such as practitioners, consultants and independent researchers. To be effective in management research therefore requires more than simply the acquisition of technical skills. It is also necessary to undertake cultural learning. This involves acquiring the attitudes, values and vocabularies that are shared by fellow researchers. In part these are, perhaps, common to all social scientists or even all scientists. But some are peculiar to those engaged in a particular specialism. Also, because management studies is associated with the practical activity of managing, managers play an important part, directly or indirectly, in influencing the contents of the problem field. Carrying out a successful piece of research and developing a successful research career in management may well depend importantly not only on understanding different research cultures but also on being able to work effectively in managerial environments.

Finally, we examine the question of whether there is anything distinctive about management research. Can it be approached in the same way as other social science disciplines? Does it utilize any unique research methods?

The field of management research

There is something problematic about defining the scope of management as a field of inquiry. Some fields have walls or fences around them that clearly mark them off from their neighbours, but others have only vestigial boundaries that make it difficult to tell where one field ends and another begins. Management studies is rather like that: there does not appear to be a strong consensus on what the field contains. It looks rather as if it is still in the process of being invented.

The ontological status of academic disciplines is similar to that of countries, in that they don't exist 'naturally': like nation-states, disciplines or subject areas have to be created, designated and defined (see Box 4.1). It is an interesting project to trace the creation and emergence of disciplines, as Coleman (1987), for example, has done for economic history, to see how and why the boundaries have been drawn as they have. Here, however, we can simply note that the process of establishing the scope and identity of management studies and management research is still very much in progress. That this is so is evident from the need expressed recently in several influential quarters to define it, clarify it, tidy it up, give it an identity and fix its position on the landscape of knowledge.

Box 4.1 The social construction of boundaries

In the winter of 1989 I was on a plane taking my first trip to Russia. It was a murky February morning as we crossed the English Channel and made our way over the European mainland. I gazed down at the sludge-green landscape 30,000 feet below, trying to figure out where we were. That must have been Rotterdam, I thought, and now we must have left the Netherlands and be over West Germany. As the journey progressed, I imagined Napoleon leading the *Grande Armée* from Paris to Moscow and marvelled at the thought that he and his troops had walked or ridden all the way there and all the way back. I was particularly struck by the 'obvious' fact that there were no national boundaries to be seen but just one continuous land mass. The familiar patchwork of states I knew from the atlas was altogether absent from the ground I could see below. I was reminded that nation-states have no natural existence but are *social constructions*.

This uncertainty over the identity of management studies arises partly because it is a relatively new field of inquiry (Economic and Social Research Council,

1993). Its recent emergence is indicated by the dates at which academic journals specializing in management first appeared. In Britain, for example, the *Journal of Management Studies* was first published in 1964 and the *British Journal of Management* as recently as 1990. In the United States the prestigious *Administrative Science Quarterly* began publication in 1956, the *Academy of Management Journal* in 1958 and the *Academy of Management Review* in 1976. The first issue of the European journal *Organization Studies* appeared in 1980. Although the leading journal in accounting research, *Accounting Review*, was first published in the United States in 1926, this seems to be an exception among management subjects. As management studies is a relative newcomer, the question of where it is to be placed among older-established subject areas and disciplines is still a matter of debate.

The content of management studies

Management is a problematic field because it seems peculiarly heterogeneous and complex. One outstanding feature is its broad scope, for it includes a wide range of subject areas or subdisciplines. It may even be an understatement to call it, as Thietart (2001, p. 1) does, 'an extremely broad area of research'. It

---

Box 4.2 What is management research?

Management research seeks to understand and explain the activity of managing, its outcomes and the contexts in which it occurs. This involves the study of the origins of managing and its ongoing development as both an intellectual field and arena of practice. The subject as a whole is concerned with exploring the role of all of those who contribute to the management process and the forces which shape its character. It seeks to produce a broad body of knowledge which will explain the underlying causes of given business situations and the means of assessing alternative courses of action. The organization of resources in order to achieve optimal performance in specific settings is a preoccupation in certain areas of the field, while in others researchers investigate the variety of ways in which managing and organizing occurs.

Its subject matter includes all the possible spheres of management and business activity and is conventionally classified around the specialist areas of, *inter alia*, accounting, finance, marketing, organizational behaviour/industrial relations, and operations research. As an academic field of inquiry it is heterogeneous, utilizing frameworks and research methods derived from adjacent disciplines, predominantly in the social sciences.

(Economic and Social Research Council, 2001,
Section F, pp. 16–17)

has recently been described as a field 'characterised by a diverse collection of sub-disciplines which have little in common, apart, that is, from an interest in a vaguely similar subject matter' (Ackroyd and Fleetwood, 2000, p. 3). The management field is thus both diverse, containing many different sub-areas, and lacking in generally agreed boundaries. This means that if we look at various listings of the content of management studies, we are likely to find that the items included tend to differ from list to list.

For example, Boxes 4.3 and 4.4 show two lists that describe the contents of the field in terms of topics or themes. Both lists are intended to indicate the research interests of users. One was produced by a funding body for management research, the Economic and Social Research Council (ESRC), as part of a policy document and is titled 'Key Themes for Management Research'. The other list appears in a business research textbook (Ticehurst and Veal, 2000) and is described as 'research areas that concern managers'. On what basis these lists were constructed is unclear. Although there is a degree of overlap between the lists they are far from uniform. However, they could be useful indicators of possible themes and topics for management research.

Box 4.3 Key themes for management research: a funding body's view

External change	Organizational change
Managerial roles	Innovation
Competitiveness	Internationalization
Large firms	Small businesses
Public sector	Education and health sectors

Source: Economic and Social Research Council (1994, p. 7)

Box 4.4 Research areas that concern managers

Clients	Legal issues	Productivity
Communication	Managerial effectiveness	Products
Competitiveness	Organizational development	Quality
Culture	Organizational environment	Sales
Finance	Performance	Staffing
Industrial relations	Policy	Strategy
Information technology	Potential clients	

Source: Ticehurst and Veal (2000, p. 7)

Box 4.5 The content of management studies

A.	B.	C.
Accounting	Accountancy	Human resources
Corporate strategy	Economics	Organization theory
Economics	HRM	Organizational
Finance	Information	behaviour
Human resource	technology	Policy/strategy
management (HRM)	Law	
Information management	Management	
International business	Marketing	
Management science	Organizational	
Marketing	behaviour	
Operations management	Quantitative methods	
Organizational behaviour		
Public-sector management		

A: Economic and Social Research Council (2001) *Postgraduate Training Guidelines*, www.csrc.ac.uk
B: Macfarlane (1997)
C: Scandura and Williams (2000)

Box 4.5 shows three further lists. These describe content in terms of subject areas or disciplines rather than topics or problem areas. The first two lists differ in detail but there is a considerable degree of agreement between them. Both include a wide range of subject matters. The third list looks anomalous, seeming to focus only on some of the key 'behavioural' areas and leaving out altogether the quantitative fields such as accounting and finance, operations management and quantitative methods. Nonetheless, all three lists indicate a range of subject areas that are frequently considered to be part of management studies.

Among the broad set of items which are often included within the field we can discern certain key divisions/groupings. One is the distinction between subject areas derived from the world of management practice (e.g. innovation, organizational change, managerial effectiveness) and those that are derived from the academic disciplines (e.g. organization theory, economics). Lupton (1984) makes this distinction in terms of the 'fields of action' and the 'fields of knowledge'. A further distinction can be seen within the subject areas or disciplines, between the 'behavioural' and the 'quantitative' areas and between the 'functional' (e.g. marketing, accounting, HRM) and the 'disciplinary' areas (e.g. economics, organizational behaviour). These distinctions are fairly crude but they do indicate ways in which the field of management studies and research has been conceptualized to date.

Activity 4.1 What do you count as management studies?

Consider the lists of subjects in Box 4.5. Which of these comes closest to your idea of management studies? How much or little do you know about areas other than your own specialism? Which areas should you investigate to broaden your awareness of the scope of management research?

The methods of management studies

Some writers have attempted to identify the common characteristics that management research displays or that they think it ought to display. However, as the content lists discussed above suggest, it seems likely that the styles and methods of research adopted in management studies will be diverse, given the broad range of subject areas it encompasses. In this section we will look briefly at the 'modes of knowledge' debate in management research, which stresses common features, and then at the predominant types of research strategy that have actually been adopted in some management subject areas.

Modes of knowledge production

It has been proposed by Gibbons *et al.* (1994) that the means for the production of knowledge in contemporary society have been organized in two main forms, Mode 1 and Mode 2. Mode 1 is the traditional academic pursuit of 'knowledge for its own sake'. It is discipline based and is largely undertaken by highly trained specialists working in universities. It is validated by peer review and approval and there is little concern with the practical implications and application of the knowledge generated. In contrast, in Mode 2, knowledge is created in the process of application. It favours group-based work involving individuals from different disciplines and user groups. Knowledge is validated in use and is transitory.

Gibbons *et al.* argue that Mode 2 is replacing Mode 1. This is partly because the nature of the resources devoted to the creation of knowledge has changed. It is no longer universities that are the main contributors. Other types of organization such as government agencies, corporations and consulting firms have also become important. In addition, there has been a growing demand for applied knowledge as global competition has intensified. Mode 2 therefore appears to be in the process of becoming the dominant form of knowledge production in modern society.

Although Gibbons *et al.*'s analysis is largely concerned with knowledge production in science and technology, their ideas have been taken up in recent debates on the nature of management research. In an influential article, Tranfield and Starkey (1998) depicted Mode 2 as the 'way forward' for management research, so giving it a strong applied focus. Huff (2000), on the other hand, has argued for the blending of the best features of both Mode 1 and Mode 2 to produce what she called Mode 1.5. Initially this was somewhat vaguely defined but involved the idea of management research adopting a halfway position between Mode 1 and Mode 2. Management research would deal with practical problems but using the theoretical and methodological orientation of Mode 1. Later Huff and Huff (2001) developed this idea in more depth by proposing a full-blown Mode 3. The main features of the three modes are summarized in Table 4.1 on the next page.

A good deal of the debate on appropriate modes of knowledge production for management represents a reworking of long-standing debates on how management research can and should be related to management practice. Berry (1995, p. 104) has argued that

> management studies have adhered too closely to the model of the exact sciences. Using the classical scientific model as a guide, management studies have accentuated the quantifiable; they have sought to establish universal laws, to formulate standardized rules. But practical management deals with unique situations, fast-paced events, and subjective reactions.

Given the special nature of management problems (Udwadia, 1986), it might well be that unconventional modes of knowledge production are needed to cope with them. We will be returning to these important questions in Chapter 8 when we examine the strategy of management inquiry known as action research.

Research strategies in management studies

We lack the systematic 'research on research' in management that would provide comprehensive evidence on the types of research strategy adopted across all the subjects of management studies. However, Table 4.2 depicts the research strategies adopted in four 'behavioural' management specialisms: policy/strategy, organization theory, organizational behaviour and human resources.

These figures are based on Scandura and Williams's (2000) content analysis of research articles appearing in three US management journals for the years 1985–87 and 1995–97. The original study analysed 774 articles, though the statistics presented in Table 4.2 are based on 556 articles. The study omits reference to a number of fields that could be considered as management studies, such as marketing, accounting and finance, and production and operations management. These authors seem to equate management studies with organizational studies. Even so, the figures shown in Table 4.2 throw some interesting light on the methodological strategies that have been favoured in some management research areas.

For example, in the areas shown, experimental research appears relatively infrequently among the research strategies that have been adopted. It is undertaken

Table 4.1 Alternative modes of knowledge production in management research.

Descriptors	Mode 1	Mode 2	Mode 3
Activity trigger	Theoretic or empirical hole	Thwarted goal ('problem')	Appreciation and critique
Participants	Homogeneous subdiscipline	Activity-centred, transdisciplinary (including Mode 1)	Diverse stakeholders (including Mode 1 and Mode 2 producers)
Goal	Truth, theoretic extension, order	Solution improvement	Future good
Methods	Pre-tested, paradigm-based	Often invented, based on experience	Collective experience, conversation
Activity site	Sheltered, 'ivory tower'	Practice	Off-site (but aware of practice)
Time horizon	Individually driven, often unimportant	Often immediate, transient	Community driven, immediate to very long term
Boundaries	Disciplinary, pure/applied, institutional	Transdisciplinary, often proprietary	Multiple modes of knowing
Beneficiaries	Individual scientists, professional groups	Firms, government bodies, etc.	Society
Quality control	Elite-dominated peer review	Utility, efficiency	Community agreement
Funding (primary source)	University, government	Business	Philanthropy? university, business, government
Dissemination	Scholarly conferences, journals	Practitioner conferences, mobility, Internet	Local to global debate and action, media report

Source: Huff and Huff (2001)

Table 4.2 Research strategies adopted in four areas of management research.

Research strategy	Management subject area				Total
	Policy/strategy	Organization theory	Organizational behaviour	Human resources	
Laboratory experiment	3	0	45	10	58
Field experiment	2	0	10	6	18
Sample survey	6	6	13	13	38
Field study	28	50	148	65	291
Archival study	52	51	26	22	151
Total	91	107	242	116	556

Source: Adapted from Scandura and Williams (2000, table 2).

Notes: 'Field study' includes case studies. 'Archival study' refers to research based on documentary records. Figures refer to published articles in which the listed strategy was predominant.

most often in organizational behaviour, reflecting the field's deep roots in psychology in the United States. Surveys are also infrequently undertaken. On the other hand, field studies, which include case studies, are popular in all four areas, and especially in organizational behaviour and human resources. Archival research using documentary sources is quite frequently used and appears to be the most favoured strategy both in the policy/strategy field and in organization theory.

The overall impression given by this profile is again one of diversity. Management research, even among these behavioural fields, displays considerable methodological variety. Had such quantitative fields as accounting, finance and operations research been included, the diversity would probably be even greater. Research in accounting and finance, for example, has been strongly based on positivist assumptions and has favoured the empirical testing of quantitative hypotheses using experimental and quasi-experimental research strategies. There has been considerable use of case studies in accounting research but less so in the area of finance (Ryan *et al.*, 2002).

Having considered these rather abstract views of management research, we can now look at the social and organizational context in which management research takes place. We can also draw on the few studies of management academics themselves to see what they can tell us about the field of management research.

Academic tribes and territories

It is tempting to assume that researchers are simply technicians. Equipped with a tool-kit of research methods, they dispassionately select and apply these to problems purely according to their suitability to the problem at hand. Yet this image of the 'rational' actor is as misleading when applied to researchers as it is more generally. To understand the ways in which researchers behave, it makes more sense to see them as members of disciplinary or quasi-disciplinary tribes. They are people with emotional as well as intellectual commitments to their fields and to the methods of investigation that prevail there. They do not simply inhabit fields; they occupy territories.

The organization of academic disciplines

In a fascinating study, Becher (1989) has traced the disciplinary boundaries within the modern university. He suggests that academics tend to identify themselves primarily with their discipline or subdiscipline, which constitutes the territory they occupy. Disciplines consist of demarcated bodies of knowledge in which a specific vocabulary of technical terms is deployed and which have their own distinctive ways of creating new knowledge. Those who identify themselves with a discipline can be thought of as a 'tribe'. Each tribe has its own way of thinking and its own way of doing work, including research. Traditionally, the pursuit of a research degree has been the way in which new members are admitted to the tribe. This involves passing on not only the tribe's skills and knowledge but also its basic beliefs, values and ways of thinking and acting – in short, the tribe's culture.

Box 4.6 Join the club

To be admitted to membership of a particular sector of the academic profession involves not only a sufficient level of technical proficiency in one's intellectual trade but also a proper measure of loyalty to one's collegial group and of adherence to its norms.

(Becher, 1989, p. 24)

Drawing partly on a framework originally proposed by Biglan (1973), Becher sets out to map disciplines in terms of two sets of coordinates. One is the character of a discipline's knowledge-generating process and the other is its social organization. Each aspect itself consists of two dimensions.

The knowledge-generating process can be thought of as either hard or soft and as pure or applied. The process is hard when members of the discipline share the same view of how research should be conducted in their field, but soft when there is little consensus and therefore many approaches to research. The natural sciences and engineering are typical hard disciplines whereas the humanities and the social sciences are typically soft. The distinction is similar to that between knowledge subjects and argument subjects (Anderson *et al.*, 1985). Knowledge subjects, such as physics, consist largely of well-established and uncontentious bodies of knowledge. Argument subjects, such as philosophy, largely comprise dissenting points of view on the subject's key issues.

If we now turn to the pure–applied distinction, the knowledge-generating process is pure when knowledge develops along a few well-defined paths in a cumulative way according to agendas set by academics. It is applied when agendas are open to the influence of many stakeholders, including professional practitioners. This tends to produce a heterogeneous set of topics of inquiry and less in the way of cumulative knowledge.

A discipline's social organization can be convergent or divergent and urban or rural. A convergent discipline is characterized by a strong sense of shared beliefs, values and purposes. Members identify strongly with the discipline and feel themselves to be members of a community. These disciplines exhibit strong cultures akin to those described by some writers on corporate culture (Deal and Kennedy, 1982). Divergent disciplines display opposite tendencies. They are characterized by diversity and variety of belief and outlook, and lack a strong sense of collective identity. Whereas convergent disciplines can breed arrogance, isolationism and intolerance, divergent ones are more relaxed, permissive and open.

The urban–rural distinction draws quite directly on our images of city and country life. Urban disciplines are densely packed, with many researchers working on relatively few widely recognized and accepted problems. Communications and competition are correspondingly intense. In rural disciplines the pace of life is slower. There, relatively few researchers are working on a wide range of problems, fewer people are engaged in communication about any one issue and the atmosphere is less competitive.

Tribes and territories in management studies

Tranfield and Starkey (1998) have applied Becher's framework to the analysis of management research. They argue that management research can be considered a soft, applied, divergent, rural field of inquiry rather than a hard, pure, convergent, urban one.

Management research can be seen as a soft field because it draws on no single ontological or epistemological framework and because it utilizes research methods and knowledge from a variety of related social science disciplines. It is an applied field because it is interested not simply in abstract theoretical knowledge but also in 'know-how'. 'It is concerned to build a body of knowledge which documents, codifies and articulates a problem and solution-set concerned with understanding and improving the practice of management' (Tranfield and Starkey, 1998, p. 346).

In terms of its social organization, management research is a divergent field. Members of the tribe lack a strong sense of collective identity and there are a great variety of outlooks and beliefs. Partly because of this, the field finds it hard to present a united front to outsiders and to vigorously promote its interests in competition with other, more convergent fields. It is also a rural field because the wide variety of problems and issues that are tackled and the varied set of research approaches that are adopted means that the people-to-problem ratio is relatively low.

Tranfield and Starkey's analysis of management research helps to clarify the character of the field. It conveys important if speculative ideas about its social and cognitive organization, its tribes and territories. Further light on these matters is cast by the few empirical studies of those who teach and research in the field, the tribe members themselves.

Macfarlane (1997) conducted a study of lecturers who teach business studies at undergraduate level. He was interested in how lecturers perceive this field, which is, of course, closely related to management studies. He used two dimensions to frame his investigation. The first is familiar from our discussion of Becher's work and concerns the knowledge structure of the field: whether it is seen as a 'hard', science-based field or as a 'soft', humanities-based field. The second refers to the aims of business studies: is it perceived in terms of being 'for business' or 'about business'? The distinction concerns the extent to which studying business should be focused on preparing the student to become a management practitioner or should be treated as a liberal discipline, akin to political or religious studies (Grey and French, 1996), in which the aim is to develop an 'external' understanding of the field rather than 'internal' expertise in its practice. The distinction parallels that between pure and applied disciplines as used by Becher.

Using a postal questionnaire, Macfarlane (1997) obtained responses from 224 lecturers at 19 institutions of higher education in Britain, a response rate of 40.3 per cent. Among the results of this study were the following:

- Nearly half of the lecturers thought business studies should be 'for business' whereas about a third thought it should be 'about business'.
- Lecturers at the 'old' (pre-1992) universities tended to prefer a science-based curriculum about business, whereas those at 'new' universities preferred a humanities-based curriculum for business.
- Attitudes were related to the nature of the lecturers' first degrees and their work experiences: those working in the 'old' universities had science-based degrees and little work experience outside academia.
- Attitudes were also related to the subject area which the lecturers taught.

Figure 4.1 depicts the management subjects according to their location within the axes of aims and knowledge structure. The four quadrants represent a 'science-based study for business', 'a science-based study about business', 'a humanities-based study for business' and 'a humanities-based study about business'. Each subject area has been placed according to the most frequently offered (modal) response to each alternative. To clarify the relationship with Tranfield and Starkey's analysis, the terms 'hard', 'soft', 'pure' and 'applied' have been added to Macfarlane's labels.

What Macfarlane's analysis demonstrates is the diversity of business/ management studies, something that is played down in Tranfield and Starkey's analysis. As can be seen, subjects within business studies can be found in, or on the borders of, nearly all the quadrants. Although the subject areas of marketing,

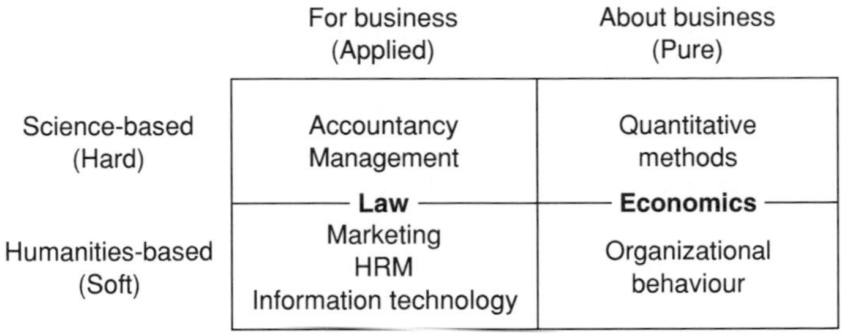

	For business (Applied)	About business (Pure)
Science-based (Hard)	Accountancy Management	Quantitative methods
	—— **Law** ——	—— **Economics** ——
Humanities-based (Soft)	Marketing HRM Information technology	Organizational behaviour

Figure 4.1 A map of the field of management research.
Source: Adapted from Macfarlane (1997, figure 2).

HRM and information technology appear to be soft and applied, the other six areas do not seem to be so readily characterized. Two of the attributes Tranfield and Starkey see as defining management research seem, on this evidence, to be exhibited by only a minority of the subjects comprising management studies. Indeed, the two areas closest to 'management' – management and organizational behaviour – do not appear to be conceived by these teachers as soft, applied subjects.

In terms of the aims of the curriculum, there is a clear division in Macfarlane's study between economics and organizational behaviour, where 'external' aims are preferred, and the remaining areas, which tend to be orientated 'for business'. The degree to which management studies is or ought to be focused on practical management problems remains unresolved. Although managers do influence management research directly and indirectly, whether that influence is too small or too great is one of the long-standing issues for debate in management studies.

A useful aspect of the 'tribes and territories' perspective is that it enables us to understand some of the difficulties that can arise when members of different disciplines try to work together. Some of the tribes have much stronger identities than others so that members will find it easy to speak to and collaborate with each other but more difficult to do so with those who identify with other tribes. Within the management-related sciences, economics seems to be unusually close-knit (Macfarlane, 1997). Other disciplines are much looser and more diverse in their outlooks, the classic case being organizational behaviour (Danieli and Thomas, 1999).

National differences and management research

Academic tribes and territories transcend national boundaries but national differences in patterns of management and management education can also be important influences on orientations to management research. Hofstede (1980b) pointed out the culturally specific nature of much management theory. Similarly, it would be wrong to assume that management research is conceptualized and can be carried out in the same way in all countries (Usunier, 1998) and that management studies is organized according to the same categories everywhere.

Given the numerical dominance and global reach of US management ideas, it is worth noting that it has features not necessarily shown elsewhere. For example, in the United States a distinction is made between organization theory (OT) and organizational behaviour (OB). There OT is focused on 'macro', large-scale issues of organization structure and tends to be the province of sociologists and organization theorists. OB deals with 'micro', smaller-scale matters of group and individual behaviour and is the province of individual and social psychologists. In Britain, however, the generic term for both macro and micro studies is organizational behaviour, a label that emerged in the 1970s to designate a new field of inquiry (Pugh *et al.*, 1975).

There are also differences between countries in methodological preferences and philosophical priorities. Historically, social science in the United States developed a strongly empirical slant with relatively little concern with fundamental epistemological issues. In Europe a broader theoretical and philosophical tradition emerged. These differences have persisted, so that top US management journals have until recently tended to be dominated by quantitative, positivist research reports.

Berry (1995) has contrasted the differing approaches to management research in the United States and France by comparing the orientation of the management schools of two of France's elite *Grandes Ecoles d'Ingénieurs* with that of the American academic system. There are noticeable differences in both the knowledge-generating process and social organization. In the French schools there is less individual competition and less employment mobility between institutions than in the United States. Berry argues that this supports a style of research that is long-term and clinically focused. The favoured research approach is close involvement with organizations entailing a one- to four-year observational period. From this, long-term cooperative relationships with scholars in other fields and with management practitioners are developed. The French tradition of management research is, he proposes, distinctive.

Is management research distinctive?

Management research embraces a wide range of subject matter which seems only to share a common concern with the notoriously vague 'management'. But apart from its interest in management, does management research display any features that distinguish it from other fields?

Easterby-Smith *et al.* (2002, p. 7) argue that management research is indeed distinctive and that it 'poses some unusual problems which are not often encountered in the broader social sciences'. These imply a need to 'rethink some of the traditional techniques and methods'. These authors also believe that management research may develop entirely new research methods. They propose three factors that make management research distinctive:

- Management practice is largely eclectic, requiring managers to work across technical, cultural and functional boundaries and to use knowledge from many disciplines. Management can thus be studied either from a single discipline or from a 'transdisciplinary' perspective.
- Managers are powerful, busy people and this can make access to organizations problematic. Even if access is granted, it may be very much on managers' terms and they may exert a strong influence over both what questions are to be researched and what methods are to be used.
- Management requires both thought and action, and the demand for practical outcomes should be taken into account by researchers.

However, as these authors acknowledge, the factors they mention are not unique to management research. Other applied fields, such as education and healthcare, are studied from several disciplinary perspectives; organizational sociologists also face problems of access; and in all applied fields there is an expectation of results that can be used. Even so, these authors believe that, taken together, these factors do pose special challenges to management researchers.

If, on the other hand, we compare management studies with one of the traditional social science disciplines such as sociology, psychology or economics, it might indeed appear distinctive. As I suggested in Chapter 2, although far from being homogeneous, these disciplines tend to have a methodological 'centre of gravity' which gives them a distinct character. Management studies, by contrast, draws on a whole range of methodological styles and traditions, which gives it a cosmopolitan flavour.

Management: a problematic problem field

The nature of management research and its relation with other fields of knowledge has been a matter for considerable debate in recent years and this seems likely to continue. What subject areas should be counted as part of the management field? Is concern with application necessarily central to it? Who and what is management research for? Is Mode 2 or possibly Mode 3 most appropriate for knowledge production in management? Is there anything distinctive about management research? Could it eventually develop new research methods? There is currently no agreed definition of management research and these issues continue to be a matter of debate (see Hodgkinson, 2001).

So far as I can see, management research uses the same research strategies and methods as other social science disciplines. The context in which management research is undertaken also has a good deal in common with other applied fields. Management research is, of course, distinctive, but largely because of the scope of its subject matter. What seems more important, though, is that it shares in the same methodological tradition as other areas of social research. There is a risk that by emphasizing the distinctiveness of a field it will become inward-looking and isolationist, cutting itself off from useful external experience. Perhaps the best way to think of management studies is, then, as a large and loosely related family with many different branches but common roots in the social science disciplines.

Activity 4.2 How do you see management research?

What do you think are the distinguishing characteristics of management as a field of inquiry? Should management research be primarily 'for' or 'about' business and other types of organization?

Key points

1   Management is a multi-subject, multidisciplinary field with few clear boundaries.
2   Management research draws on a highly diverse range of research strategies and methods.
3   Subject areas within management studies tend to differ in their profiles of research strategies and methods.
4   Becoming a management researcher requires cultural as well as technical learning, partly because of the need for collaboration across subject areas.
5   Management research draws on the same strategies and methods as the basic social science disciplines.

Key reading

Easterby-Smith, M., Thorpe, R. and Lowe, A. (2002) *Management Research: An Introduction*, London: Sage.
Hodgkinson, G.P. (ed.) (2001) 'Facing the Future: The Nature and Purpose of Management Research Re-assessed', *British Journal of Management*, 12, Special Issue.

Further reading

Bryman, A. (ed.) (1988) *Doing Research in Organizations*, London: Routledge.
Bryman, A. (1989) *Research Methods and Organization Studies*, London: Unwin Hyman.
Daft, R.L. (1983) 'Learning the Craft of Organizational Research', *Academy of Management Review*, 8, pp. 539–46.
Ghauri, P., Grønhaug, K. and Kristianslund, I. (1995) *Research Methods in Business Studies: A Practical Guide*, Hemel Hempstead: Prentice Hall.
Hussey, J. and Hussey, R. (1997) *Business Research: A Practical Guide for Undergraduate and Postgraduate Students*, Basingstoke, UK: Macmillan.
Kervin, J.B. (1992) *Methods for Business Research*, New York: HarperCollins.
Remenyi, D., Williams, B., Money, A. and Swartz, E. (1998) *Doing Research in Business and Management: An Introduction to Process and Method*, London: Sage.

Ryan, B., Scapens, R.W. and Theobold, M. (2002) *Research Method and Methodology in Finance and Accounting*, London: Thomson.

Saunders, M., Lewis, P. and Thornhill, A. (1997) *Research Methods for Business Students*, London: Pitman.

Smith, N.C. and Dainty, P. (eds) (1991) *The Management Research Handbook*, London: Routledge.

Thietart, R.-A. (2001) *Doing Management Research: A Comprehensive Guide*, London: Sage.

Ticehurst, G.W. and Veal, A.J. (2000) *Business Research Methods: A Managerial Approach*, Frenchs Forest, NSW: Pearson.

Wass, V.J. and Wells, P.E. (eds) (1994) *Principles and Practice in Business and Management Research*, Aldershot, UK: Dartmouth.

Zikmund, W.G. (1994) *Business Research Methods*, Fort Worth, TX: Dryden Press.

5   Problem identification

Identifying problems and evaluating their suitability for research is a high priority for researchers. We need to know where to look for problems and how to carry out an effective search. We also want to be reasonably sure that any problem we choose to study is worthy of the effort. Nobody wants to spend years heading for a destination that no one wanted to reach in the first place. Although it is not possible to give a definitive answer to the question of what makes for a worthwhile research topic, I can offer some useful pointers that will increase the chances of making a wise choice.

Entering the problem field

People begin their research studies in varying states of readiness. Some arrive with a definite research problem in mind while others have little more than a few vague ideas. In either case there is usually a good deal of work to be done to advance to the point at which there is a clearly stated and researchable problem.

Beginning a research degree with a definite question or topic in mind might seem to be an advantage, but it is not always possible to be sure from the start that the first idea is the best idea. There is a danger of becoming locked on to a problem before there has been sufficient exploration of the field and careful evaluation of the proposed topic. This can lead to a false start. If, however, you are unsure of what exactly to study, that need not be a cause for too much concern. It is not unusual to begin in a fog. A certain amount of wandering around is inevitable before it is possible to find one's bearings and gain a sense of direction. It is necessary to tolerate uncertainty at the beginning of a project, starting out with a broad view, scanning for a range of possibilities and then narrowing down to a specific focus. It sounds easy but of course it isn't, and your supervisor's guidance will be essential.

If you look at a sample of the journals in your field, you will see that they are typically filled with reports of completed research. The reassuring aspect of this is that it provides clear evidence that research is possible! But what many students find problematic is where to start, how to find a topic to research. Even more important is the question of how to find a good topic for research. There are two main issues we need to consider:

Box 5.1 Floundering around is not unusual

Research involves

> a great deal of floundering around in the empirical world. Somewhere and somehow in the process of floundering, the research worker will get ideas. On largely intuitive grounds he [*sic*] will reject most of his ideas and will accept others as the basis for extended work.
>
> American Psychological Association Education
> and Training Board (1959), cited in
> Allen (1981, p. 11)

---

1   What *sources* can we consult in order to identify potentially researchable problems?
2   What *criteria* should be applied to a problem to help us decide whether it is a viable research topic?

Sources of problems

Finding a problem to research may seem deceptively simple. The world is full of problems and the world of business and management has its fair share. Yet many, perhaps most, students find this a considerable headache. Identifying an appropriate topic with reasonable speed is, as Howard and Sharp (1983, p. 22) say, 'one of the most common problems encountered in student research'. Problem-finding can itself be a problem.

Researchable problems can arise from any or all of the following:

Personal interest

One source of ideas is the problems and issues that you find personally interesting and significant, but before resources can be devoted to studying a problem, someone else usually has to give approval. As the ethos expressed in Merton's CUDOS indicates, research is a collective enterprise and projects have to be related to the collective concerns of the research community. So, while a personal concern with a research topic on the part of the researcher is often necessary for it to be pursued, it is seldom sufficient. The topic typically has to fit in with other researchers' agendas.

Existing problem agendas

One place to find worthwhile problems is in the existing research literature. It used to be something of a joke that research papers would typically end with the well-worn phrase 'further research is needed'. Many papers do indeed point the way to further work needed to carry investigation of the topic further. Of particular value are review papers which summarize the state of play in a particular field and then set out an explicit agenda for further research. You should keep a special watch for these papers, for, apart from their signposting of current research needs, they also serve as literature reviews, which can be very helpful indeed when you are conducting your own review.

A second source of problems is what Lupton (1984) called 'the fields of action', the everyday world of managers and other organizational practitioners. Professional and management journals can be useful sources, although more direct familiarity with current management concerns can be had through contacts with managers and management organizations, such as the Chartered Management Institute (CMI), the Chartered Institute of Marketing (CIM) and the Chartered Institute of Personnel and Development (CIPD). Involvement with managers and other employees through teaching and during consulting assignments can also provide valuable insights into management issues and problems.

Box 5.2 So you think you've got problems!

During a transatlantic flight to Canada I struck up a conversation with the passenger in the adjoining seat, who happened to be a retired professor of biology. As we took our in-flight meal he told me that when he had taken his PhD some forty years previously, the topic of his research had been 'bacterial processes in human sewage sludge'. Fortunately for my digestion, he left the details of his fieldwork to my imagination!

Novel problem agendas

The truly innovative researchers have tended to be those who have created entirely new research agendas of their own making. Doing so requires considerable curiosity, creativity and originality of thought, and necessarily entails higher risks than working with pre-established agendas does. It is likely to be more difficult to have research accepted either at the initiation stage or when the results are available.

Normally, research students are likely to be working on the safer ground of established issues, extending and developing previous work rather than striking out in entirely new directions. This need not discourage anyone from pursuing bold, original ideas and new avenues of inquiry. However, it is important to be realistic and to be guided by more experienced colleagues because of the risks of failure that often accompany pioneering work.

Reviewing the literature

Reviewing the literature on a topic is sometimes regarded by novice researchers as a ritual, a chore that has to be endured before getting on to the real business of the research. However, a careful and thorough literature review is essential in order to provide a solid foundation for the main project. The purpose of a literature review is to establish the current state of knowledge in the field. It will therefore be a significant contribution to the dissertation or thesis and will usually be included in it as a prelude to the report of the empirical work.

Familiarity with previous work is necessary both to provide ideas for future research and to ensure that earlier studies are not unwittingly repeated. A problem field consists very largely of the literature that has accumulated about it. The material there can not only tell you what has already been said on the topic but also provide examples of how it has been researched by other investigators. Sometimes a prior study may stand as an exemplar for the intended work and so provide a direct comparison with it. These studies can be enormously helpful in giving advance appreciation of the problems and possibilities that are likely to arise in one's own fieldwork.

Types of review

There are two main types of literature review, the exploratory review and the synoptic review.

The exploratory review

As the name indicates, the exploratory review is intended to provide a broad appreciation of the content of the problem field. It involves a 'let's see what's there' approach and the aim is secure breadth rather than depth. Although some sources will be read in full, many others will simply be noted and stockpiled for later consultation as required. The exploratory review seeks to answer two main questions:

- *What aspects of the topic are covered?* For example, does the literature include both theoretical and empirical papers? From what angles has the topic been examined? What disciplines have been interested in the topic? What have been the main questions and themes of research to date? Which appear to be the key contributions?
- *How big is the literature?* At one extreme, it may be difficult to find any previous literature if the topic is novel or unusual enough. At the other, there may be a vast amount of material possibly stretching back over decades. Whatever the outcome, it is important to try to establish the size of the literature at an early stage. One way of estimating this is by conducting a keyword search on one of the electronic databases that hold abstracts of articles in the management field, such as ABI-INFORM (see Box 5.3).

By the end of the exploratory review, you should have a good general feel for the size and scope of your problem field.

**Box 5.3 How big is the literature? Example keyword search
results**

Keyword	*Hits*
Capital asset pricing	28
Cognitive maps	8
Corporate governance	1,016
Customer relationship marketing	33
Emotional intelligence	60
Globalization	2,716
International HRM	2
Leadership	4,531
Lean production	41
Multi-criteria decision-making	7
Organizational creativity	2
Strategic groups	8
Transformational leadership	34
Virtual organization	20

Source: ABI-INFORM for the period January 2000–June 2002. Search
conducted on 3 December 2002

The synoptic review

Unlike that of the exploratory review, the purpose of the synoptic review is to
provide a concise but accurate overview of all the material that appears to be
relevant to your chosen topic. This includes both substantive material, dealing
with the topic content, and methodological material, concerned with the methods
of research that have been used so far. Depending on the size and scope of the
literature, carrying out the synoptic review can be a major undertaking in itself.

The synoptic review should aim to be both descriptive and evaluative. It
should summarize previous studies but also attempt to show how that body of
work could be extended and improved in terms of both content and method.
By demonstrating 'gaps' in the literature, you open up spaces which your own
research may be able to fill.

Literature sources

The range of sources available today is enormous, and texts are increasingly
available in electronic as well as hard-copy formats. Access to a good library,
where detailed advice can be obtained on what is available and how to access it,
is essential. Since library staff are important gatekeepers who can be of tremend-
ous help to researchers, it is worth taking care to treat them accordingly.

For management research, sources are likely to include books, reports and papers or articles published in the academic and professional journals. Journals are likely to prove particularly useful because they contain more up-to-date material than appears in books. You will also find that the authors of books have often published their material in compressed form as one or more journal papers, so giving more concise access to their ideas.

Conducting the review

Carrying out a literature review involves two elements: finding appropriate literature, and processing the literature.

Finding the literature

A good way to start is by asking your tutor or supervisor to give you a starter list of key articles. The reference lists appended to those papers will then provide further leads, which in turn will lead to more. With the advent of electronic archives, literature-searching has become a research method in itself. Various technical books and articles are available which offer formalized procedures for literature-searching (Fink, 1998; Gash, 1989; Hart, 1998; Helmericks *et al.*, 1991).

Alongside these procedures, the value of informal, random methods should not be ignored. Time spent wandering the library stacks browsing the contents of the shelves can be time well spent. Informal methods are probably of most value for exploratory searches where openness to new ideas from unexpected sources is to be valued. Formal methods are particularly appropriate for the synoptic review.

During the search it is worth looking out for three particularly important kinds of contribution. I refer here to papers, though they could, of course, be books or other forms of publication:

- *Review papers*. These are themselves synoptic literature reviews. If recent examples of these exist for your topic, they can give an instant overview and so save you considerable time when creating your own. Examples of such papers are those by Pettigrew (1992) on top management research, Legge (1988) on HRM and Lyles (1990) on strategy. Many review papers discuss both the content of the field and methodological issues, but some focus specifically on methods. These can be especially valuable when you are designing your own project. Lengnick-Hall's (1995) review of sexual harassment research is an example. The *International Journal of Management Reviews* specializes in publishing state-of-the-art review articles in a variety of management fields.
- *Star papers*. These papers are cited repeatedly in the literature and represent foundational or particularly influential contributions. They constitute the literature that everyone working in the field is aware of. Review papers may themselves be star papers.

• *Model papers*. Some reports of empirical projects may be exemplars of the kind of study you have in mind. Your intended study will probably be different in scale, scope or context, but might adopt the same research strategy and address the same or similar questions as the exemplar. These papers can serve as a model for your own project. If the design of your research is close enough to the model study, it may be considered as a replication of it.

Processing the literature

The amount of literature available on different topics varies enormously. Box 5.3 shows the number of articles held in one of the electronic archives for a selection of management topics. While some topics are represented by only a handful of articles, others have several thousand. If hardly anything has been written about your topic, you are probably facing a problem of underload. More likely, however, is that a good deal has been produced and your problem is one of overload. In this case it is necessary to be selective in deciding what to read and how to read it.

On the matter of how to read, the important point is not to try to read everything from start to finish. That kind of 'study reading' should be reserved for key sources only (see Box 5.4). So far as what to read is concerned, I suggest you pay special attention to the kinds of contributions mentioned above: review papers, star papers and model papers. Weed out irrelevant material but do not destroy it, or your references to it, at this stage. What seems irrelevant and unimportant now may not seem so in a few months' time.

Box 5.4 Four types of reading

1   Skim reading: rapid scanning of the entire source.
2   Index reading: using the index to locate specific items and reading only the sections referring to those items.
3   Top-and-tailing: reading the introduction and conclusion of the whole work or of each chapter.
4   Study reading: close and repeated reading.

One way of organizing your material is by means of a relevance funnel (Figure 5.1a). The funnel is divided into three zones. The innermost zone represents literature that is very close to your topic. It includes, for example, model papers. The intermediate zone represents material that is directly relevant but not quite so close. The outer zone represents material that is relevant but more remote. The area beyond the mouth of the funnel contains the irrelevant material. The size of the areas enclosed by each zone reflects the expected relative sizes of each subset of articles: we expect relatively few closely related papers, rather more at the next level and even more as the degree of relevance decreases.

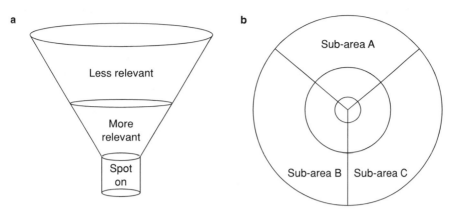

Figure 5.1 Organizing research literature by relevance funnel.

For example, suppose your topic is 'Leadership in small high-technology firms in Britain'. Papers on exactly that would be placed at the lower tip of the funnel. The same but in, say, China or Spain would be placed in the intermediate zone. Studies of leadership in large firms might be placed in the outer zone, together with those on leadership in politics. The process of deciding where to place material in the funnel can be valuable in itself. Of course, nothing is fixed by this process and material may be moved from one zone to another as the study progresses and becomes clearer.

Where a topic is complex and draws on several distinct literatures, the funnels can be combined into a relevance diagram such as that in Figure 5.1b. A literature review of 'Organizational change and culture in banking', for example, might be organized using three funnels, one each for the literature on organizational change, organizational culture and the banking industry.

A final point is that you must keep full references of all the published works you consult. If you take a word-for-word copy of a sentence or paragraph from such a source for quotation later in your own work, be sure to note the page number on which it appears. If you don't, you will probably discover two things:

1   You're bound to want to quote that material when the time comes to write up your work.
2   When you attempt to consult the original source to retrieve the page reference, it will probably have disappeared!

Selecting a problem

Unfortunately, few researchers, even experienced ones, have an entirely free hand in choosing their research topics. For experienced researchers undertaking projects that require substantial funding, grant-awarding bodies have to be convinced that their money is being wisely spent. Research students' proposals have to be approved by the academic authorities in their institution. Even so-called personal research, requiring few or no additional resources beyond those of the investigator, will normally be undertaken with publication in mind and so the question of whether anyone is likely to be interested in the work cannot be ignored. Unless they are exceptionally rich and/or exceptionally famous, everyone has to account to somebody in order to get a project launched.

Criteria for selecting problems

The two main criteria that are applied to potential problems in order to decide whether to select them for research are value and feasibility. If you are required to submit a research proposal before being admitted to your degree course, these criteria will almost certainly be high on the list of the evaluators. Both need to be convincingly met if resources are to be allocated to a specific project.

Value

The essential question here is 'To what extent is this problem worth researching?' Unless this question is answered positively, the subsequent issue of feasibility need not be considered. There is not much point in working out how to do something that isn't worth doing! However, figuring out what *is* worth researching is not necessarily easy.

Nobody wants to carry out trivial research but it is important to keep the matter of the value of a project in perspective. Most degree research is seen as part of an educational enterprise in which developing research skills is as important as the actual outcomes of the study. You do not need to feel that you must conduct earth-shattering research. You should feel comfortable with a modest contribution but it must at least be a contribution of some kind.

Feasibility

The key question here is 'Can the problem be researched?' Because a problem is regarded as highly significant, that does not mean that it can be researched. Practical considerations loom large here. Feasibility considerations include:

- *Availability of data.* To be researchable, relevant data must be either already in existence, such as statistical records, or able to be generated by such means as interviews, questionnaires and observations. For some problems, data exist but are inaccessible to researchers. Individual government census records, for example, are inaccessible for 100 years after their collection. Research on how juries reach their verdicts is also unavailable in Britain, where jury deliberations are protected by law from scrutiny. Corporate records may also be inaccessible for reasons of commercial security. The likelihood of being able to secure appropriate data must be considered at the planning stage.

- *Can the research plan be implemented?* Some research strategies, such as the experiment, may require the random allocation of subjects to groups. This may be difficult or impossible to achieve because of practical constraints. Studies of the effectiveness of different teaching methods, for example, ideally require students to be randomly allocated to groups. One group is exposed to what, on theoretical grounds, is believed to be a more effective teaching method and the second group to a less effective method. But this creates the possibility that one group may be unfairly disadvantaged. Not many students and their parents are likely to be willing to participate in an experiment which could lead to exam failure for the sake of testing a new teaching method.
- *Is there enough time?* Most research operates within a fixed time schedule. In degree research this is at most two or three years. Can the project be implemented within the prevailing time constraints?
- *Are the appropriate research skills available?* It would be unwise to undertake research that requires skills you do not have and that you do not expect to be able to acquire. For example, if you lack sufficient statistical expertise, it might be unwise to embark on elaborate multivariate studies. Similarly, if you are uncomfortable working with the uncertainties of studying a strange social group at close hand, this type of ethnographic research might best be avoided. On the other hand, you might see such projects as opportunities that provide you with the incentive to develop new skills.
- *Is there enough money?* Few research degree studies can be allocated significant resources for travel, printing and postage of questionnaires, taped interview transcriptions, special laboratory facilities, and so on. Working out a realistic budget for your research project may be difficult but is an essential aspect of research planning.
- *What degree of risk can be accepted?* All research entails some risk, and the more innovative the project, the more risky it is likely to be. Some research is personally risky. The sociologist Roy Wallis (1977) was pursued for some years by disgruntled Scientologists after he had undertaken research on their activities. A more likely possibility in management research is the risk of producing insignificant or obvious findings. It is to guard against this prospect that projects should be designed with symmetry of outcomes in mind.

Symmetry of outcomes

Because research is an inherently risky business, sometimes things are going to go wrong. To reduce this possibility we need to build some protection into our work, rather as rock climbers do when they rope themselves to a firm anchorage. If they do slip, they do not fall too far and are able to regain their hold and complete their climb. In research, one way of doing this is by trying to ensure that the problem is studied in such a way that the project will yield worthwhile findings whatever happens. This 'symmetry of outcomes' is clearly a desirable feature of research designs because it provides some insurance against the consequences of unexpected outcomes.

In fields that have been little studied, this 'win–win' outcome is not too difficult to achieve. When little or nothing is known about a topic, almost anything that is discovered will be valuable, assuming, of course, that the topic itself is regarded as worth researching. In well-researched fields, however, it is more difficult to ensure a positive outcome. If the field has been heavily researched, it may be difficult even to find a worthwhile topic.

Researchers are encouraged to build symmetry into their studies so that whatever results they produce will be sufficiently newsworthy. Quite how this can be achieved is difficult to say in the abstract. The question you have to ask yourself is: 'If my results do not turn out as expected, will I still have something worthwhile to say?' If the answer is 'No', then you are clearly at greater risk than if it is 'Yes'. One way of approaching the problem is by devising a fall-back strategy that indicates how symmetry will be achieved if the main plan goes wrong.

What makes for worthwhile research?

As we saw in Chapter 1, a completed piece of research can be judged in terms of the significance of the topic or problem, the validity of the findings or results, and the extent to which the investigators report their work in sufficient detail to enable a reader to judge the project's significance and validity. The first issue is clearly crucial, for however valid a study's findings are, and however explicitly the research is reported, the end product will still be regarded as inadequate if the problem itself is seen to be trivial or unimportant. We therefore need to ask on what grounds a topic is to be judged significant or interesting and what factors help researchers to identify such problems.

What makes a problem interesting?

In a difficult but classic paper that is well worth serious study, Davis (1971) has explored the factors which lead social theories and the theorists who create them to be regarded as 'interesting'. Interesting theories and theorists tend to be remembered while the uninteresting are forgotten. Although he deals with theories and with some of the most prominent theorists in social science, his arguments can also be applied to research propositions, the central claims which researchers make about the issue they are investigating.

Propositions assert something about the world and can be broadly divided into those which assert that some single phenomenon has particular characteristics and those which assert a particular kind of relationship between several phenomena. An example of the former might be 'managerial work consists of six distinct activities'. An example of the latter might be 'the larger a firm is, the less innovative it is'. In other words, propositions refer to discrete descriptions and to relational descriptions, two of the basic elements of research we introduced in Chapter 1.

The key point we can take from Davis's paper is that propositions are neither *intrinsically* interesting nor *intrinsically* uninteresting. The quality of being interesting or otherwise is *attributed* to a proposition by the audience to which it is directed. In scholarly research, that audience is the fellow members of the research community to which the researcher belongs, and their judgement is made in terms of whatever is currently believed about the matter to which the proposition relates. Propositions are thus warranted by those with the authority to issue such warrants. One consequence of this is that if a proposition is regarded by an investigator as interesting, but not by the warranting authorities, it may be difficult or impossible to have it accepted as a worthwhile research topic. It is partly for this reason that it is important to be thoroughly familiar with previous research on a topic when trying to identify an acceptable problem.

Box 5.5 Elements of the interesting

Single phenomena

1 *Organization*

   a   What seems to be a disorganized (unstructured) phenomenon is in reality an organized (structured) phenomenon.
       Example: the behaviour of task groups of any kind progresses through a common set of stages.

   b   What seems to be an organized (structured) phenomenon is in reality a disorganized (unstructured) phenomenon.
       Example: organizational decision processes are anarchic rather than rational.

2 *Composition*

   a   What seem to be assorted, heterogeneous phenomena are in reality composed of a single element.
       Example: magic and science are based on the same operating principles.

   b   What seems to be a single, homogeneous phenomenon is in reality composed of assorted, heterogeneous elements.
       Example: the psychological individual is not a unity but consists of several interacting selves.

3 *Abstraction*

   a   What seems to be an individual phenomenon is in reality a holistic phenomenon.
       Example: suicide is determined by social rather than psychological forces.

b   What seems to be a holistic phenomenon is in reality an individual phenomenon.
Example: crime is a product of individual irresponsibility rather
than social conditions.

4   *Generalization*

a   What seems to be a local phenomenon is in reality a general
phenomenon.
Example: tribal rituals are as common in 'modern' societies as
they are in 'traditional' ones.
b   What seems to be a general phenomenon is in reality a local one.
Example: management is not a recognized activity in all industrial societies, only in certain countries.

5   *Stabilization*

a   What seems to be a stable and unchanging phenomenon is in
reality unstable and changing.
Example: the universe is expanding rather than existing in a steady
state.
b   What seems to be an unstable and changing phenomenon is in
reality stable and unchanging.
Example: football hooliganism in Britain is no more extensive or
severe than it was a century ago.

6   *Function*

a   What seems to be a phenomenon that functions ineffectively as a
means to the attainment of an end is in reality a phenomenon that
functions effectively.
Example: trade unions promote management control rather than
obstruct it.
b   What seems to be a phenomenon that functions effectively as a
means to the attainment of an end is in reality a phenomenon that
functions ineffectively.
Example: performance-related pay impairs performance rather than
improving it.

7   *Evaluation*

a   What seems to be a bad phenomenon is in reality a good one.
Example: psychological stress promotes achievement.

b What seems to be a good phenomenon is in reality a bad one.
Example: agricultural aid to Third World nations increases their economic dependence.

Multiple phenomena

8 *Co-relation*

a What seem to be unrelated phenomena (independent) are in reality related (interdependent).
Example: an organization's structure is related to the nature of its core technology.

b What seem to be related phenomena (interdependent) are in reality unrelated (independent).
Example: an organization's structure has no bearing on its performance.

9 *Coexistence*

a What seem to be phenomena which can exist together are in reality ones which cannot exist together.
Example: managers cannot be both successful and effective.

b What seem to be phenomena which cannot exist together are in reality ones which can.
Example: workers' control and economic efficiency are compatible.

10 *Co-variation*

a What seems to be a positive co-variation between phenomena is in reality a negative co-variation.
Example: as wealth increases, happiness decreases.

b What seems to be a negative co-variation between phenomena is in reality a positive co-variation.
Example: longer prison sentences increase the likelihood of re-offending rather than reducing it.

11 *Opposition*

a What seem to be similar (nearly identical) phenomena are in reality opposite phenomena.
Example: human behaviour is unlike animal behaviour because it is subjectively meaningful.

b What seem to be opposite phenomena are in reality similar (nearly identical) phenomena.

> *Example*: totalitarian and democratic systems of government both perpetuate rule by elites.
>
> 12   *Causation*
>
>   a   What seems to be the independent phenomenon (variable) in a causal relation is in reality the dependent phenomenon.
>   *Example*: attitudes are a consequence of one's behaviour rather than a cause of it.
>   b   What seems to be the dependent phenomenon (variable) in a causal relation is in reality the independent phenomenon.
>   *Example*: 'It is not the consciousness of men which determines their social being but their social being which determines their consciousness' (Marx).

In general, Davis argues, for a proposition to be warranted as interesting, it has to deny the assumptions of the audience to which it is directed. Such propositions thus assert that 'what seems to be the case is not the case', or 'what is accepted as the case is not the case'. If, on the other hand, the proposition asserts something that is already accepted, this is likely to lead to the judgement of 'That's obvious!' Or if it asserts something for which the audience holds no beliefs at all, the response may be 'That's irrelevant!' Finally, if the proposition denies everything the audience believes about the phenomenon, this may lead to the judgement 'That's absurd!' Interesting propositions tend to be those that deny part but not all of the audience's assumptions.

Box 5.6 The nature of 'interesting' propositions

1   Whether a proposition is considered 'interesting' depends on the assumptions of the audience to which it is directed.
2   'Interesting' propositions deny some of an audience's assumptions about a topic.
3   The common element of 'interesting' propositions is:
              What seems to be the case is really not the case.
    Or   What is accepted as the case is actually not the case.

So, for example, if as a research student in business and management you propose research to show that some firms are more profitable than others, that seems likely to be judged obvious; to investigate the properties of galaxies might well be regarded as irrelevant; to show that all firms are equally profitable might be regarded as absurd. If, however, you proposed to investigate the proposition that a firm's profitability depends on the industry experience of its chief execut-ive, that *might* be regarded as interesting. It all depends.

Activity 5.1 Assert your own interesting propositions

In his paper, Davis describes 12 general forms of the interesting. I have listed these in Box 5.5 together with illustrative examples. Try to identify some major propositions that have been made in your research field and see if you can locate them within this typology.

Davis argues that being interesting is not, therefore, a mysterious matter, for we can learn how to create interesting propositions for ourselves: 'If we come to understand the process by which interesting theories are generated, we will not have to continue to do what has been done up till now – leave the "interesting" to the "inspired"' (1971, p. 312).

How are 'interesting' problems identified?

Campbell *et al.* (1982) carried out a study to identify the factors that distinguished between 'significant' and 'not-so-significant' research in the field of organizations. They commented that 'we simply do not know how "innovative" and productive investigators generate their innovative and productive research questions' (1982, p. 91), but their research was intended to provide some clues.

To this end, they asked 29 scholars to identify two of their own research projects: one that they regarded as significant, in the sense that it had received recognition as a contribution to their field by other scholars, and one tactfully called 'not-so-significant' that had received less or possibly no recognition. These latter were ones of which the researchers were not especially proud and which they probably preferred to forget – which comfortingly demonstrates that not even experienced scholars always get it right!

The factors associated with significant research were:

1   Investigators were actively involved in networks of researchers rather than isolated in their studies.
2   A research idea, method and an opportunity converged.
3   The topic had a high intrinsic interest and the researchers had a strong intuitive belief in the value of the topic.
4   The research displayed a concern with theory and explanation.
5   The research had a real-world flavour.

Not-so-significant research, by contrast, was associated with:

1   researchers who had an expedient outlook, doing 'quick-and-dirty' research;
2   concern with methods and techniques dominating substantive issues ('methodolatry' – see Chapter 1);
3   low motivation, often because the topic had been imposed;
4   lack of theoretical orientation.

Preparing a research proposal

A key stage in the planning of research is the production of a research proposal. This document should provide a fairly detailed overview of all the stages of the project. An example specification is shown in Box 5.7.

Box 5.7 An example specification for a research proposal

A research proposal, prepared in consultation with a supervisor, will include:

1   a description of the research problem;
2   evidence of its academic suitability;
3   the conceptual framework for the research;
4   a justification of the research methods;
5   a timetable;
6   a budget, together with any sources of funding.

Source: Doctoral Programme brochure, Manchester Business School, University of Manchester

---

The preparation of a comprehensive research proposal is a significant task that takes considerable effort and patience but this is time well invested. The proposal serves several important purposes:

- It forces the investigator to address all the main issues associated with a project and so helps avoid missing key items.
- It encourages a holistic view of the project, so enabling both problematic and beneficial synergies to be anticipated before work begins.
- It enables the proposed research to be communicated to interested parties such as supervisory bodies, ethics committees, potential sponsors, and so on.

The proposal brings together the substantive and methodological aspects of the project with the practical operational ones. At this stage, for example, detailed thought will have to be given to the financing of the work. A budget should be prepared showing the main items of expenditure that are anticipated. Time planning is also important and a chart showing the main stages of the project and their likely time-scales should be included.

Problem statements

Formulating a statement of the research question or problem that is clear and accurate is a crucial step in research. Sometimes, of course, the problem becomes clear only as the study progresses, but you should work to achieve as much clarity as you can from the start. It may seem surprising but it is possible to reach the end of a research project with its aim still being obscure. It can be safely assumed that if it is unclear to you, it will almost certainly be unclear to everyone else.

Activity 5.2 Is your research problem clear?

A good test of whether you are clear in your own mind about your research problem is to see if you can state it accurately in a single sentence. Try to do this using no more than 50 words. Test the result for intelligibility with colleagues and your supervisor. Repeat as necessary. Later you will need to apply the same treatment to the title of your study but using perhaps 5 to 10 words. Condensing the central theme of your research into a small space involves a lot of thought and effort but is an essential process.

A key question that arises at this point is how the research topic should be presented. Is it necessary to couch the project's aims in terms of a set of hypotheses? The answer depends on the style of research being adopted. Given the broad view of research adopted here, a formal statement of hypotheses will only be strictly necessary if a hypothetico-deductive approach, with hypothesis-testing at its heart, is being used. Otherwise, a clear statement of the research problem is generally sufficient.

Activity 5.3 The interesting-problem generator

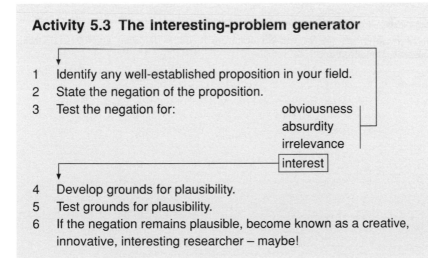

1   Identify any well-established proposition in your field.
2   State the negation of the proposition.
3   Test the negation for: obviousness
                                     absurdity
                                     irrelevance
                                     interest

4   Develop grounds for plausibility.
5   Test grounds for plausibility.
6   If the negation remains plausible, become known as a creative, innovative, interesting researcher – maybe!

Key points

1   Uncertainty about identifying suitable research problems is common in degree research.
2   The literature review should be treated as a significant part of the project itself rather than as a minor prelude or chore.
3   A research problem must be practically feasible and meet at least minimum conditions of interest or value.
4   What counts as an 'interesting' problem is relative to audience interests.
5   Design your study to produce a 'win–win' outcome if possible.

Key reading

Campbell, J.P., Daft, R.L. and Hulin, C.L. (1982) *What to Study? Generating and Developing Research Questions*, Beverly Hills, CA: Sage.
Davis, M.S. (1971) 'That's Interesting! Towards a Phenomenology of Sociology and a Sociology of Phenomenology', *Philosophy of Social Science*, 1, pp. 309–44.
Saunders, M. and Lewis, P. (1997) 'Great Ideas and Blind Alleys? A Review of the Literature on Starting Research', *Management Learning*, 28, pp. 283–99.

Further reading

Fink, A. (1998) *Conducting Research Literature Reviews: From Paper to the Internet*, London: Sage.
Hart, C. (2001) *Doing a Literature Search: A Comprehensive Guide for the Social Sciences*, London: Sage.
Howard, K. and Sharp, J.A. (1983) *The Management of a Student Research Project*, Aldershot, UK: Gower.
Kelly, M. (1998) 'Writing a Research Proposal', in C. Seale (ed.) *Researching Society and Culture*, London: Sage, pp. 111–22.
Locke, L.F., Spirduso, W.W. and Silverman, S.J. (1998) *Reading and Understanding Research*, London: Sage.

6　Research ethics

1　A management researcher is invited by a tobacco company to tender for a major research contract for the study of employee behaviour in its factories. The project will almost certainly have a highly positive effect on the researcher's professional reputation. But she believes that nicotine is a dangerous, addictive drug and that the manufacture and sale of tobacco products is immoral, and hence is reluctant to carry out work funded by the sale of tobacco.

2　During a study of the job satisfaction of police constables, a researcher interviews an officer at her police station about what she likes and dislikes about the job. The officer has been assured by the interviewer that anything she says will remain confidential. As the researcher is leaving the building after completing the interview, the station sergeant hails him jovially and says, 'I see you've been interviewing Constable Briggs. I expect she's been telling you about the difficulty she has getting along with her male colleagues.'

3　A researcher is called in by a top manager to study the effects of an innovative change programme that has recently been implemented, at great cost and with much publicity, at the manager's insistence. The research shows that the programme has had little or no effect. The manager angrily instructs the researcher not to publish the study even though the researcher had said at the start that freedom to publish was a condition of doing the work.

These three vignettes illustrate some of the ways in which ethical issues can emerge in the course of doing research. By its very nature, all social research has ethical implications and management research is no exception. Although it is unlikely that management researchers will have to face the dramatic moral problems that arise from natural science research, such as the uses of nuclear energy or the implications of human cloning, they still need to be ethically aware. On the one hand, they must take care not to cause harm to those they study. But it is also in their own interests to be alert for ethical pitfalls in their research in order to avoid being hurt themselves. In addition, unethical work is likely to reflect badly on the reputation of a researcher's institution and the discipline which he or she represents.

To draw attention to ethical considerations does not mean, of course, that research students are presumed to be morally incompetent or less caring and honest than the rest of the population. Explicit attention to ethics is necessary both because researchers often encounter difficult moral dilemmas which cannot be readily resolved, and because in research, ethical problems are not necessarily easy to spot. Researchers may find themselves taken unawares when suddenly confronted with a situation that requires an ethical response and behave inappropriately. Forewarned is, as they say, forearmed. In this chapter we will therefore consider why ethical problems arise in management research, the ways in which they manifest themselves at each stage of the research process, and ways of managing them.

Activity 6.1 Making ethical decisions

Put yourself in the shoes of the researchers in the three vignettes above. What would you have done in their situation?

Ethics in research

What are ethics?

Ethics are moral principles that are intended to guide a person's behaviour in society. Professional ethics are more narrowly concerned with regulating behaviour in the context of a specific occupation such as medicine. When codified, these principles serve to guide practitioners when dealing with the ethical implications of their work.

Much of this guidance is straightforward and it can often be followed without difficulty. Indeed, it may amount to little more than a restatement of general moral principles that are widely accepted in the wider society. Difficulties arise, however, when the application of moral principles in a specific situation has conflicting implications – when following one principle entails breaking another. In research, this happens when methodological procedures which are seen as desirable or obligatory by the research community in order to advance knowledge contravene the ethics of society or the personal ethical commitments of the researcher. Then researchers face an ethical dilemma: to live up to the requirements of being a good researcher or to maintain their self-respect and standing as a good citizen.

For example, in the second vignette presented above, the researcher is being asked to violate the guarantee of confidentiality that has been given to the constable. There is no ethical dilemma in this case; people are expected to keep their promises and there is no difficulty in following this moral requirement here. Suppose, however, that the person asking the question of the researcher had been a high court judge demanding to know what the constable had said during the interview and that the penalty for refusing to answer were a jail sentence for

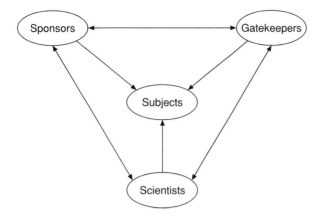

Figure 6.1 The social context of social inquiry.

contempt of court? Now the researcher faces an ethical dilemma: society requires him to keep his promise to the constable but it also requires him to obey the law.

Barnes (1979) argues that ethical problems in social research arise out of the relationships between four interested parties: the researchers, the research subjects, the research sponsors and the gatekeepers who control access to the research subjects (Figure 6.1). Each group has the power to influence the course of a research project and each has its own ideas and expectations of both desirable and undesirable outcomes. Not all these groups will necessarily be represented in every study. Questionnaire surveys may, for example, be delivered direct to research subjects without the intervention of gatekeepers. Studies within organizations, on the other hand, typically require access to be granted and usually cannot be undertaken without the cooperation of gatekeepers.

Activity 6.2 CUDOS and ethics

Look back at the CUDOS framework of values that underpin scientific research (Chapter 3). How might the application of these ideals lead to ethical dilemmas in management research?

Managing ethical issues

Ethical problems cannot be avoided in social research, so it is important to find appropriate ways of handling them. One way is by looking to the philosophy of ethics for a well-reasoned approach. Another is to look at the pragmatic solutions that have been adopted by researchers themselves as they have encountered ethical problems during the course of their studies.

Philosophical approaches

The problem of what is to count as good or right conduct has been a matter of philosophical discussion since at least the time of Aristotle. Various answers have been proposed, but two important and contrasting approaches are those which argue for the possibility of universally applicable, general ethical rules and those which deny such a possibility.

Universal ethics

If there were agreed general moral rules, ethical uncertainties would not occur. Everyone would know what is right and wrong. In effect, human behaviour would be subject to ethical laws which everyone ought to obey. They might not actually obey such rules, but the character of moral action would at least be clear and moral decision-making would be unproblematic. If, for example, 'lying is always wrong', then any research which required the deliberate and calculated telling of lies would be unethical.

Although the idea of universal ethics is appealing in both its simplicity (rules apply to everyone at all times in all places) and its dramatic import, it is also problematic. One key difficulty is that posed by contradictions: two or more ethical universals may lead to an impasse if they are applied simultaneously. If 'killing is always wrong' and 'keeping promises is always right', what am I to do if I promise my friend I will keep his secrets and he then tells me that one of them is that he is a serial killer? Should I hand him over to the police and so prevent further murders? If one rule is obeyed, the other is transgressed.

Situation ethics

Perhaps in the example just given we might conclude that it would be right to hand him over and that 'keeping promises is not always right'. Circumstances, it would seem, alter cases. We might argue that it all depends on the situation, perhaps adding that while moral rules should be applied in general, there are always exceptions to the rule. This is the position known as situation ethics. Ethical principles are fixed but what actually counts as ethical conduct becomes contingent. Under these assumptions we have to continually negotiate ethically satisfactory conduct with our consciences, seeking morally acceptable outcomes as each new situation arises.

Pragmatic approaches

In practice, researchers often have to resolve ethical dilemmas for themselves. Where there is risk of harm to subjects this has to be balanced against the potential benefits to be derived from the research. As Bailey *et al.* (1995) point out, researchers tend to differ in their views. Some believe in giving priority to the rights of subjects, others in giving priority to the pursuit of knowledge.

Box 6.1 The uncommon language of researcher and citizen

Researcher	*Citizen*
Subjects	People
Respondents	Individuals
Cases	Persons
Organisms	Human beings
Units	Men and women
Covert observation	Spying
Hoaxing	Tricking
Non-disclosure of purposes	Lying, patronizing
Neutral	Amoral, immoral
Objective	Uncaring, unfeeling

Subjects first

Some researchers believe that if there is a conflict of interest between researchers and subjects, then the subjects' interests should be respected at the expense of the researchers'. On this view, research should never be undertaken if those involved are to be put at risk of harm without their consent, are likely to have their privacy violated, or are to be deceived. Where such outcomes are likely, research must be forgone no matter how important or attractive it is to the research community.

Warwick (1975) expresses this point of view when he argues that 'social scientists ought to stop lying'. Deception in research is, in his view, unethical and unjustified irrespective of whether the research is intended to help oppressed groups or simply to advance knowledge. He argues that if deception is seen to be acceptable within the research community, there is a danger of encouraging its use everywhere, so helping to undermine society. Therefore he calls for a permanent moratorium on deceptive research.

Knowledge first

Others believe that it sometimes is justifiable to carry out research that places research subjects at risk without their knowledge or consent. It is argued that the likely benefits of the research to the community or the public's right to know outweigh any negative impacts on research subjects. This argument is sometimes applied to the undercover study of powerful groups who wish to avoid scrutiny. Holdaway (1983), for example, adopted this position to justify his covert study of the British police.

On this view, the ends are held to justify the means. A difficulty with this position is that researchers often act as judge and jury in their own case, so it can be argued that such decisions, if they are morally justifiable at all, should at least be made by an independent party applying a clearly stated and coherent set of ethical principles.

Ethical codes

One way of attempting to regulate researchers' behaviour is by means of professional codes of ethics. Such codes are formulated by professional associations for the guidance of their members and set out the profession's view on acceptable and unacceptable research practices. In addition, many universities have instituted ethics committees which scrutinize research plans and proposals to ensure that they meet required ethical standards.

The (American) Academy of Management publishes a Code of Ethical Conduct which includes a section on research. The preamble to the code outlines academy members' responsibilities. These include responsibility to managerial knowledge, where 'prudence in research design, human subject use, confidentiality, result

---

Box 6.2 Management researchers' code of ethics

The research of Academy members should be done honestly, have a clear purpose, show respect for the rights of all individuals and organizations, efficiently use resources, and advance knowledge in the field.

(p. 1296)

It is the duty of Academy members to preserve and protect the privacy, dignity, well-being, and freedom of research participants. This duty requires both careful research design and informed consent from all participants. Risk and the possibility of harm to research participants must be carefully considered and, to the extent possible, these must be minimized. When there is a degree of risk or potential harm inherent in the research, potential participants – organizations as well as individuals – must be informed.

(p. 1297)

Deception should be minimized and, when necessary, the degree and effects must be mitigated as much as possible. Researchers should carefully weigh the gains achieved against the cost in human dignity. To the extent that concealment or deception is necessary, the researcher must provide a full and accurate explanation to participants at the conclusion of the study, including counselling, if appropriate.

(p. 1297)

Extracts from Academy of Management (2000)

reporting, and proper attribution of work is a necessity' (2000, p. 1296). The code itself deals with the need for honesty in the conduct of research; the need for rigour in the design, execution and reporting of studies; the protection of research participants; the fair treatment of manuscripts submitted for journal publication; and accurate self-representation when bidding for research contracts and grants. As yet, the British Academy of Management has not produced an ethical code, but organizations representing certain related disciplines, such as the British Sociological Association and the British Psychological Society, provide extensive guidelines which are available to members and non-members alike.

Although each professional association produces its own code, social researchers in different fields tend to face the same sorts of methodological and ethical problems, so the different codes tend to have much in common. Codes typically deal with such matters as the rights of research subjects in relation to protection from harm, participation in research, and privacy.

Protection from harm

In some fields of medical and biological research, participants may well run the risk of permanent physical harm or even death. Although physical harm is unlikely in management research, participants may be exposed to the risk of psychological and social harm. Researchers are generally expected to minimize such risks, to secure informed consent where the risks are significant, and to take steps to protect participants from harm both during the data construction phase and after the study has been completed and published.

Informed consent

A key element in most research codes is the duty placed on the researcher to secure the *informed consent* of those who are intended as the subjects of or participants in the research. The principle of informed consent was formulated in 1947 by American judges at the end of the Nuremberg Medical Trial and has become known as the Nuremberg Code. Article 1 of the code states:

> The voluntary consent of the human subject is absolutely essential. This means that the person involved should have legal capacity to give consent; should be so situated as to be able to exercise free power of choice, without the intervention of any element of force, fraud, deceit, duress, over-reaching, or other ulterior form of constraint or coercion; and should have sufficient knowledge and comprehension of the elements of the subject matter involved as to enable him to make an understanding and enlightened decision.
> (International Military Tribunal, 1949, p. 181)

To be able to give informed consent, persons must be competent to make decisions, be in a position to volunteer participation freely, be given full information upon which to base their decision, and fully understand the decision situation. People must be provided with sufficient information to enable them to decide whether they wish to participate in the research, and it is the responsibility of the researcher to give this information.

Box 6.3 Sociologists' code of ethics

2) The statement does not . . . provide a set of recipes for resolving ethical choices or dilemmas, but recognises that it will be necessary to make such choices on the basis of principles and values, and the (often conflicting) interests of those involved.

13) Sociologists have a responsibility to ensure that the physical, social and psychological well-being of research participants is not adversely affected by the research. They should strive to protect the rights of those they study, their interests, sensitivities and privacy, while recognising the difficulty of balancing potentially conflicting interests.

14) Because sociologists study the relatively powerless as well as those more powerful than themselves, research relationships are frequently characterised by disparities of power and status. Despite this, research relationships should be characterised, whenever possible, by trust and integrity.

32) . . . covert methods violate the principles of informed consent and may invade the privacy of those being studied. . . . Participant or non-participant observation in non-public spaces or experimental manipulation of research participants without their knowledge should be resorted to only where it is impossible to use other methods to obtain essential data.

Extracts from British Sociological Association (2002)

In many disciplines the full implementation of the principle of informed consent is difficult and sometimes impossible to realize. Studies of people suffering from severe mental illness, for example, require participation from those who are not regarded as competent to make such decisions. The ethics of such studies therefore requires special treatment. There are also circumstances in which obtaining informed consent seems unnecessary or at least impractical. For example, a study of the number of people entering a shopping centre at different times of the day seems to fall into this category.

In management research, difficulties over informed consent can arise in a variety of ways. Where students are 'invited' by their teacher to participate as research subjects in, for example, studies of small-group behaviour, there may be significant doubts as to the reality of their freedom of choice. Similarly, company employees who are 'encouraged' by management to cooperate with research investigations may experience a sense of coercion along the lines of 'All those in favour say "yes". All those against say "I resign".' On the other hand, where personal data are already in the public domain, seeking informed consent to use those data is deemed unnecessary. For example, the analysis of statements made by heads of companies in annual reports does not require the informed consent of those concerned.

Deception

The principle of informed consent rules out the involvement of persons in research investigations without their knowledge and agreement. This creates a significant dilemma for many researchers since they know that people are likely to alter their behaviour when they are aware that they are being studied. To deal with this methodological problem of 'reactivity', researchers may wish to conduct covert, 'deceptive' research. Codes of ethics usually have great difficulty with this dilemma. While wishing to uphold the principle of informed consent they also make exceptions to permit deceptive research. The issue remains controversial.

Privacy

Researchers are expected to respect persons' rights to privacy. Broadly speaking, the right to privacy means that individuals should be able to decide what information about themselves they wish to reveal to or withhold from others. Violations of privacy thus include obtaining personal information without the individual's consent as well as the release of such information to third parties.

People are likely to be reluctant to provide researchers with information if they think that in doing so they are exposing themselves to the risk of harm. That harm may be psychological, in the form of embarrassment or stress, or could entail financial hardship and damage to employment and career prospects, as many corporate 'whistle-blowers' have found. To reduce these risks, researchers may offer their informants guarantees of confidentiality, anonymity or both.

Confidentiality applies to information provided by research subjects and means that this information will not be revealed to third parties without the provider's consent. So, for example, while the researcher's report may summarize what most people said during an interview survey, individual interview transcripts will not be published in full or in part.

Anonymity applies to the identities of those who provide information. The implication of a guarantee of anonymity is that although the information provided may be published, the identity of the provider will not be. So, for example, verbatim extracts from an interview may be published but without attribution.

In some cases the researcher will not know the names of those who provide data. Postal surveys which ask people to return questionnaires without any means of identification are of this kind. Subsequent protection of anonymity is then not an issue. However, the researcher may know the identities of informants, particularly in studies involving fieldwork in organizations. In such cases, protection of anonymity may require some care. Merely omitting names from research reports may be insufficient. Quotes attributed to 'the Chief Executive' in a write-up of a company case study are unlikely to do much to safeguard the informant's anonymity.

Box 6.4 Psychologists' code of ethics

3. Obtaining consent

Psychologists shall normally carry out investigations or interventions only with the valid consent of participants, having taken all reasonable steps to ensure that they have adequately understood the nature of the investigation or intervention and its anticipated consequences.

Deception

The issue of deception caused the Committee considerable problems. To many outside the psychology profession, and to some within it, the idea of deceiving the participants in one's research is seen as quite inappropriate. . . . However, since there are very many psychological processes that are modifiable by individuals if they are aware that they are being studied, the statement of the research hypothesis in advance of the collection of data would make much psychological research impossible. . . . While the Committee wishes to urge all psychologists to seek to supply as full information as possible to those taking part in their research, it concluded that the central principle was the reaction of participants when deception was revealed. If this led to discomfort, anger or objections from the participants, then the deception was inappropriate. The Committee hopes that such a principle protects the dignity of the participants while allowing valuable psychological research to be conducted.

Extracts from British Psychological Society (2000)

Limitations of codes of ethics

Codes of ethics can perform a useful function by alerting researchers to the ethical implications of their work. Management researchers should certainly acquaint themselves with the Academy of Management code or with that provided by the appropriate professional association. Even so, ethical codes have two significant limitations:

1 *They usually lack teeth.* As Homan (1991) has observed, professional associations in the social sciences are in a weak position to enforce codes of practice and back them with significant sanctions, since membership is not obligatory for all practitioners.
2 *They are often permissive.* The prescriptions in codes of ethics rarely insist that certain practices *must* be followed. Instead they tend to offer recommendations that *should* be followed, normally, if circumstances allow, etc. Codes are often presented as guidelines rather than rules.

If codes of ethics give the impression of being rather half-hearted, this may be because they have been produced less from moral conviction than from professional expediency (Homan, 1991). At worst they might be seen as public relations exercises which give the appearance of ethical propriety to research while actually ruling little or nothing out. More charitably, it is often the case that ethical problems in social research are complex and that there is no consensus among professionals about appropriate courses of action. If, as some philosophers have argued, right conduct cannot be guaranteed by following general moral rules but is situationally determined, it is no wonder that the professional associations' ethics committees have so much difficulty in formulating clear-cut codes of practice for social and management research.

A case study in research ethics: Milgram's research on obedience to authority

One of the best-known examples of social research to have given rise to ethical controversy is that carried out in the 1960s by the American psychologist Stanley Milgram at Yale University. His work has been variously described as 'classic', 'famous', 'controversial' and 'notorious' (Miller, 1986).

Milgram conducted a series of experiments that were intended to illuminate the processes associated with obedience to authority. In part these studies were motivated by a desire to understand the kind of behaviour which resulted in the systematic extermination of millions of people in the Nazi death-camps during the Second World War. This activity required the obedience of 'ordinary people' to the murderous commands of their superiors. Milgram (1963, p. 371) described the project as follows:

> This article describes a procedure for the study of destructive obedience in the laboratory. It consists of ordering a naïve S[ubject] to administer increasingly severe punishment to a victim in the context of a learning experiment. Punishment is administered by means of a shock generator with 30 graded switches ranging from Slight Shock to Danger: Severe Shock. The victim is a confederate of the E[xperimenter]. The primary dependent variable is the maximum shock the S is willing to administer before he refuses to continue further.

The experimental procedure

In order to study obedience, an experimental apparatus was constructed that would enable the researchers to measure the extent of subjects' conformity to commands. This apparatus consisted of a realistic-looking but fake electric shock generator comprising a control panel linked to an 'electric chair'. The control panel had a row of 30 switches each marked with a voltage level ranging from 15 to 450 volts. Labels under groups of four switches ran from 'Slight Shock' at one end to 'Danger: Severe Shock' near the other. The last two switches were marked 'XXX' to denote indescribable levels of shock.

The subjects, recruited by newspaper advertisements, were told that they were participating in a 'learning experiment' designed to assess the effect of punishment on memory. In this experiment, one of the subjects would act as the teacher and the other as the learner. The teacher would be seated at the control panel. The learner, or 'victim' as Milgram called him, would be strapped into the electric chair in an adjoining room. The teacher would read out a set of word-pairs and then re-read the first word of one pair followed by four alternatives. The learner was to press one of four buttons to indicate which of the four alternatives matched the word in the original pair. The buttons lit a display on the control panel showing the teacher whether the learner had answered correctly.

The subjects were told that each time the learner signalled a wrong answer the teacher was to administer a shock by pressing a switch on the shock-generator. The shock levels were to be increased progressively so that each time the learner gave a wrong answer a stronger shock would be administered. The teacher was to announce the shock level to the learner before administering it.

Each subject was introduced to a 'fellow participant' who was in fact an associate of the researcher. The participants drew lots to decide who would be the teacher and who would be the learner. This process was rigged so that the experimenter's associate always became the learner and the subjects always became the teacher. To convince the subjects that the shock generator was genuine they were connected to the machine and given a small shock. They were also told that the shocks the learner would receive could be 'extremely painful'.

The experimenter's associate had been told that during the experiment he should give correct answers to only one question in four. When the teacher announced a shock level of 300 volts, the associate was to pound the walls of the room and cease giving answers to subsequent questions. The teacher, on the other hand, was told to treat a no answer as a wrong answer and administer the next level of shock whenever the learner failed to respond to a question. Above 315 volts the learner was told to remain silent.

The experiment was conducted by a male experimenter who wore a grey technician's coat and who remained impassive and stern. He issued standard commands to the subject in response to any expressions of unwillingness to continue. Such expressions usually began at the point when the learner pounded the walls. The commands were issued in the following order:

1 'Please continue/Please go on.'
2 'The experiment requires that you continue.'
3 'It is absolutely essential that you continue.'
4 'You have no other choice, you *must* go on.'

If the subject refused to continue after the first command, the second command was issued, and so on. The behaviour of each subject was recorded on tape and they were observed through one-way mirrors.

The results of the experiment

The first experiment involved 40 male subjects aged 20–50. A modest monetary incentive to participate was offered ($4.00) but it was made clear that this was to be kept by the subjects irrespective of how they behaved during the experiment.

All 40 subjects continued to administer shocks to the level of 300 volts, the point at which the learner pounds the wall of the room and ceases to respond to further questions. Fourteen subjects refused to continue, despite the experimenter's commands, at various points between 315 and 450 volts. Twenty-six (65 per cent) of the subjects administered shocks up to the highest level – 450 volts, two switches beyond the label 'Danger: Severe Shock'.

Most subjects displayed signs of considerable tension and nervousness:

> The procedure created extreme levels of nervous tension in some S[ubject]s. Profuse sweating, trembling, and stuttering were typical expressions of this emotional disturbance. . . . In a large number of cases the degree of tension reached extremes that are rarely seen in sociopsychological laboratory studies. Subjects were observed to sweat, tremble, stutter, bite their lips, groan, and dig their fingernails into their flesh. These were characteristic rather than exceptional responses to the experiment.
>
> (Milgram, 1963, pp. 371, 375)

One observer reported:

> I observed a mature and initially poised businessman enter the laboratory smiling and confident. Within 20 minutes he was reduced to a twitching, stuttering wreck, who was rapidly approaching a point of nervous collapse. He constantly pulled on his earlobe, and twisted his hands. At one point he pushed his fist into his forehead and muttered: 'Oh God, let's stop it!' And yet he continued to respond to every word of the experimenter, and obeyed to the end.
>
> (Milgram, 1963, p. 377)

In general, when faced with the choice of inflicting extreme pain on a fellow human being or of defying the experimenter by ignoring his commands, the subjects obeyed authority.

Post-experiment procedures

On completion of each session the subjects were interviewed. Afterwards,

> procedures were undertaken to assure that the subject would leave the laboratory in a state of well being. A friendly reconciliation was arranged between the subject and the victim, and an effort was made to reduce any tensions that arose as a result of the experiment.
>
> (Milgram, 1963, p. 374)

Was the study ethical?

Various objections to this study have been made on ethical grounds (see, for example, Baumrind, 1964):

1   By deceiving the subjects about the purpose of the research, the genuineness of the equipment, the identity of the victim, and the means used to allocate roles of teacher and learner, the research violated the expectation of trust between professional experts and lay members of the public.
2   Subjects were exposed to extreme levels of stress without their consent.
3   The post-experiment procedures cannot be taken to compensate for the distress caused to the subjects.
4   The subjects may have suffered long-term damage to their self-esteem since the fact that they had believed themselves to be inflicting pain in obedience to orders cannot be overturned.
5   The risk of damage to subjects cannot be justified in terms of the significance of the results as a contribution to knowledge.

In defence of his study, Milgram (1964) replied that:

1   The extreme reactions of the subjects had not been intended and were not expected. Subjects could not therefore have been warned in advance.
2   A follow-up questionnaire showed that 84 per cent of the subjects said they were glad to have participated in the experiment.
3   The subjects were never exposed to real danger or injurious effects.
4   The subjects were able to gain valuable insights into their own behaviour.
5   During the experiment the subjects retained their ethical capacity to choose whether or not to obey. They were not forced to obey.
6   It is necessary to accept the risk of unexpected outcomes in research or give up scientific inquiry.

Activity 6.3 Ethical evaluation

You are a member of a university ethics committee which evaluates proposals for research studies. The committee has received a proposal from a group of researchers within the university to replicate Milgram's obedience experiment as described above.

- What ethical issues are raised by the proposal?
- What are the arguments in favour of approving the proposal?
- What are the arguments in favour of rejecting the proposal?
- What would your decision be on whether to allow the research to go ahead?

Key points

1   All research projects have ethical implications. It is up to researchers to be ethically aware and accept responsibility for whatever ethical choices they make.
2   Researchers must familiarize themselves with the legal and ethical requirements of their field and any institutional mechanisms for vetting research proposals.
3   Guarantees of reward, confidentiality and anonymity that are given to research subjects must be honoured.

Key reading

Homan, R. (1991) *The Ethics of Social Research*, London: Longman.

Further reading

Barnes, J.A. (1979) *Who Should Know What? Social Science, Privacy and Ethics*, Harmondsworth, UK: Penguin.

Baumrind, D. (1964) 'Some Thoughts on Ethics of Research: After Reading Milgram's "Behavioral Study of Obedience"', *American Psychologist*, 19, pp. 421–3.

Bok, S. (1978) 'Deceptive Social Science Research', in *Lying: Moral Choice in Public and Private Life*, New York: Pantheon, pp. 182–202.

Colman, A.M. (1987) 'Obedience and Cruelty: Are Most People Potential Killers?', in *Facts, Fallacies and Frauds in Psychology*, London: Hutchinson, pp. 81–108.

Kelman, H.C. (1965) 'Manipulation of Human Behaviour: An Ethical Dilemma for the Social Scientist', *Journal of Social Issues*, 21, pp. 31–46.

Milgram, S. (1963) 'Behavioral Study of Obedience', *Journal of Abnormal and Social Psychology*, 67, pp. 371–8.

Milgram, S. (1964) 'Issues in the Study of Obedience: A Reply to Baumrind', *American Psychologist*, 19, pp. 848–52.

Miller, A.G. (1986) *The Obedience Experiments: A Case Study of Controversy in Social Science*, Westport, CT: Praeger.

Mirvis, P.H. and Seashore, S.E. (1979) 'Being Ethical in Organizational Research', *American Psychologist*, 34, pp. 766–80.

Pinder, C.C. (1977) 'Concerning the Application of Human Motivation Theories in Organizational Settings', *Academy of Management Review*, 2, pp. 384–97.

Tymchuk, A.J. (1982) 'Strategies for Resolving Value Dilemmas, *American Behavioral Scientist*, 26, pp. 159–75.

Warwick, D.P. (1975) 'Social Scientists Ought to Stop Lying', *Psychology Today*, February, pp. 38–40, 105–6.

7   Research strategies

The experiment and survey

In this and the following chapter, I introduce the major research strategies used in management research. We begin with two strategies that are associated with variable analysis, the experiment and the survey. In Chapter 8 we discuss the case study, ethnography and action research. But we begin with the topic of sampling.

Selecting units for study

During the course of designing our study we have to make many methodological decisions about both what to study and how to study it. A well-formulated problem should indicate what sorts of entities we expect to treat as sources of data: perhaps firms or other organizations; perhaps individuals, such as chief executives, middle managers or technical specialists; perhaps financial datasets or company accounts. In addition, we need to decide:

• how these units should be selected;
• how many units should be selected.

How these questions are answered depends partly on the aims of the research. If the intention is to make empirical generalizations, then we need to consider using methods of sampling that will support this aim. Where generalization is not an issue, alternative approaches can be used.

What sampling methods are available?

Given our limited resources, we can never study the whole world but only parts of it. The parts we select for examination are known as the cases, sampling units or units of analysis. They are often individual people but could be other phenomena: groups, organizations, industries, documents, processes, events and even time periods. The total set of elements we are interested in is called the population. Defining the population we wish to study is an important prelude to being able to draw samples from it, but this can be problematic. The term 'manager', for example, is notoriously vague and it is often unclear as to which job titles should be included under this label. In practice it may be difficult to decide who in an organization should be included in a listing of its managers. Similarly, it can be difficult to allocate firms to sector or industry categories.

There are two general methods of sampling: probability and non-probability. Probability methods are those in which all population units have an equal probability (or, strictly speaking, a known probability) of selection. Samples are drawn at random from a list of all the population units known as a sampling frame. Non-probability sampling does not involve random selection and so may produce biased samples that are unrepresentative. This may or may not be a problem, depending on the aims of the research.

Probability methods

The general aim of probability sampling is to obtain a subset of a population that is representative of it. Such samples can be regarded as a kind of surrogate for a population. However, a sample's characteristics will rarely coincide exactly with those found in the population. This 'sampling error' is present whenever samples are used to infer population values.

Box 7.1 What is a probability sample?

A sample is a small-scale representation – a kind of miniature model – of the population from which it was selected. Because it includes merely a part, not all, of the parent population, it can never be an exact replica of that population. But in many respects it will resemble it closely, and it is this resemblance that makes sampling so useful in the study of populations too large to survey in their entirety: the proportions, ratios, averages and other similar measures computed from the sample are likely to correspond to those of the parent population.

(Hedges, 1978, p. 57)

Representativeness is usually aimed for by means of the random selection of population units for inclusion in the study. Methods of random selection include:

- *Simple random sampling.* Ideally, a complete list of the population units is required (the sampling frame). Each unit is then given a number. A second set of numbers is then 'pulled out of the hat' (by reference to a table of random numbers). Units are selected in accordance with the correspondence of their numbers with those picked at random.
- *Systematic random sampling.* This is a simpler method of random sampling. To select a sample of a given size, the sampling fraction is calculated: sample size/population size. For instance, the sampling fraction for a sample of 10 from a population of 100 is 1/10. In this case, following random selection of

one of the first ten units listed in the sampling frame, every tenth unit thereafter is selected.

- *Stratified random sampling.* The logic behind stratified sampling is to use known characteristics of the population during sampling in order to increase the likelihood of selecting a representative sample. For example, suppose we wish to draw a sample of 20 individuals from a population of 100 executives consisting of 50 women and 50 men. Simple random sampling could produce a skewed or even a single-sex sample. Stratified sampling means that we divide the population into two groups, male and female, and draw random samples from within these subgroups. This ensures that women and men will be represented in the sample in proportion to their preponderance in the population. Stratified sampling thus increases the likelihood that a sample will be representative.

  Stratified sampling is more complex than simple random sampling. It requires knowledge of which variables are important from the point of view of the aims of the research. In addition, the sampling frame must contain information on these stratifying variables for each unit.

- *Cluster sampling.* Also known as area sampling, this method can be used when no complete sampling frame exists for the population of interest and where it would be impractical to create one. It involves random sampling of units at various levels. For example, a sample of managers might be drawn by first drawing a random sample of geographical areas. Within the selected areas a random sample of organizations is chosen. Finally, within the selected organizations a random sample of managers is identified.

Non-probability methods

Where empirical generalization is the aim, probability sampling is desirable from a statistical point of view because the theory of statistical inference assumes that data are derived from such samples. However, in practice, studies drawing on data from random samples are the exception rather than the rule in management research (Freeman, 1986). Non-random samples are often the only practical alternative. Although their adequacy as a basis for generalization is always in question, this does not diminish their importance for research purposes.

- *Quota sampling.* Like stratified sampling, the intention of quota sampling is to use information about the population's characteristics to improve the likelihood of drawing a representative sample. A specific number (a quota) of population members with specified characteristics are chosen. But, unlike in stratified sampling, strictly random selection procedures are not used. For example, an interviewer may simply be asked to select 'ten young males and ten young females', so allowing the interviewer's preferences to enter, consciously or, more probably, unconsciously, into the selection process. This can result in a biased sample.

- *Availability/convenience sampling.* Sometimes this is just a respectable-sounding term meaning that your sample includes anyone you could get! This approach may produce samples consisting of volunteers, who are, by definition, self-selected. In some types of management research, students, such as those taking management courses, may be more or less willingly recruited as research subjects. Given practical constraints, it may be necessary and desirable to use this method, particularly for pilot and exploratory studies.

- *Purposive sampling.* Where the researcher possesses sufficient knowledge, it may be possible to select one or a few units because they have characteristics relevant to the objectives of the study. For example, in political election studies a particular electoral district may be known on the basis of previous experience to be a reliable indicator of national voting intentions. More generally, exceptional or unusual cases may be selected for intensive examination either in their own right or as a prelude to a wider study.

- *Theoretical sampling.* This method is closely associated with the grounded theory approach developed by Glaser and Strauss (1967). The intention is to develop theories of social processes as they are being studied in the field. As theoretical categories and propositions emerge, the researcher's attention is directed towards data that will test, develop and extend the theory. The sampling of units for observation takes place throughout the fieldwork and is theoretically rather than statistically driven. As Locke (2001, p. 55) says, 'The rationale of theoretical sampling, then, is to direct all data gathering efforts towards gathering information that will best support development of the theoretical framework.'

How many units are needed?

The question 'How many units are needed?' is difficult to answer in the abstract. At a minimum, the obvious answer is at least one – or possibly, and non-obviously, less than one (see March *et al.*, 1991)! The case-study strategy, for example, may entail investigation of a single case, although larger numbers are needed for comparative work.

In survey research, by contrast, relatively large numbers of units will be required. Sample sizes are likely to be influenced by both technical and practical considerations. On the technical side, as sample size increases, the magnitude of sampling errors decreases, although at a diminishing rate. How much error is acceptable will influence decisions about ideal sample size. Also, various kinds of statistical analysis cannot be undertaken without sufficient cases being available. The number of subgroups that will be analysed separately is a key consideration. A size of 50–100 for the smallest subgroup has been recommended (Hoinville *et al.*, 1978, p. 61). In practical terms, funding constraints are likely to limit sample sizes and these are likely to be quite tight in research degree studies.

In my experience, samples of around 200 cases usually give sufficient scope for analysis of survey data. Others suggest either lower minimum limits, perhaps

100 or even 30 (Bailey, 1994, p. 97), or higher ones, perhaps 1,000 (Hoinville *et al.*, 1978, p. 61). At the upper end, 5,000 cases has been suggested as a maximum for most purposes by Hoinville *et al.* (1978, p. 61), although these authors are writing in the context of large-scale government surveys. Many survey organizations use no more than about 2,000–2,500 cases (de Vaus, 1990, p. 73; Marshall, 1998, p. 576) but even those numbers are likely to be beyond the reach of the research student. A general rule of thumb is: 'As few as you must, as many as you can.'

Problems with sampling

It is tempting to believe that large sample sizes ensure that a sample will be representative, but this is not necessarily so, as the *Literary Digest* fiasco shows (Box 7.2). Described by Shipman (1988, p. 58) as 'the greatest blunder in survey history', it shows that even gigantic samples do not guarantee representation.

Box 7.2 There's safety in numbers?

The *Literary Digest* magazine sent a postal questionnaire to a sample of 10 million American voters in an attempt to predict the outcome of the 1936 US presidential election. The magazine predicted that Landon, the Republican candidate, would win. In fact, he lost to the Democrat, Roosevelt. The error was attributed to various factors, including (a) a 20 per cent response rate, and (b) the fact that telephone directories were used as the sampling frame, which excluded many poorer voters who tended to vote Democrat. Even responses from 2 million voters could not guarantee an accurate result.

Source: Moser (1967). See also Squire (1988)

It is also important to note that random sampling does not *guarantee* a sample's representativeness. It makes it probable but not certain. If, for example, you were to draw a simple random sample of 100 firms from a population of 200 in which 50 per cent were manufacturing companies and 50 per cent were retailers, it is probable that your sample would contain approximately equal numbers of each. But it could still turn out that the sample contained all 100 firms from the same industry. Improbable events are not expected to occur very often but that does not mean that they can never occur at all.

A further difficulty is the absence or inadequacy of sampling frames. Frequently, complete listings of population units do not exist and substitutes must be used. Surveys of managers in Britain, for example, have often been based on the membership lists of management organizations such as the Chartered Management Institute. Since the population from which the samples have been selected is restricted to those managers who happen to be members, so are the inferences that can be drawn from the surveys. There have been a number of surveys of managers in Britain but none gives a strictly representative picture because no complete sampling frame exists. Even where sampling frames do exist, they may be inaccurate, out of date or expensive to obtain.

Statisticians tend to make a song and dance about sampling that you may find intimidating but this needs to be resisted. Although the basic principles need to be understood, the more technical aspects of sampling theory and methodology are most likely to be relevant to large-scale survey projects and when dealing with purely quantitative datasets. In research degree studies in management, as in other kinds of social research, reliance is increasingly being placed on availability samples. As Punch has noted (1998, p. 105), 'Very often indeed, the researcher must take whatever sample is available.' It is perhaps worth noting that doctors make significant medical decisions on the basis of blood samples that are not drawn using strict statistical probability methods. In sampling, as elsewhere in research, ingenuity – not to mention a strong stomach – is often required in order to make progress.

Experimental designs

Like so much research terminology, the term 'experiment' is used with several meanings. It may be used to refer to any systematic test or trial of some new technique or the implementation of an innovation. However, from the point of view of research design, its most important meaning is as the classical controlled experiment.

The experiment is often seen as a symbol of true scientific method. Although experimental research is the exception rather than the rule in management studies, other strategies draw on the logic of the experiment. It is for this reason, rather than because you are likely to carry out a full-blown experiment in your own research, that it is important to understand the thinking behind experimental designs.

The logic of the experiment

The experiment is based on two basic assumptions:

1   The world is to be conceived of as a set of interrelated variables.
2   The aim of research is to identify causal connections between variables.

Experimental designs are those which seek to make possible the identification of causal connections between variables with high degrees of confidence. At its simplest, the experiment deals with two variables. The researcher's problem is to establish whether these variables are causally related. Typically, the researcher will have a theoretically derived hypothesis which states that changes in the values of one variable cause concomitant changes in the values of another. The variable that is thought to be causing the changes is called the independent variable; the variable that is being changed by it is called the dependent variable, because its values are, or are hypothesized to be, dependent on those of the independent variable.

To establish whether the independent and dependent variables are causally related, the experiment focuses upon two factors, comparison and control. The aim is to compare changes in the values of the independent variable with changes in the values of the dependent variable while controlling for the effects of other, extraneous variables. Experimental design aims to isolate the dependent variable from all potential causal influences except the independent variable, so that any variation in the dependent variable can only be attributed to the independent variable.

To see how this might, and might not, be achieved, we will examine some alternative experimental designs. In the accompanying diagrams, each row indic-ates how the researcher intends to study a group of research subjects. The row is divided into three time periods designated as T1, T2, T3. According to the nature of the design, observations are to be made to measure the dependent vari-able during one or more of these periods. Exposure to the independent variable is referred to as the treatment, which always occurs before the final observations since presumed causes must precede presumed effects.

Pseudo-experiments

Pseudo-experiments are those designs that claim to be able to establish causal relationships among variables but which fail to do so. Campbell and Stanley (1963) give examples of several types of what they call 'pre-experimental' designs.

The one-group post-test

T = time period	T1	T2	T3
Group 1		Treatment	Observation

The main features of this design are:

1   One group is observed after exposure to a treatment (the independent variable).
2   The condition of the group (the dependent variable) is attributed to the effects of the treatment.

For example, a group of managers graduate with MBAs and secure highly paid jobs. The business school claims that its MBA has caused their career success. Here the MBA programme is the independent variable and the managers' jobs are the dependent variable. The difficulty with this design is that it does not eliminate the possibility that something other than the treatment caused the observed effects: maybe the managers held just as good jobs before taking the MBA. Because the design does not require any observations of the value of the dependent variable to be taken before the treatment is applied, we cannot even tell whether the dependent variable has changed, still less that it has done so because of the treatment.

The one-group pre-test/post-test

	T1	T2	T3
Group 1	Observation	Treatment	Observation

In this design the group is measured on the dependent variable both before and after the treatment, hence 'pre-test/post-test'. Differences between the 'before' and 'after' measures are taken to indicate that the treatment has caused changes in the dependent variable. As with the previous design, alternative explanations are not ruled out. These can include:

- *History.* An external event, other than the treatment, may have happened between the times of the first and last measurement; and that event may have caused the value of the dependent variable to change.
- *Maturation.* An internal process may have been under way that changed the value of the dependent variable.
- *Testing.* Changes in the dependent variable may be due to a learning effect; the second application of the measure of the dependent variable may itself result in changed outcomes.
- *Instrumentation.* The procedures used to measure the dependent variable may have changed between the times when the first and second set of observations are made; this might in itself have produced different results.

The static group comparison

	T1	T2	T3
Group 1		Treatment	Observation
Group 2			Observation

Here two groups are compared with each other in terms of the value of the dependent variable, one group having received the treatment and the other not having done so. If the values of the dependent variable differ for the groups, it is inferred that this difference reflects the effects of the treatment. The difficulty here is that there is no guarantee that the two groups were similar *before* one of them was exposed to the treatment: observed differences may be a consequence of the way the members of the groups were selected.

The classical experiment

	T1	T2	T3
Random Group 1	Observation	Treatment	Observation
Random Group 2	Observation		Observation

The classical experimental design serves to overcome the difficulties associated with these pseudo-experimental designs. The subjects of the experiment are randomly assigned to two groups. The value of the dependent variable is measured for both groups at T1. During T2, one group, the experimental group, receives the treatment while the other group, the control group, does not. At T3, measures of the dependent variable are again taken for both groups. A statistical procedure known as the 'analysis of variance' (see p. 124) is used to assess the probability that the differences between the groups are due to the different treatments rather than chance.

Quasi-experiments

Quasi-experiments are designs that follow the spirit if not the letter of the classical controlled experiment. These designs attempt to realize the goals of comparison and control but do so in a partial way. So, for example, the control group logic

---

Box 7.3 Experimenting without visible means of support

In social research, and especially in psychology, the experiment is associated with the use of expensive and elaborate laboratory facilities such as those used by Milgram (1963) in his obedience studies. But there is one kind of experiment that requires nothing of this kind: the thought experiment. Hypotheses are tested by running imagined experiments, using the logic of comparison and control to explore possible outcomes under different conditions. Historians, for example, cannot re-run history to see what might have happened if a key event or circumstance had been different. But they can try to estimate the effects of such counterfactual conditions by providing a reasoned argument based on knowledge of the behavioural dispositions of the historical actors. Thought experiments are a part of our everyday reasoning capacity, in which we make disciplined use of the imagination to project the consequences of our own and others' actions. As such, they not only are indispensable to the craft of research but also have the advantage that they can be conducted at virtually no cost other than the expenditure of brainpower.

may be followed, seeking to find closely comparable groups but without the random assignment of subjects to groups or groups to treatments. Or the groups may be exposed to different conditions of the independent variable but without the experimenter being able to manipulate it at will.

Problems with experiments

The validity of experimental findings is threatened by several factors. Following Campbell and Stanley (1963), we have already identified *history, maturation, testing, instrumentation* and *selection*. In principle, these can be warded off by adopting the classical experimental design. But further problems arise from the reactive nature of the laboratory experiment and the subtle influence of experimenter effects (Jung, 1971). These difficulties are much more difficult, and perhaps impossible, to overcome.

Reactivity and the experiment

Critics of the experiment argue that because experiments are artificial situations, people react to them in artificial ways. In the social sciences, experiments are conducted with human beings rather than on atoms and molecules, and people interpret experimental situations and behave accordingly. For example, some critics of Milgram's obedience studies (see Chapter 6) claimed that his results were invalid because the subjects would not have really believed that they were hurting anyone. They continued to administer shocks only because they believed they were participating in a psychological hoax, a claim that Milgram (1964) denied.

Orne (1962) has argued that many laboratory experiments have implicit 'demand characteristics'. Participants seem to make sense of the situation by anticipating the sorts of behaviour they think the experiment demands of them. They then supply that behaviour. For example, if participants in a group experiment think that the investigator is trying to study conflict, they may spend a lot of time arguing, irrespective of the experimenter's intentions.

The artificiality of the laboratory experimental situation raises questions about both the internal and the external validity of results. Equally problematic are the unintended effects of the experimenter's expectations on the experiment's outcomes.

Experimenter effects

Experimenter effects are the ways in which the researcher may influence the behaviour of participants in experiments in ways that neither are aware of and which significantly affect experimental outcomes. Rosenthal (1966) conducted a series of studies designed to assess the impact of experimenters' expectations on the outcomes of experiments. Generally, when experimenters expected a particular outcome they found it, even when the groups they were working with were identical. It seems that the experimenters' expectations about outcomes were conveyed more or less subtly to the experimental subjects. The implication is that outcomes may be effects generated by the experimenter rather than by the independent variables introduced into the experiment.

Box 7.4 Example experiments in management studies

Bloomfield, R. and O'Hara, M. (1999) 'Market Transparency: Who Wins and Who Loses?', *Review of Financial Studies*, 12, pp. 5–35.

Copeland, T.E. and Friedman, D. (1987) 'The Effect of Sequential Information Arrival on Asset Prices: An Experimental Study', *Journal of Finance*, 42, pp. 763–97.

Flood, M., Huisman, R., Koedjik, K. and Mahieu, R. (1999) 'Quote Disclosure and Price Discovery in Multiple-Dealer Financial Markets', *Review of Financial Studies*, 12, pp. 37–59.

Lam, S.S.K. and Schaubroeck, J. (2000) 'The Role of Locus of Control in Reactions to Being Promoted and to Being Passed Over: A Quasi Experiment', *Academy of Management Journal*, 43, pp. 66–79.

McEvoy, G.M. (1997) 'Organizational Change and Outdoor Management Education', *Human Resource Management*, 36, pp. 235–50.

Punnett, B.J. (1988) 'Designing Field Experiments for Management Research outside North America', *International Studies of Management and Organization*, 18 (3), pp. 44–54.

Seers, A. and Woodruff, S. (1997) 'Temporal Pacing in Taskforces: Group Development or Deadline Pressure', *Journal of Management*, 23, pp. 169–87.

Wayne, S. and Ferris, G.R. (1990) 'Influence Tactics, Affect and Exchange Quality in Supervisor–Subordinate Interactions: A Laboratory Experiment and Field Study', *Journal of Applied Psychology*, 75, pp. 461–8.

When is an experiment appropriate?

The logic of the experiment has a wide range of applications but the use of experimental research designs is less common. The classical experiment imposes methodological constraints that are often difficult or impossible to meet in the social sciences. Laboratory experiments may require elaborate facilities, allocation of research subjects to experimental and control groups can be problematic, and the management of an experimental study may well be beyond the resources of a single researcher working alone. Quasi-experiments, however, offer considerable opportunities for ingenious designs.

The experiment works best with clear hypotheses and readily quantifiable variables. This often means that the issues explored through the strategy of the experiment are derived from a well-developed theory. The experimental strategy is likely to be appropriate, then, when it is possible to test formal hypotheses using quantified measures.

Activity 7.1 Design your own experiment

A simple motivation theory predicts that the more you reward people for output, the more they will produce. Imagine that you could use a group of your fellow students as research subjects. How would you set about testing this proposition using an experimental strategy?

- How would you define and measure the independent and dependent variables?
- How would you control the effects of other variables?
- How would you brief the subjects on their participation in the experiment?

The survey

The nature and uses of surveys

A survey can be used to gather information on a wide variety of topics, but a key distinction is between surveys that are intended only to yield descriptions of the characteristics of a population and those which aim to test explanatory propositions. Government and commercial surveys are frequently designed with the former objective in mind whereas management researchers are more concerned with the latter.

A survey which aims to obtain information from all the members of a defined population is known as a census. Where the population is very large (e.g. as in a national census), costs are correspondingly high. A more usual type of survey is the sample survey, which uses information from a subset of the population as a basis for estimating population values or parameters. Since generalization from the sample is usually aimed for, the adequacy of the sampling process is of fundamental importance.

Methods of delivery

The traditional methods of conducting a survey are by means of postal, self-completion questionnaires and by interviewing. Telephone interviews are also frequently used in opinion polling and market research. Many studies combine these methods in an attempt to offset the disadvantages of relying on one method alone. With the advent of the Internet and the spread of personal computers, a new type of survey has emerged, the Internet survey, in which questions are delivered via the Web. Each method has certain advantages and disadvantages.

Table 7.1 Methods of delivering a survey: strengths and weaknesses.

	Interview	Mail	Telephone	Internet
Response rate	High	Medium/low	High	Medium/low
Response quality	High	Medium	High	Medium/high
Sample size	Small	Large	Medium	Medium/high
Dispersed groups	Poor	Good	Good	Good
Unit cost	High	Low	Medium	Medium/high

Table 7.1 provides a tentative comparison of these methods of delivery. In practice, the appropriateness of each of these methods has to be judged in terms of the specific nature of the project and the skills and other resources available to carry it out — all part of the craftwork of research.

Postal, self-completion surveys

Self-completion questionnaires are those which respondents are expected to answer alone, without the assistance of an interviewer. Because they are delivered by post and completed unaided, they are a relatively cheap survey instrument. However, the self-completion questionnaire has to be a 'self-sufficient' document: because the researcher is not on hand to clarify unclear questions and to motivate the recipient to participate in the survey, great care must be taken to deal with these issues in print in order to minimize threats to response quality.

Because of its low costs, the questionnaire can be used to reach large samples. It may also be the only practical way of reaching geographically dispersed or socially inaccessible groups. However, it often suffers from relatively low response rates. On average, rates of around 40–50 per cent may be expected. It is sobering to realize that the most likely destination for a postal questionnaire is the waste bin. Low levels of response offset cost advantages and are likely to result in biased samples.

A further problem is that the self-completion questionnaire can be unwieldy if the target group contains many subgroups each of which is required to be asked specific questions. It may also be unsuited for the investigation of some complex and sensitive topics.

Face-to-face interview surveys

After the self-completion questionnaire, the interview is probably the most widely used survey method. Many surveys combine a large-scale postal survey with a smaller interview study of members of the same population. Normally some interview work is required as a prelude to the design of self-completion questionnaires.

The advantages and disadvantages of the face-to-face interview mirror those of the self-completion questionnaire. Its advantages include higher response rates, better control of response, and the capacity to deal with complex, sensitive topics. The presence of an interviewer can serve to motivate potential respondents to participate and to maintain their interest over what may be a lengthy series of questions. Interviewers can also control the order in which questions are answered and clarify unclear terms or ambiguous questions. Where topics are complex and difficult to reduce to a concise set of questions and where the issues are sensitive, interviewing may be the only practical survey approach.

The disadvantages of the face-to-face interview include its relatively high cost to both interviewers and interviewees since one or other is usually involved in travel. It also requires the researcher to possess interviewing expertise in addition to the skills of questionnaire design. Finally, the presence of an interviewer, while introducing flexibility, also opens up the possibility that interviewer bias will distort the data.

Telephone interview surveys

Telephone surveys stand somewhere between postal questionnaires and face-to-face interviewing. Like face-to-face interviews, they require interviewing expertise in a situation that is made more difficult by the absence of visual feedback. However, they are economical since they avoid travel costs. They are also the fastest means of carrying out a survey, provided that those contacted can be persuaded to participate. By comparison, questionnaires may take weeks to be returned and face-to-face interviews may need to be arranged well in advance.

Internet surveys

Although a Web-based survey might seem to be an attractive option, like the more traditional methods it involves both costs and benefits. For example, computer technology enables automatic sequencing. When, following an answer to a question, the respondent needs to be directed to another part of the questionnaire, this can be done automatically. Similarly, automatic validation of answers can be given: if the respondent gives a response that is out of range, this can be indicated with a request for another try.

However, the limited experience with Internet surveys to date indicates that they are not obviously superior to more traditional means. Their use is, of course, restricted to populations that can be reached by Web access, and where e-mail directories do not exist, random sampling is problematic. In particular, Web-based surveys are vulnerable to technical problems at the design and implementation stage, particularly in the hands of inexperienced users (Schonlau *et al.*, 2002).

Objectives of survey design

In general, the two key objectives when designing surveys are to:

- *Maximize the quantity of response.* As the example of the *Literary Digest* fiasco shows, a large responding sample is not necessarily a representative sample. Nonetheless, survey researchers are concerned to maximize the number of questionnaires returned and so achieve a high response rate (defined as the number of respondents participating in the survey as a percentage of those contacted). Each unreturned questionnaire represents a cost, and statistical analysis is likely to be inhibited if the number of cases falls below a minimum.

• *Maximize the quality of response.* Even a large number of returned questionnaires will not be of great value if the quality of the responses is low. There are at least four elements of response quality:

1 Have all the questions been correctly understood by the respondent?
2 Can all answers be correctly understood by the analyst?
3 Have all questions been answered in the correct mode? For example, if the respondents are asked to circle a number or tick a box to indicate an answer, then have they done this and not done other things that may make it impossible to be sure what their answer is?
4 Have all relevant questions been answered? Respondents may be routed to different parts of the questionnaire depending on their answers to certain questions. If some questions have been overlooked or if sections that are not appropriate have been filled in, this detracts from the response quality.

These objectives are interrelated. For example, if the questions are difficult to understand, recipients may give up trying to complete the questionnaire and this will depress response rates. To achieve these objectives the researcher must pay careful attention to the design of the survey and especially to question design, questionnaire layout and survey administration. Because question design is so crucial, I will deal with this in detail in Chapter 9.

Questionnaire layout refers to the visual impact of the questionnaire or interview schedule. With postal surveys this can have an important impact on response rates. With interview schedules, good layout can make the interviewer's tasks much easier and reduce the likelihood of interviewer error. A postal questionnaire should:

• *Be visually attractive.* It must be easy on the eye and have a businesslike appearance.
• *Look short.* Careful layout can keep the number of pages to a minimum. Grouping the questions into sections and numbering them within sections can reduce the impression of there being many questions. Instead of the last question appearing as Q.150 it could be given as J.15.
• *Look interesting.* The main problem is getting people to start completing the questionnaire. It may be necessary to put an interest-grabbing question at the start of the questionnaire even if the information it asks for is not really required. Avoid asking for personal or background details at the start, such as name, age, sex, address, occupation, and so on. This is information most people have written on forms hundreds of times, and the last thing we want

to do is to give the impression that this is yet another boring form-filling exercise.

- *Be easy to complete.* Clear instructions must be given indicating how to give answers (tick, write in, and so on) and what sequence of questions to follow.
- *Be easy to return.* Although postal questionnaires will usually be sent out with a prepaid return envelope, always place the return address on the questionnaire itself. Prepaid envelopes can be mislaid and there is nothing likely to frustrate respondents more than having spent considerable time completing a questionnaire only to discover that they have no way of returning it.

The key point to keep in mind is that while the survey may be a source of important data for us, it may be seen by its recipients as simply a source of irritation. It is up to the researcher to ensure that recipients are engaged by the survey rather than alienated by it.

Conducting a survey

Box 7.5 shows the main stages in the conduct of a survey once the topic of investigation has been decided. Whatever the method of delivery adopted, the same care needs to be devoted to the survey's design. During the design process, the following questions have to be answered:

Box 7.5 Stages in conducting a survey

1 Define population.
2 Obtain/construct sampling frame.
3 Decide sample size.
4 Choose sampling method.
5 Define survey content.
6 Decide method(s) of delivery: self-completion questionnaire, face-to-face interview, telephone interview, Internet survey.
7 Design survey instruments: questionnaires, interview schedules.
8 Design incentives: financial, material, normative.
9 Conduct pilot study.
10 Amend survey methods.
11 Deliver survey.
12 Edit responses.
13 Analyse and interpret results.
14 Prepare presentation and feedback.

- *Who will be contacted?* The population to be contacted must be defined as clearly as possible. A sampling frame must then be obtained, or created by the researcher if it does not already exist. For example, company listings such as the *Times 1000* may be adequate for generating samples of larger firms, but a list of chief executives of small and medium-sized enterprises (SMEs) in a particular city may have to be created from scratch. The sample size and sampling method must be decided, taking into account technical and practical considerations.

- *What information will be requested?* Once the overall topic of the survey has been established, this must be broken down into areas and sub-areas and finally into questions and scales (see Chapter 9). Content decisions are made by reference to previous studies, to the theoretical framework of the research, and to the study's research questions. How much information can be sought with a reasonable expectation of cooperation from respondents is a matter of judgement in individual cases. Surveys dealing with topics that are of high interest to the survey population may be more successful in making demands on respondents than those that are perceived to be of marginal or no interest.
- *How will it be obtained?* Will the survey use self-completion questionnaires, interviews, telephone contact or the Internet? Combinations of methods are possible. One useful approach is to use a small-scale interview programme in conjunction with a large-scale questionnaire survey. Some interviewing with population members and others knowledgeable about the topic is usually necessary during the process of specifying content. A trial run with the survey questionnaire or interview schedule is essential before launching the main study, using a small sample of the population. Ten to twenty cases is likely to be sufficient, but even the feedback one person can provide can be extremely valuable in revealing flaws in the questions.

  Thought also needs to be given to what incentives might be offered to induce those surveyed to participate. The completion of questionnaires and participation in interviews involves costs for the subjects. Their time is always taken and sometimes there may be psychological costs such as anxiety and boredom. Financial incentives, such as small cash rewards, and material incentives, such as gifts, have sometimes been used in commercial surveys. Academic studies are more likely to have to rely on 'normative' incentives or 'friendly persuasion'. The offer of a summary (not the entirety) of the survey's results may prove effective. Making the survey interesting and easy to follow will also help motivate respondents to participate. Simply demanding participation without offering anything in return is unlikely to be much help.
- *How will it be analysed?* Where questions have required written answers (open questions) rather than 'ticks in boxes' (pre-coded questions), those answers will need to be categorized and coded. Coding involves the construction of answer categories for each question and the allocation of numerals to identify each category and so render the data machine-readable. This qualitative analysis precedes statistical analysis of the data (see Chapter 12). Completed questionnaires may also require some editing to check that the

Table 7.2 An example data matrix, survey of staff: seven cases, six variables.

Case number	Variable 1: Age	Variable 2: Sex	Variable 3: Job title	Variable 4: Company size	Variable 5: Qualification	Variable 6: Function
001	1	1	3	2	2	3
002	1	2	2	4	1	4
003	3	2	1	1	2	1
004	2	1	2	3	1	1
005	3	1	1	2	1	2
006	1	2	3	4	2	3
007	2	1	2	1	1	4

Codes: V1 Age: <21 = 1, 21–40 = 2, >40 = 3
V2 Sex: Female = 1, Male = 2
V3 Job title: Director = 1, Manager = 2, Supervisor = 3
V4 Company size: Very large = 1, Large = 2, Medium = 3, Small = 4
V5 Qualification: MBA = 1, No MBA = 2
V6 Function: Finance = 1, HRM = 2, Production = 3, Marketing = 4

contents are complete. Partially completed or illegible questionnaires may need to be removed from the study at this stage.

Survey data are usually organized in the form of a data matrix before computer processing (see Table 7.2). In the data matrix each case is allocated to a row and a variable to each column. Each row contains the data on all the variables included in the survey for each case. The intersection of the rows and columns contains the value of a variable for a specific case. The entries in the first row, for example, indicate that this manager (case 001) is under 21 years of age, is female, a supervisor, in a large company, has no MBA and works in production.

Data from a survey will typically be analysed using a statistical package such as SPSS or Minitab (see Chapter 12). Statistical packages usually accept data in the form of a data matrix. The analytical procedures that are likely to be used need to be reviewed during the design stage of the survey because they may affect decisions on sample size. Survey data are typically analysed using frequency distributions, cross-tabulations and correlational analyses.

Problems with surveys

Obtaining representative samples

Surveys typically rely on samples of the population as sources of data. To the extent that researchers wish to generalize from survey results, the degree to which their samples are representative of the populations from which they are drawn is crucial. Because most surveys experience non-response, the responding sample cannot be assumed to be a random selection from the population even if the original, target sample was. Researchers can try to assess how representative the responding sample is by comparing its key characteristics with those of the target sample. For example, a survey of companies might compare the two samples in terms of company size, industry and geographical location and assess the degree to which they match.

Box 7.6 Caution: survey in progress

Survey literature abounds with portentous conclusions based on faulty inferences from insufficient evidence misguidedly collected and wrongly assembled.

(Oppenheim, 1992, p. 7)

Obtaining valid answers

Answers to survey questions may be invalid owing to a variety of factors. Questions may be misunderstood, answers may be inaccurate or falsified for various reasons, and interviewers may influence respondents' answers in subtle, unintended ways. Coping with these problems is a major concern when designing surveys. We will examine them in more depth in Chapter 9 together with possible ways of dealing with them.

Mail surveys have a further drawback. Strictly speaking, we do not know who answered the questionnaire, or what condition they were in when they did so. Researchers tend to assume, often implicitly, that each of their questionnaires is completed in a quiet room, during working hours, by the person to whom it was sent, who is fully awake, has good recall, is interested in the survey topic, and is not under the influence of mood-altering substances. These assumptions cannot necessarily be relied on.

Other problems

Survey methods have been subjected to a number of additional criticisms. De Vaus (1990) lists and comments on 10 issues. Several of these are related to the criticisms of variable analysis I mentioned in Chapter 3. How serious these problems are and the extent to which they can be solved or ameliorated continues to be a matter of debate.

When is a survey appropriate?

Large-scale surveys are relatively rare in management studies except for those carried out by government and commercial research organizations. Resource constraints and the organizationally focused nature of much management research may partly account for this, together with a more general move away from survey methodology in some social sciences in recent decades. Smaller-scale survey

---

Box 7.7 Example surveys in management studies

Chaston, I., Badger, B. and Sadler-Smith, E. (2001) 'Organizational Learning: An Empirical Assessment of Process in Small U.K. Manufacturing Firms', *Journal of Small Business Management*, 39, pp. 139–51.

Clarke, R.N., Conyon, M.J. and Peck, S.I. (1998) 'Corporate Governance and Directors' Remuneration: Views from the Top', *Business Strategy Review*, 9 (4), pp. 21–30.

Cui, G. and Liu, Q. (2001) 'Executive Insights: Emerging Market Segments in a Transitional Economy: A Study of Urban Consumers in China', *Journal of International Marketing*, 9, pp. 84–106.

Cully, M., Woodland, S., O'Reilly, A. and Dix, G. (1999) *Britain at Work: As Depicted by the 1998 Workplace Employee Relations Survey*, London: Routledge.

Gersick, C.J.G., Bartunek, J.M. and Dutton, J.E. (2000) 'Learning from Academia: The Importance of Relationships in Professional Life', *Academy of Management Journal*, 43, pp. 1026–44.

Hofstede, G. (1980a) *Culture's Consequences: International Differences in Work-Related Values*, Beverly Hills, CA: Sage.

Konrad, A.M. and Mangel, R. (2000) 'The Impact of Work–Life Programs on Firm Productivity', *Strategic Management Journal*, 21, pp. 1225–37.

Lane, N. (2000) 'The Management Implications of Women's Employment Disadvantage in a Female-Dominated Profession: A Study of NHS Nursing', *Journal of Management Studies*, 37, pp. 705–31.

Leong, S.W., Sheth, J.N. and Tan, C.T. (1993) 'An Empirical Study of the Scientific Styles of Marketing Academics', *European Journal of Marketing*, 28 (8/9), pp. 12–26.

Marshall, R.S. and Boush, D.M. (2001) 'Dynamic Decision-Making: A Cross-cultural Comparison of U.S. and Peruvian Export Managers', *Journal of International Business Studies*, 32, pp. 873–93.

Murtha, T.P., Lenway, S.A. and Bagozzi, R.P. (1998) 'Global Mind-Sets and Cognitive Shift in a Complex Multinational Corporation', *Strategic Management Journal*, 19, pp. 97–114.

---

studies of managers and other employees within organizations are more realistic for degree research.

For the survey to be effective, the investigator needs a well worked out theoretical scheme or analytical framework to inform design decisions. The survey is relatively inflexible, particularly when using self-completion questionnaires. Knowing which questions are worth asking before the survey is launched is therefore vital. Exploratory and pilot work is normally required. Adequate sampling frames must also be either available or able to be constructed by the investigator.

Activity 7.2 Conduct your own survey

1 Design 20–25 questions on the topic of 'Your Leisure Interests and Activities' for distribution to a small 'availability' sample of your friends and colleagues.
2 Organize your set of questions as a self-completion questionnaire. Suggested procedure:

- Decide the general topics to be covered, e.g. sports, hobbies, cultural pursuits, etc.
- Divide the topics into sub-topics.
- Formulate questions that address each sub-topic. Include both pre-coded and open questions.
- Decide the order of presentation of topics, sub-topics and questions.
- Construct the layout of the questionnaire.

3 Fill out your own answers to the questions to see how well the questionnaire works.
4 Ask 10–20 people to complete the questionnaire.
5 Enter the data from each questionnaire as a row in a data matrix in preparation for analysis.

Key points

1 From within the framework of variable analysis, the controlled experiment offers the only way of making strong claims about causal relations.
2 Explanatory surveys substitute statistical controls for experimental controls but the underlying logic is the same as for the experiment.

Key reading

de Vaus, D.A. (1990) *Surveys in Social Research*, London: Routledge.
Griffin, R. and Kacmar, K.M. (1991) 'Laboratory Research in Management: Misconceptions and Missed Opportunities', *Journal of Organizational Behavior*, 12, pp. 301–11.

Further reading

The experiment

Campbell, D.T. (1979) 'Reforms as Experiments', in J. Bynner and K.M. Stribley (eds) *Social Research: Principles and Procedures*, Harlow, UK: Longman, pp. 79–112.

Campbell, D.T. and Stanley, J.C. (1963) *Experimental and Quasi-experimental Designs for Research*, Chicago: Rand McNally.

Evan, W.M. (1971) *Organizational Experiments: Laboratory and Field Research*, New York: Harper and Row.

Field, A. and Hole, G. (2002) *How to Design and Report Experiments*, London: Sage.

Jung, J. (1971) *The Experimenter's Dilemma*, New York: Harper and Row.

Punnett, B.J. (1988) 'Designing Field Experiments for Management Research outside North America', *International Studies of Management and Organization*, 18, pp. 44–54.

Strube, M. (1994) 'Experimentation as Reality', *Journal of Applied Behavioral Science*, 30, pp. 402–7.

The survey

Czaya, R. and Blair, J. (1995) *Designing Surveys*, London: Sage.

Fink, A. and Kosecoff, J. (1998) *How to Conduct Surveys: A Step-by-Step Guide*, London: Sage.

Goyder, J.C. (1988) *The Silent Majority: Nonrespondents in Sample Surveys*, Oxford: Polity Press.

Hoinville, G., Jowell, R. and associates (1978) *Survey Research Practice*, London: Heinemann.

Lavrakas, P.J. (1995) *Telephone Survey Methods: Sampling, Selection and Supervision*, London: Sage.

Litwin, M.S. (1995) *How to Measure Survey Reliability and Validity*, Thousand Oaks, CA: Sage.

Oppenheim, A.N. (2000) *Questionnaire Design, Interviewing and Attitude Measurement*, London: Continuum.

8 Research strategies

The case study, ethnography and action research

In this chapter I introduce three further important research strategies that are often used in management studies: the case study, ethnography and action research. They differ from the experiment and survey in that they all focus on the intensive study of one, or a few, cases in natural settings. The researcher's experience of implementing these strategies will be very different from that of the laboratory experimenter or the survey researcher. Those approaches do not require and may well forbid any close contact between the investigator and those being studied. Adoption of any one of the strategies reviewed in this chapter, however, will usually bring the researcher and the researched into immediate contact, with all the problems and opportunities that such meetings bring.

The case study

Research based on case studies has been of growing importance in the management field and is often the preferred strategy for research degree work in such fields as organization, strategy, marketing and accounting. However, from a methodological point of view the approach has attracted considerable criticism and it continues to attract debate.

What is a case study?

A case study can be defined as 'the detailed examination of a single example of a class of phenomena' (Abercrombie *et al.*, 2000, p. 41) or as 'a research design that takes as its subject a single case or a few selected examples of a social entity' (Marshall, 1998, p. 56). As a research strategy, the case study aims for the intensive examination of one or a small number of instances of the units of interest. These units may be of any kind, but in management research they are often organizations or departments within them. They could, however, be larger units such as industries, smaller units such as work groups, or even single individuals such as organizational leaders (see, for example, Kets de Vries, 1996). Units need not be entities, for events and processes, such as managerial decisions, may also be researched using this strategy.

Box 8.1 What is a case study?

It is a way of organising social data so as to preserve the unitary character of the social object being studied. Expressed somewhat differently, it is an approach which views any social unit as a whole.

(Goode and Hatt, 1952, p. 331)

As a working definition we may characterise a case study as a detailed examination of an event (or series of related events) which the analyst believes exhibits (or exhibit) the operation of some identified general theoretical principle.

(Mitchell, 1983, p. 192)

... a general term widely used, especially in the social and behavioural sciences, to refer to the description and analysis of a particular entity (object, person, group, event, state, condition, process or whatever). Such singular entities are usually natural occurrences with definable boundaries, although they exist and function within a context of surrounding circumstances.

(Bromley, 1986, pp. 7–8)

A case study is an empirical inquiry that investigates a contemporary phenomenon within its real-life context; when the boundaries between phenomenon and context are not clearly evident; and in which multiple sources of evidence are used.

(Yin, 1989, p. 23)

Types of case study

Case-study designs may be distinguished in terms of their purposes and the number of cases involved.

Uses for the case study

In general, case studies may be used for three main purposes. Where little or nothing is known about the phenomenon of interest, an intensive study of one or a small number of instances of it can be undertaken in order to produce detailed descriptions of typical cases. These descriptive case studies may then form the basis for the construction of explanatory theories and hypotheses. For example, Mintzberg's (1973) study *The Nature of Managerial Work* was based on his doctoral research, which was largely concerned to describe the work activities of five chief executives.

More usually, especially in research degree studies, case studies are used for explanatory purposes. These include both theory-building and theory-testing. Case studies can be particularly useful for producing theory. Because a case study entails detailed investigation of a complex entity or process, it can generate theoretical insights that are closely grounded in real experience, in contrast to more speculative 'armchair' theorizing. As Eisenhardt (1989) argues, case studies can yield theories that are novel, utilizing concepts that are strongly validated by their close contact with empirical reality. High-quality theories which provide convincing explanations are therefore a possibility with case-study research, although the best way of generating them using this strategy continues to be debated (see Dyer and Wilkins, 1991; Eisenhardt, 1991).

Box 8.2 What is an explanatory case study?

An explanatory case study consists of: a) an accurate rendition of the facts of the case, b) some consideration of alternative explanations of these facts, and c) a conclusion based on the single explanation that appears most congruent with the facts.

(Yin, 1981, p. 61)

For theory-testing, the theory or competing theories must predict the characteristics and/or behaviour of a specific instance. The study of a single case may then be sufficient to support the theory, or possibly even to refute it. As de Vaus (2001, p. 223) puts it:

> The difference between the theory testing and theory building approaches is that in the former we *begin* with a set of quite specific propositions and then see if these work in real world situations. In the theory building model we begin with only a question and perhaps a basic proposition, look at real cases and *end* up with a more specific theory or set of propositions *as a result* of examining actual cases.

Single and multiple case studies

The classic application of the case-study strategy is to a single case. Dyer and Wilkins (1991) argue that the in-depth investigation of one case is the essence of case-study research, since it enables deep understanding and rich theory construction, whereas multiple case studies seem less likely to yield the same quality of understanding and theorizing. Many of the classic case studies in management, they suggest, were based on one or at most two cases.

Yin (1994) proposes three rationales for the single case study. A well-formulated theory may enable the deduction of a situation that would provide a critical test of the theory's propositions. A single, critical case study would then be appropriate. Second, extreme or unique cases may occur which justify study in their own right. Third, where a topic has not been previously investigated, a single case study may serve a revelatory purpose, opening up an unresearched area.

Depending on the scale of the entity being studied and the time available for studying it, a single case may be all that can feasibly be researched. But the use of multiple cases brings certain advantages. In particular, it may be possible to select contrasting cases so as to approximate a quasi-experimental design, one case having been exposed to some condition while the other, near-identical case, has not.

The logic of adopting a multi-case design differs from that of survey sampling. When the aim of the study is descriptive, cases are chosen so that they will reflect the varied attributes of the population from which they are drawn. The approach is akin to that of stratified sampling although the aim is not that of producing a statistically representative sample. When theory-testing is the goal, the selection of cases follows a replication logic (Yin, 1994) rather than a sampling logic. Cases are selected either because they are predicted to display the same characteristics (literal replication) or because they are predicted to exhibit different ones (theoretical replication). The study of the cases may support the theoretical propositions or may diverge from expectations, so requiring revision of the theory.

If multiple cases are to be studied, how many should there be? This is a difficult question to answer because there are both practical and theoretical considerations to be taken into account. As we have seen, for some purposes only a single case is likely to be available or required. Where multiple cases are considered desirable, a rule of thumb suggests that between four and ten cases is usually sufficient (Eisenhardt, 1989).

Problems with case studies

Case studies and those who undertake them have long been the object of criticism by those who see the qualitative investigation of one or a few cases as an inadequate or inappropriate strategy of inquiry. Indeed, there has been talk of a 'case study crisis' (Yin, 1981). Such critiques arise in part from epistemological differences between the protagonists, which are themselves reflected in preferences for either quantitative or qualitative styles of research. Defenders of the case study have responded in kind, so producing a lively methodological debate that is far from over.

This debate has focused on two main sets of issues: the extent to which case studies can produce rigorous data and so yield findings of high internal validity, and the problem of generalization or external validity. The latter has proved by far to be the more troublesome.

Internal validity

Case studies have been criticized for using ill-defined methods of data collection, for the likelihood of investigator bias influencing what is observed and reported, and for the impossibility of replication. In part, these points are based on a misunderstanding of the case study, equating it with observational fieldwork, where such issues have been important. Even so, advocates of the case study have found it necessary to address these criticisms.

As Stoecker (1991) has indicated, there have been two types of response. One has been to show that these problems are by no means restricted to the case study but are typical of all forms of social research. The absence of bias, for example, cannot be guaranteed even in rigorously designed and conducted laboratory experiments (see Jung, 1971). Second, procedures have been developed which are intended to strengthen the internal validity of the case study. Triangulation, or the use of multiple methods of data construction, is one possibility advocated by Bromley (1986) and Yin (1994). Yin also suggests a number of additional ways in which a case study's internal validity can be enhanced.

External validity

Critics of case studies argue that since it is impossible to generalize from a single case, such research is inherently flawed. At best, a case study can only be used for exploratory purposes, to generate hypotheses for investigation by other means. Its role is therefore secondary and perhaps even relatively trivial in comparison with that of the survey or experiment.

There have been several lines of response to this criticism. Stake (1995) argues that the main concern of case study research is 'particularization' rather than generalization (see Box 8.3). Others argue that even if generalization from a single case is not possible, such studies can still be valuable. We have already seen that case studies can serve as sources of theory. In addition, Punch (1998) points out that a case may be sufficiently complex, unusual, interesting or misunderstood to warrant study of itself without any aspiration to generalization. Also, March *et al.* (1991) have shown that it is possible to learn useful lessons from samples of one – or even fewer!

Box 8.3 What's so great about generalization?

The real business of a case study is particularization, not generalization. We take a particular case and come to know it well, not primarily as to how it is different from others but what it is, what it does. There is emphasis on uniqueness, and that implies knowledge of others that the case is different from, but the first emphasis is on understanding the case itself.

(Stake, 1995, p. 8)

A second line argues that some kind of generalization from case studies is possible. Yin (1994) argues that while case-study results cannot be generalized to populations or universes (statistical generalization), they can be generalized to theoretical propositions (analytical generalization). Punch (1998, p. 154) adds that the derivation of new concepts is another way in which a case study can yield 'generalisable results'. What seems to be meant by these claims is that an analyst may derive general *theoretical* propositions and *concepts* from the study of a specific case. But these are not empirical generalizations. Indeed, I would argue that they are not generalizations at all.

In my view, these claims for generalization of case studies amount to saying that they can be used for theory-building, as Eisenhardt (1989) suggests. This seems to me to be better described as a process of analytical or inductive *inference* rather than one of generalization. As Bechhofer and Paterson (2000, p. 48) say, 'In a strictly statistical sense, we cannot generalise at all from a case study.' There are, as ever in research, exceptions. It certainly seems reasonable to generalize from a sample of one to a population of identical cases or near-identical cases. Reports of road tests of the latest model of a mass-produced car are of this kind. But in general, and as common sense suggests, it is necessary to be cautious about making empirical generalizations on the basis of the study of only one or a few cases. It would be easy to get the impression that some case-study researchers feel the need to cling on to the notion that their work

Activity 8.1 Analyse a case study

Find an example of a published research case study (not a teaching case) in your field. How have the following issues been dealt with by the researcher(s):

- *Justification*. Why was this strategy adopted? Is it appropriate to the problem? Was the intention to describe, explain or both?
- *Selection*. How many cases were used? How were they selected? Why these cases? If access to a site was required, how was this obtained?
- *Ethics*. Was it necessary to disguise the identity of the case(s)? Were there any other ethical difficulties?
- *Data*. What data were obtained? From what sources were they obtained? By what methods?
- *Analysis*. How were the data organized and summarized? Was cross-case analysis possible?
- *Presentation*. Has a coherent and convincing account of the study been written? How has the presentation been organized?

can be generalized for fear of loss of respectability in the eyes of positivists (Lee, 1985).

In the course of dealing with criticisms of the case-study strategy there has been a tendency to codify procedures for researching cases, so making the approach more explicit and more accessible. Yin's (1994) *Case Study Research: Design and Methods* is an influential example of this proceduralizing trend; it provides comprehensive guidance on how to carry out case studies from origination to writing up. However, as with any elaboration of research methods, it is as well to be aware of the dangers mentioned in Chapter 1 of falling into methodolatry; in research, slavishly following procedures is no substitute for applying imaginative intelligence.

Box 8.4 Example case studies in management research

Blau, P.M. (1955) *The Dynamics of Bureaucracy*, Chicago: University of Chicago Press.
Crozier, M. (1964) *The Bureaucratic Phenomenon*, London: Tavistock.
Dalton, M. (1959) *Men Who Manage*, New York: Wiley.
Dore, R. (1973) *British Factory–Japanese Factory*, London: Allen & Unwin.
Gouldner, A.W. (1954) *Patterns of Industrial Bureaucracy*, Glencoe, IL: Free Press.
Kanter, R.M. (1977) *Men and Women of the Corporation*, New York: Basic Books.
Lupton, T. (1963) *On the Shop Floor*, Oxford: Pergamon.
Pettigrew, A. (1985) *The Awakening Giant: Continuity and Change in ICI*, Oxford: Blackwell.
Watson, T.J. (2001) *In Search of Management: Culture, Chaos and Control in Managerial Work*, London: Thomson.

Ethnography

Fully fledged ethnographies have been uncommon in management research but some of the most informative studies in the field have been products of ethnography. Moreover, ethnographic methods have been increasingly used in the study of management and organization. Ethnography has thus become an important strategy for research in management studies.

What is ethnography?

The term 'ethnography' refers to 'folk' (ethno) description (graphy). Ethnographers are interested in describing and understanding unfamiliar cultures and ways of life. To do this they use ethnographic methods of investigation, especially field observation, and the end products of their research are written up as ethnographies. Ethnography can therefore be thought of as a label both for a research process and for a research product; ethnographers *do* ethnography in order to produce *an* ethnography.

Box 8.5 What is ethnography?

In practical terms, *ethnography* usually refers to forms of social research having a substantial number of the following features:

- a strong emphasis on exploring the nature of particular social phenomena, rather than setting out to test hypotheses about them
- a tendency to work primarily with 'unstructured' data, that is, data that have not been coded at the point of data collection in terms of a closed set of analytic categories
- investigation of a small number of cases, perhaps just one, in detail
- analysis of data that involves explicit interpretation of the meanings and functions of human actions, the product of which mainly takes the form of verbal descriptions and explanations, with quantification and statistical analysis playing a subordinate role at most.

(Atkinson and Hammersley, 1994, p. 248)

As a research strategy, ethnography originated in the field of cultural anthropology. Anthropology began as the study of small-scale, 'primitive' societies and these usually had to be approached from scratch, without the prior knowledge and understanding that were available when researching a familiar society such as one's own. The ethnographic strategy therefore centred on 'total immersion', whereby the investigator would live among those being studied, learn their language and observe their day-to-day life. After a period of fieldwork often lasting several years, the ethnographer would gradually become familiar with the meanings attached to the social practices and customs being observed. The aim of 'classical' ethnography was to produce a comprehensive description of a society's structure and culture.

Today the ethnographic strategy not only is used by anthropologists to study 'traditional' societies but also has been adopted by both sociologists and anthropologists to study aspects of modern life. However, the greater scale and complexity of urban industrial societies has encouraged the study of subgroups or subcultures rather than whole societies. Full-blown ethnographies in the classical style are impractical but the methods and orientation of the ethnographer can still be applied. Indeed, in some usages 'ethnographic' has become almost synonymous with the adoption of qualitative methods regardless of the objectives of the work.

Within management research, ethnography is often organizationally based. Rosen (1991) has highlighted the differences between more traditional ethnography and organizational ethnography. Unlike traditional ethnography, organizational ethnography focuses on behaviour and belief in the relatively restricted and specialized setting of a formal organization rather than in the general milieu of society. Behaviour in organizations takes place in settings which contain various tensions arising from the wider society, such as ethnic, religious, sexual and political differences and conflicting economic interests. Organizational culture is thus likely to be 'rough-edged and contested' (Rosen, 1991, p. 4). The organizational ethnographer also has a different relationship with those studied: traditional ethnographers enter another culture as outsiders whereas organizational ethnographers mainly study members of their own culture.

Box 8.6 What is organizational ethnography?

The ethnographer's method of collecting data is to live among those who are the data. He or she tries to learn the subjects' rules for organizational life, to interact with them for a frequency and duration of time 'sufficient' to understand how and why they construct their social world as it is and to explain it to others.

(Rosen, 1991, p. 5)

The collection of 'inside accounts' of organizational research edited by Bryman (1988b) provides many insights into the problems and possibilities of ethnographic research in organizational settings. It includes a chapter by Bresnen (1988) describing his doctoral research on construction-project organizations.

Ethnography in management studies

Once something of a rarity, ethnographic studies have become more common in management research. They tend to have focused on three broad and overlapping topics: organizational cultures, organizational processes and organizational employee groups.

Organizational cultures

The studies by Smircich (1983) and Kunda (1992) are good examples of ethnographic research on organizational culture. Smircich spent six weeks observing the top management group of an insurance company in order to identify the shared meanings that gave the group its distinctive character. She observed the executives in a variety of organizational settings and held conversational interviews with each of them. Her data consisted of her field notes, organizational documents, taped conversations and her experience.

Box 8.7 Examples of ethnographic research in management studies

Ahrens, T. (1997) 'Talking Accounting: An Ethnography of Management Knowledge in British and German Brewers', *Accounting, Organizations and Society*, 22, pp. 617–37.

Al-Maskati, H.H. (1995) 'Participants' Strategies in Management Learning Events: An Ethnographic Study of Five Bank Training Programmes', unpublished PhD thesis, University of Manchester.

Alvesson, M. (1994) 'Talking in Organizations: Managing Identity and Impression in an Advertising Agency', *Organization Studies*, 15, pp. 535–63.

Brooks, I. and Bate, P. (1994) 'The Problems of Effecting Change within the British Civil Service: A Cultural Perspective', *British Journal of Management*, 5, pp. 177–90.

Dalton, M. (1959) *Men Who Manage*, New York: Wiley.

Dubinskas, F. (ed.) (1988) *Making Time: Ethnographies of High-Technology Organizations*, Philadelphia, PA: Temple University Press.

Fox, S. (1992) 'Self-Knowledge and Personal Change: The Reported Experience of Managers in Part-Time Management Education', unpublished PhD thesis, University of Manchester.

Hodson, R. (2001) 'Disorganized, Unilateral and Participative Organizations: New Insights from the Ethnographic Literature', *Industrial Relations*, 40, pp. 204–30.

Hyde, P. and Thomas, A.B. (2002) 'Organizational Defences Revisited: Systems and Contexts', *Journal of Managerial Psychology*, 17, pp. 408–21.

Jackall, R. (1988) *Moral Mazes: The World of Corporate Managers*, Oxford: Oxford University Press.

Kunda, G. (1992) *Engineering Culture: Control and Commitment in a High Tech Corporation*, Philadelphia, PA: Temple University Press.

Lupton, T. (1963) *On the Shop Floor*, Oxford: Pergamon.

Monder, R. (1996) 'Uncovering the Management Process: An Ethnographic Approach', *British Journal of Management*, 7, pp. 35–44.

Rosen, M. (1985) 'Breakfast at Spiro's: Dramaturgy and Dominance', *Journal of Management*, 11 (2), pp. 31–48.

Sambrook, S. (2001) 'HRD as an Emergent and Negotiated Evolution: An Ethnographic Case Study in the British National Health Service', *Human Resource Development Quarterly*, 12, pp. 169–93.

Sharpe, D.R. (1988) 'Shop Floor Practices under Changing Forms of Managerial Control: A Comparative Ethnographic Study', unpublished PhD thesis, University of Manchester.

Turner, B.A. (1971) *Exploring the Industrial Subculture*, London: Macmillan.

Watson, T.J. (1994) *In Search of Management: Culture, Chaos and Control in Managerial Work*, London: Routledge.

Kunda's doctoral research was undertaken against the backdrop of growing theoretical and practical interest in corporate cultures and their functioning. His fieldwork was carried out in the Engineering Division of High Technologies Corporation, a large manufacturer of high-technology products. Over a 12-month period Kunda spent three to five days a week on-site as a participant observer. He undertook an extensive series of conversational interviews with staff members and also drew on documentary sources. His book includes a useful appendix in which he provides an interesting reflective account of how he approached and conducted the study.

Organizational processes

Ethnographic studies of organizational processes have included those examining organizational change, executive succession, shop-floor behaviour and management learning. For example, Lupton investigated the phenomenon of 'output restriction' by workers as one of a series of ethnographic studies in factories (Cunnison, 1982; Emmett and Morgan, 1982). Lupton was employed as a full-time worker in two establishments. Each workplace was studied for a six-month period using open participant observation (see Chapter 10). The research was the basis for his doctoral thesis (Lupton, 1959), which was later published in book form (Lupton, 1963).

In the field of management learning Al-Maskati (1995; Thomas and Al-Maskati, 1997) adopted ethnographic techniques for her doctoral study of participants' experiences in five training programmes for bank employees. She used both participant and non-participant observation, formal and informal interviewing, open-ended questionnaires and documents to obtain data. Periods spent in the field were relatively short compared to those used in classical ethnography, ranging from four days to two weeks. However, her aim was not to produce an ethnography of the programmes. Her interest was more specific, focusing on participants' behaviour as teachers and learners and its effects on the learning process.

Organizational employee groups

Ethnographic studies of employees include those of managers (Dalton, 1959; Jackall, 1988; Watson, 1994a), shop-floor workers (Beynon, 1973; Lupton, 1963; Sharpe, 1988), shop stewards (Batstone *et al.*, 1977) and other groups.

Dalton's classic study *Men Who Manage* (1959) is all the more remarkable because Dalton was not a professional researcher but a regular employee at the time he began his investigations. An interest in the 'unofficial' rather than the 'official' versions of how organizations are managed led him to engage in covert participant observation over many years. Much of the work was carried out while he was an employee at one company, but he checked out his observations at other sites. His methods of data construction were intended to be unobtrusive, to better enable him to penetrate behind organizational façades: informal interviews, off-site note-taking and the cultivation of 'intimates' who could be relied upon to supply him with inaccessible information and who would not blow his cover. He published a detailed account of his research methods (Dalton, 1964).

More recently, Watson spent a year as an open participant observer at a plant of a telecommunications manufacturing company. An experienced management researcher and academic, Watson worked on developing a scheme of management competencies for the company while simultaneously pursuing his own research interests. His principal method of obtaining data was through informal dialogue with his fellow managers. The study vividly describes and analyses their 'way of working life'. Watson's reflections on doing ethnographic management research appear in several papers (Watson, 1994c, 1995) as well as in the book reporting the research (Watson, 1994a).

Doing ethnographic research

The earliest ethnographers were adventurers who went in search of 'exotic' peoples in 'strange' lands. Modern ethnography retains some of this adventurous character. The ethnographer embarks on a journey into the 'real' world with all the uncertainties and surprises that that entails. No specific methodological route

---

Box 8.8 Finding your way in ethnography

Ironically, reaching a destination in ethnography often means taking false paths, coming up against dead ends or detours, and sometimes losing the way altogether.

(Fetterman, 1998, p. ix)

Ethnographers set out to show how social action in one world makes sense from the point of view of another. Such work requires an intensive personal involvement, an abandonment of traditional scientific control, an improvisational style to meet situations not of the researcher's making, and an ability to learn from a long series of mistakes.

(Agar, 1986, p. 12)

Ethnographic research involves feeling one's way in confusing circumstances, struggling to make sense of ambiguous messages, reading signals, looking around, listening all the time, coping with conflicts and struggling to achieve tasks through establishing and maintaining a network of relationships. But this is what we all do all the time as human beings.

(Watson, 1994a, p. 8)

map is available to help find the way; experience in the field and immersion in the tradition of ethnographic work contribute a great deal to the development of competence. Nonetheless, some general guidelines can be offered to those who wish to follow the ethnographic trail.

The adoption of a rigorous attitude is as vital in ethnography as in other styles of research. Despite the open-ended nature of ethnographic research, it is important to adopt a planned approach. Four preparatory requirements for the intending organizational ethnographer have been suggested by Rosen (1991):

1   *Contextual anchoring*. Familiarize yourself with the conceptual frameworks deployed in socio-cultural studies and with a cross section of classic ethnographic studies.
2   *Field practice*. Undertake a brief study in an unfamiliar setting before embarking on more extensive work.
3   *Language learning*. Learn the local organizational language, which in management research will often be that of business.
4   *Industry knowledge*. Acquire a working knowledge of the industry in which the organization operates.

Box 8.9   What do ethnographers do?

In its most characteristic form it involves the ethnographer participating, overtly or covertly, in people's daily lives for an extended period of time, watching what happens, listening to what is said, asking questions – in fact, collecting whatever data are available to throw light on the issues that are the focus of the research.

(Hammersley and Atkinson, 1995, pp. 1–2)

Fetterman (1998) has provided a valuable guide to the various stages of an ethnographic project. He points out that the researcher should enter the field 'with an open mind, not an empty head' (1998, p. 1). Before starting the fieldwork the ethnographer must have 'a problem, a research design, specific data collection techniques, tools for analysis, and a specific writing style' (1998, p. 1).

Once a problem has been identified, the key stages are:

•   *Fieldwork* is the most characteristic part of any ethnographic study. 'The most important element of fieldwork is being there – to observe, to ask seemingly stupid but insightful questions, and to write down what is seen and heard' (Fetterman, 1998, p. 9). Although classical ethnography requires from six months to two years of fieldwork, less time can be appropriate for work in a familiar culture. Fieldwork begins with a familiarization period in which to learn the language and acquire a basic understanding of the setting.

Then themes, problems, and gaps in current understanding are identified. A theoretical rather than random sampling strategy will often be used to focus attention on particular events and processes. Unlike in most research, data collection and analysis cannot be separated. They begin simultaneously and continue throughout the fieldwork. Data must be organized and referred to as they are being collected. The decision to leave the setting is often dictated by pragmatic criteria – running out of time and/or money – but ideally should be made when it is evident that 'enough data have been gathered to describe the culture or problem convincingly and to say something significant about it' (Fetterman, 1998, p. 10). The occurrence of repetitive findings and diminishing yields from the field can indicate that fieldwork should cease.

• *Formal analysis* may require as much time as has been spent on the fieldwork. The organization of the data and writing of field notes should be undertaken as a continual process during fieldwork. The aim of analysis is to 'draw an overall picture of how a system works' (Fetterman, 1998, p. 11) from all the bits and pieces of evidence that have been obtained.

• *Writing the ethnography* is a major task. It may take the form of a full-blown ethnography or an ethnographically informed report. The success of the ethnography is to be judged in terms of the degree to which it rings true to others in the field setting. They must recognize the descriptions as accurate even if they disagree with the analyst's interpretations and conclusions. Analysts' explanations do not have to be constructed from within the frame of reference of the natives.

Doing ethnography may appear to be an especially challenging prospect, but it is encouraging to know, as Wolcott (1975, p. 116) put it, that 'there is a bit of ethnographic talent in each of us'.

Problems with ethnography

As interest in ethnographic research has grown, so have disagreements about the nature and status of ethnographic practice. Here we highlight three key issues.

Mere common sense?

One problem that has faced those wishing to adopt an ethnographic strategy in management research has been that of its methodological legitimacy. In a field historically dominated by positivism, the 'scientific' status of ethnographic research has been called into question. Its essentially everyday methods of obtaining data, with the researcher participating in social life in much the same way as any individual does, can be seen by some critics as an indication of its unsophisticated and common-sense character. Such methods are seen as incompatible with scientific rigour: indeed, scientific methods are held to exist precisely because common-sense methods are deficient.

Recognizing the continuity between such everyday methods and those of the ethnographer, Sanday (1979) has proposed a distinction between 'ethnography' and 'paradigmatic ethnography'. The former is what cultural rapporteurs such as journalists and novelists do. Paradigmatic ethnography, on the other hand, is undertaken by professional scholars. It involves the same kinds of observational methods but the process is informed by a theoretical approach to the study of culture. In general, ethnography can be seen as a rigorous enterprise that is theoretically informed whereas everyday ethnography is not.

Telling it like it is?

One attraction of ethnography has been its claim to get close to social realities in a way that is impossible with the artificial experiments and remote surveys favoured by positivists. The description of cultures is the central aim of ethnography rather than the testing of hypotheses derived from a-priori theories. Committed to a naturalistic epistemology, the ethnographer goes to the scene of action, observes what takes place there and returns to 'tell it like it is'. Ethnography might thus be seen as a way of producing more valid descriptions of the social world than is possible using a positivist approach.

However, as Hammersley and Atkinson (1995) point out, this view of ethnography shares some important assumptions with positivism. It assumes that there is an independent social reality that can be known objectively, and that observers can and should be value free. But both these assumptions have been critiqued from a range of viewpoints including constructionism, post-structuralism and critical theory. For example, constructionists argue that all accounts, whether by everyday actors or highly trained ethnographers, are constructions and not simply faithful reflections of external reality (Golden-Biddle and Locke, 1993). Also, some critical theorists advocate politically committed research, rejecting the goal of describing the world as necessarily worthwhile in itself.

Hammersley and Atkinson's view is that although neither positivism nor naturalism can offer absolute grounds for accepting knowledge claims, the radical relativism implied by some of these critiques must also be rejected. The epistemological status of ethnography continues to be debated and remains problematic – but so, of course, do all the alternatives!

How valid are ethnographic studies?

The issues here are much the same as those affecting case studies. Questions of internal validity concern the extent to which the ethnographer influences the events being witnessed, especially given the extended periods of engagement that are often involved. One attempt to deal with this is by adopting a reflexive approach (Hammersley and Atkinson, 1995). The ethnographer attempts to monitor his or her impact upon the setting and includes a personal account as part of his or her research report. Unlike positivists, who 'write themselves out of the story', reflexive ethnographers ensure that the reader is aware of their part in constructing it. However, there is no easy answer to the fact that ethnographic accounts are filtered through the distorting lens of the ethnographer's individuality. As Kunda (1992, p. 271) says, 'Ultimately, the researcher must take authority, ask the reader for a leap of faith, and perhaps do battle with critics.'

Activity 8.2 Designing an ethnographic study

You have decided to undertake an ethnographic study of 'daily life' in your study environment or workplace. Prepare a brief research plan incorporating answers to the following questions:

- Who would you want to observe? Which role-holders?
- Which events and processes would you want to observe?
- Would observing these present any special difficulties?

Action research

Research in policy-related fields such as management is often carried out in the belief that the results will be applied to help to solve important practical problems. Not surprisingly, many management researchers are interested not simply in understanding how things are managed but also in how they might be managed differently. But doing 'useful' research is not as straightforward as it might seem: researchers and practitioners can easily become isolated from each other (Heller, 1986; Lawler, 1985; Rynes *et al.*, 2001). In this section we examine action research as a strategy that seeks to increase the likelihood that management research and management practice interconnect.

Although action research approaches may not be suitable for research degree work because of the skills and risks involved, all management researchers need to be aware of this important research strategy. As we noted earlier, something very similar to action research has recently been advocated as the 'way forward' for management research in the UK (Tranfield and Starkey, 1998).

What is action research?

The term 'action research' was coined in 1944 by Kurt Lewin, a social psychologist. Lewin was keenly interested in the possibility of using social science to tackle social problems. He saw the direct involvement of social scientists with real-world issues as having a twofold pay-off. First, insights derived from the established body of social scientific knowledge could serve to guide practical changes in social arrangements and policies. Second, social science knowledge would itself change and develop as a result of experiments with real situations;

social science is supposed to be about the social world so acting upon it and seeing what happens is an essential part of developing a true, empirical social science. Action research could therefore be seen as a – or perhaps the – means of integrating social science with social practice.

Box 8.10 What is action research?

Action research aims to contribute *both* to the practical concerns of people in an immediate problematic situation and to the goals of social science by joint collaboration within a mutually acceptable ethical framework.

(Rapoport, 1970, p. 499)

Action research simultaneously assists in practical problem-solving and expands scientific knowledge, as well as enhances the competencies of the respective actors, being performed collaboratively in an immediate situation using data feedback in a cyclical process aiming at an increased understanding of a given social situation, primarily applicable for the understanding of change processes in social systems and undertaken within a mutually acceptable ethical framework.

(Hult and Lennung, 1980, p. 247)

The idea of action research has been much elaborated since Lewin's original formulation. A review in the mid-1980s (Peters and Robinson, 1984) indicated broad agreement among action researchers on its key characteristics. Action research focused on practical problems rather than being driven purely by the theoretical interests of social scientists; involved the investigator acting within and upon the settings being researched rather than remaining detached from them; and was undertaken collaboratively with those experiencing the problem rather than being carried out solely by 'experts'.

According to Dickens and Watkins (1999, p. 127), action research has now become 'an umbrella term for a shower of activities intended to foster change on the group, organizational and societal levels'. This 'shower' includes six 'action inquiry technologies' identified by Brooks and Watkins (1994): [classical] action research, participatory research, action learning, action science, developmental action inquiry and cooperative inquiry. These approaches are described in more detail and usefully summarized in tabular form in a paper by Raelin (1999). They overlap in complex ways but generally share the central action research idea of simultaneously developing knowledge and implementing change. Not all of them, however, are concerned to produce conventional research outputs in the form of dissertations or published reports. Partly because of this, they are problematic as potential strategies for research students.

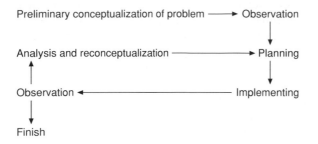

Figure 8.1 The classical action research cycle.

Doing action research

In what has become known as 'classical' action research, a fairly well-defined sequence of activities takes place (see Figure 8.1). Lewin envisaged an iterative process of investigation and action so that action research projects proceed cyclically. The conclusions from each stage of the research become the basis for initiating actions, and the effects of these become the focus of the next stage of the research. Ideally, this cycle is repeated until a satisfactory solution to the problem is arrived at. However, the problem as originally conceived may need to be rethought as the project progresses. As in much research, what was initially believed to be the main source of difficulty may not be the problem at all. One of the most significant outcomes may be a better understanding of what the real problem is all about.

Lewin described the process of action research as 'a spiral of steps each of which is composed of a circle of planning, action and fact-finding about the result of the action' (1946, p. 38). Following a preliminary formulation of the problem, data are collected and analysed in order to create an action plan. This plan is implemented and further observations made to assess how satisfactorily it has been implemented and to assess its effects. If the problem has been dealt with adequately, the project terminates. If not, there may need to be further analysis and a rethinking of the problem. The cycle of planning, acting and observing results is repeated as long as is necessary.

Given the collaborative nature of action research, both professional social scientists and non-specialists will work together throughout the cycle. Where the project focuses upon an organization it is likely to be managed and undertaken by a team. For example, in Mumford's (1995) ETHICS methodology, a steering group is established consisting of external social scientists, representatives of management, internal technical experts and operatives. (ETHICS stands for Effective Technical and Human Implementation of Computer Systems.) Action research is inherently participatory (Whyte, 1991) although collaborative relationships between academics and practitioners can prove difficult to create and sustain.

Rapoport (1970) identified three dilemmas in action research related to issues of ethics, goals and initiatives. Ethical problems include whether to be involved with organizations engaged in 'unethical' businesses such as arms manufacturing or tobacco products; the protection of participants' interests during data collection and the publication of findings; bias arising through over-involvement; and being used by a sponsor as a weapon in organizational politics. Goal dilemmas arise from action research's dual agenda, aiming for both practical and scientific outcomes. Over-emphasis on the practical can lead to mere fact-finding whereas over-emphasis on the scientific can mean that projects cease to be relevant or even intelligible to organizational members. Finally, the dilemma of initiatives refers to the process whereby problems are defined. In the service-orientated model the client defines the problem and the researcher helps to solve it. But this often proves problematic, for the client's version of the problem may be wide of the mark. The researcher then faces the dilemma of trying to help the client but in relation to a redefined problem. This can be especially awkward if the redefined problem turns out to be the client him- or herself! Carter's (1971) experiences with evaluation studies give some insight into how researcher–client relationships can deteriorate when results do not meet clients' expectations.

Problems with action research

Action research has been the object of considerable criticism. In part this reflects the by now familiar debate between positivists and constructionists that surrounds much social and management research. The status of action research as 'science' capable of contributing in any meaningful way to knowledge has been questioned, as has its ability actually to promote change. In addition, and from a more pragmatic point of view, action research can be a problematic strategy for research degree studies.

Can action research deliver the goods?

Action research has claimed to be able to serve both the needs of science, for knowledge, and those of practitioners, for solutions to practical problems, but it has sometimes been suggested that it actually tends to produce knowledge without action or action without knowledge (Foster, 1972). It is difficult to assess the overall effectiveness of action research in promoting change, as there have been few systematic overviews of the outcomes of action research projects. Ahmad (1985) followed up a number of studies for the purposes of her doctoral research. She concluded that the practice of action research was a poor reflection of the theory and that the theory was too idealistic and ambitious to be viable.

Because action research projects are typically pursued with a single client organization they are, in effect, case studies. Commitment to fieldwork in natural settings also means that action research adopts some features of ethnographic research. The epistemological questions about the capacity of action research to contribute to science are therefore similar to those associated with case studies and ethnography. So, for example, action research has been dubbed unscientific because it is too bound up with the immediate and particularistic concerns of single organizations and not enough concerned with the rigorous testing of hypotheses derived from general theory. The arguments have been reviewed by Susman and Evered (1978), who propose that action research adopts a different epistemology to normal science and so cannot be judged on positivist terms (see also De Cock, 1994). Action research, some proponents claim, is based on a constructionist epistemology. Because actors constitute their shared realities, they must also be involved in interpreting and changing them (Peters and Robinson, 1984). Action research on this view is anti-positivist and less interested in meeting positivist criteria of adequacy than in developing its own 'epistemology of practice' (Schön, 1983).

Is action research too risky?

Action research has great potential for integrating research activities with managerial practice, but it carries higher risks for the researcher than conventional studies because control of the research is shared with others, who are outside the academic community. Instead of being able to carry out a controlled investigation, in which the involvement of organizational members is restricted to authorizing access, gatekeeping, and passively providing data, the action researcher demands much more from them and is, in turn, open to greater demands from them. While the traditional researcher seeks cooperation from research subjects, the action researcher seeks collaboration with research partners. Additional demands are therefore placed on the investigator, who must be 'organization-wise' in the manner of a consultant (Eden and Huxham, 1996) and possess the skills and temperament of the change agent.

The significance of these factors is likely to vary from case to case and according to the type of action inquiry being undertaken. While they need not necessarily deter students from adopting the action research strategy, they do indicate that extra support may be required. Even more than is usually the case with research, action research is not an undertaking to be entered into lightly.

Is action research appropriate for research-degree studies?

Action research is an appropriate strategy when the researcher wishes to be involved in contributing to and analysing ongoing change activities within organizations. However, it may not be appropriate for research-degree students unless they are part of an experienced team (Eden and Huxham, 1996). Even then, there is likely to be greater uncertainty about outcomes than in more conventional forms of research, and the skills of the organizational consultant or change agent are likely to be required in addition to conventional research skills. For these reasons, research students should consider the following questions before committing themselves to this strategy:

- Are you able to join an ongoing project or one that is about to start? Can you join an experienced action research team? It may be unwise to attempt to initiate action research yourself.
- Will you be able to deal effectively with the challenges arising from close and lengthy engagement with a 'strange' organization and its members?
- Will the nature of the project be likely to prevent or restrict publication of your findings?
- Will uncertainties over time-scales and outcomes be compatible with the constraints imposed by your own circumstances?

Box 8.11 Examples of action research studies in management

Avison, D.E. (1997) 'Action Research in Information Systems', in G. McKenzie, J. Powell and R. Usher (eds) *Understanding Social Research: Perspectives on Methodology and Practice*, London: Falmer Press, pp. 196–209.

Barker, S.B. and Barker, R.T. (1994) 'Managing Change in an Interdisciplinary Inpatient Unit: An Action Research Approach', *Journal of Mental Health Administration*, 21, pp. 80–91.

Gaffney, M.M. and Walton, R.E. (1989) 'Research, Action and Participation', *American Behavioral Scientist*, 32, pp. 582–611.

Jaques, E. (1951) *The Changing Culture of a Factory*, London: Tavistock.

Maclure, R. and Bassey, M. (1991) 'Participatory Action Research in Togo: An Inquiry into Maize Storage Systems', in W.F. Whyte (ed.) *Participatory Action Research*, Newbury Park, CA: Sage, pp. 190–209.

Pasmore, W. and Friedlander, F. (1982) 'An Action Research Programme for Increasing Employee Involvement in Problem-Solving', *Administrative Science Quarterly*, 27, pp. 343–62.

Whyte, W.F., Greenwood, D.J. and Lazes, P. (1989) 'Saving Jobs in Industry: The Xerox Corporation', *American Behavioral Scientist*, 32, pp. 513–51.

Key points

1 The case study, ethnography and action research tend to focus on the intensive study of one or a few cases.

2 The potential gains of depth, verisimilitude and richness often have to be traded off against likely losses in parsimony, replicability and generalization.

3 The adoption of these strategies typically requires the researcher to possess fieldwork skills that are seldom needed for experiments and surveys.

Key reading

The case study

Eisenhardt, K.M. (1989) 'Building Theories from Case Study Research', *Academy of Management Review*, 14, pp. 532–50.

Stake, R.E. (1994) 'Case Studies', in N.K. Denzin and Y.S. Lincoln (eds) *Handbook of Qualitative Research*, Thousand Oaks, CA: Sage, pp. 236–47.

Stoecker, R. (1991) 'Evaluating and Rethinking the Case Study', *Sociological Review*, 39, pp. 88–112.

Ethnography

Fetterman, D.M. (1998) *Ethnography: Step by Step*, Thousand Oaks, CA: Sage.

Hammersley, M. and Atkinson, P. (1995) *Ethnography: Principles in Practice*, London: Routledge.

Rosen, M. (1991) 'Coming to Terms with the Field: Understanding and Doing Organizational Ethnography', *Journal of Management Studies*, 28, pp. 1–24.

Action research

Dickens, L. and Watkins, K. (1999) 'Action Research: Rethinking Lewin', *Management Learning*, 30, pp. 127–40.

Thomas, A.B. (2003) 'The Social Sciences: Can They Help Managers?', in *Controversies in Management: Issues, Debates, Answers*, London: Routledge, pp. 74–96.

Whyte, W.F. (ed.) (1991) *Participatory Action Research*, Newbury Park, CA: Sage.

Further reading

The case study

Gummesson, E. (1991) *Qualitative Methods in Management Research*, Newbury Park, CA: Sage.

Humphrey, C. and Scapens, R.W. (1996) 'Theories and Case Studies of Organizational Accounting Practices: Limitation or Liberation', *Accounting, Auditing and Accountability Journal*, 9 (4), pp. 86–106.

McCutcheon, D.M. and Meredith, J.R. (1993) 'Conducting Case Study Research in Operating Management', *Journal of Operations Management*, 11, pp. 239–56.

Mitchell, J.C. (1983) 'Case and Situation Analysis', *Sociological Review*, 31, pp. 187–211.

Numagami, T. (1998) 'The Infeasibility of Invariant Laws in Management Studies: A Reflective Dialogue in Defence of Case Studies', *Organization Science*, 9, pp. 2–15.

Otley, D.T. and Berry, A.J. (1994) 'Case Study Research in Management Accounting and Control', *Management Accounting Research*, 5, pp. 45–66.

Smith, N.C. (1991) 'The Case-Study: A Vital yet Misunderstood Research Method for Management', in N.C. Smith and P. Dainty (eds) *The Management Research Handbook*, London: Routledge, pp. 145–58.

Stake, R.E. (1995) *The Art of Case Study Research*, London: Sage.

Yin, R.K. (1994) *Case Study Research: Design and Methods*, London: Sage.

Ethnography

Agar, M.H. (1986) *Speaking of Ethnography*, Beverly Hills, CA: Sage.

Bate, S.P. (1997) 'Whatever Happened to Organizational Anthropology? A Review of the Field of Organizational Ethnography and Anthropological Studies', *Human Relations*, 30, pp. 1147–75.

D'Iribarne, P. (1996/97) 'The Usefulness of an Ethnographic Approach to the International Comparison of Organizations', *International Studies of Management and Organization*, 26 (4), pp. 30–47.

LeCompte, M.D. and Schensul, J.J. (1999) *Designing and Conducting Ethnographic Research*, Walnut Creek, CA: AltaMira Press.

Linstead, S. (1997) 'The Social Anthropology of Management', *British Journal of Management*, 8, pp. 85–98.

Mariampolski, H. (1999) 'The Power of Ethnography', *Journal of the Market Research Society*, 41, pp. 75–86.

Russell, B.H. (2002) *Research Methods in Anthropology*, Walnut Creek, CA: AltaMira Press.

Schwartzman, H.B. (1993) *Ethnography in Organizations*, Newbury Park, CA: Sage.

Van Maanen, J. (1979) 'The Fact of Fiction in Organizational Ethnography', *Administrative Science Quarterly*, 24, pp. 539–50.

Walsh, D. (1998) 'Doing Ethnography', in C. Seale (ed.) *Researching Society and Culture*, London: Sage, pp. 217–32.

Action research

Baburoglu, O.N. and Ravn, I. (1992) 'Normative Action Research', *Organization Studies*, 13, pp. 19–34.

Brooks, A. and Watkins, K. (eds) (1994) *The Emerging Power of Action Inquiry Technologies*, San Francisco: Jossey-Bass.

Greenwood, D.J. and Levin, M. (1998) *Introduction to Action Research: Social Research for Social Change*, London: Sage.

Peters, M. and Robinson, V. (1984) 'The Origins and Status of Action Research', *Journal of Applied Behavioral Science*, 20, pp. 113–24.

Reason, P. and Bradbury, H. (eds) (2000) *Handbook of Action Research*, London: Sage.

Stringer, E.T. (1999) *Action Research: A Handbook for Practitioners*, London: Sage.

Warmington, A. (1980) 'Action Research: Its Methods and Its Implications', *Journal of Applied Systems Analysis*, 7, pp. 23–39.

Whyte, W.F. (ed.) (1991) *Participatory Action Research*, Newbury Park, CA: Sage.

9   Data construction by asking questions

If there is one thing that distinguishes the social sciences from natural science, it is that while both rely on questions to guide inquiry, only social scientists ask questions in order to produce data. We may want to know about atoms and molecules, but asking them how and why they behave as they do is not an option. But with people, questioning is the most important way of discovering the contents of their inner world.

Asking questions by means of questionnaires and interviews is something that has been closely associated with the survey. Although questioning may take place when one is following alternative strategies, such as ethnography, the survey is the only approach that relies exclusively on questions to generate data. In this chapter we shall be mainly concerned with questioning in surveys by means of postal questionnaires and interviewing, although I shall also refer to interviews in ethnographic studies.

Questioning processes are an aspect of social research in which the constructed character of data is at its most visible. Particularly in the interview, it is difficult to maintain the idea that data are simply being 'collected' like stones from a beach. Even so, a good deal of conventional methodological prescription concerning questioning procedures is based on the positivist conception of data, as we shall see.

Questioning data: straight questions, crooked answers?

Obtaining information from our fellow human beings by means of asking questions would seem to be a straightforward process. We do it every day and it seems to work. Yet when researchers have set out to conduct surveys systematically, things have seldom worked out so nicely. Criticisms of the survey as a method of obtaining data have been legion. In surveys it seems that what appear to the researcher to be straight questions all too often produce crooked answers.

For example, Foddy (1993), whose excellent analysis has provided much of the material in this section, has identified ten significant problems associated with survey questions:

* Respondents commonly misinterpret questions.
* Respondents often answer questions even when it appears that they know very little about the topic.

- Small changes in wording sometimes produce major changes in the distribution of responses.
- Answers to earlier questions can affect respondents' answers to later questions.
- Changing the order in which response options are presented sometimes affects respondents' answers.
- Respondents' answers are sometimes affected by the question format *per se*.
- Factual questions sometimes elicit invalid answers.
- The cultural context in which a question is presented often has an impact on the way respondents interpret and answer questions.
- The relationship between what respondents say they do and what they actually do is not always very strong.
- Respondents' attitudes, beliefs, opinions, habits and interests often seem to be extraordinarily unstable.

Although not all of these problems can be directly attributed to the way in which questions have been asked, many of them seem to stem directly from the assumptions researchers make about the questioning process – assumptions that are embedded in their theories and models of questioning. We need to take a close look at what is going on beneath the surface of this seemingly simple matter of asking questions. Perhaps what look like straight questions are not quite so straight after all.

Theories of questioning

The pragmatic orientation of much writing on social research methods has meant that issues associated with the use of questions have often been treated in an a-theoretical fashion. Indeed, much of the advice on questionnaire design is more a product of experience than it is the application of empirically validated theory or an explicit epistemological position. Yet decisions about the methods to be used to question people (the phrasing of questions, the vocabulary to use, the order in which they are asked, and so on) are always based on theoretical assumptions of some kind.

Positivist, stimulus–response model

The traditional approach to questioning in social research has been based on positivist/behaviourist assumptions. Questions are treated as 'stimuli' which are applied to 'respondents'. The underlying methodological prescription of this stimulus–response model is that the stimuli, including the conditions in which questions are asked, must be kept constant. Differences among respondents in the answers they give must be real and not attributable to differences in the questions asked or the conditions in which they are asked. This position is summed up in the Principle of Invariance of Stimuli: to produce a response that validly differentiates one respondent from another, the stimulus to which they are exposed must be identical. This means that ideally:

1   Questions must always be presented to respondents exactly as written, word for word.
2   Questions must always be presented in the same order.
3   The conditions in which the questions are answered must be held constant.

It is therefore assumed that:

1   It is possible to identify one form of question wording that has the same meaning for all respondents. Questions must be standardized so that the same wording is presented to everyone. In interviews, the interviewer must always read out the questions as they are written, without alteration.
2   A single order of questions will invoke the same context of meaning for everyone. Questionnaire respondents are assumed to answer questions in the order in which they are presented and not, for example, by starting at the end and working backwards. Interviewers are required to deliver questions in sequence as they appear on the interview schedule.
3   It is possible to ensure that the physical conditions in which the interviews are held and the behaviour of the interviewer do not vary for different interviewees.
4   Pilot work can identify standardized questions and a fixed question order. Where interviewing is being used, it is assumed that interviewers can be trained to standardize their behaviour.

Clearly, these conditions can never be fully realized. From an alternative perspective the model might appear somewhat impractical and even absurd. Even so, it has nonetheless been used to guide the design of questioning procedures in much survey research.

Constructionist, symbolic interactionist model

Under constructionist assumptions, questions are not stimuli but meaningful utterances. Meanings are intended by the questioner and may or may not be understood by the listener in the way intended. Questions are open to interpretation, and the way they are interpreted influences the way they are answered. Answers are also open to interpretation. Both questions and answers may be misinterpreted, so giving rise to misunderstandings. From this point of view, the question–answer sequence is an act of communication in which meanings, rather than stimuli, are exchanged.

This process of communication by questioning is depicted in Figure 9.1. A questioner asks a question of a respondent (a term we will retain for the sake of convenience despite its stimulus–response connotations). The respondent formulates an answer and presents it to the questioner. Between questioner and respondent there is a semi-permeable barrier which permits words and other expressions of meaning (gestures, facial expressions, and so on) to be exchanged between the parties, but which prevents either having direct access to the meanings

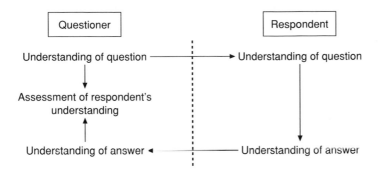

Figure 9.1 Communication by questioning.

of the other. To put it more colloquially, neither can see inside the other person's head to read the thoughts and meanings that reside within. The principal medium used to send messages across this barrier is, of course, language.

The conditions for valid communication to take place are that:

1   The questioner must have a clear understanding of what the intended meaning of the question is. If the questioner does not understand the question, then the answer is unlikely to be understood.
2   The respondent must understand the question to have the same meaning as the questioner understands it to have. If the respondent misunderstands the question, then any answer given will be an answer not to the question asked but to the question as the respondent understands it.
3   The respondent must be able to formulate an answer that accurately conveys his or her meaning. Even if the respondent shares the meaning of the question with the questioner, the answer given may not accurately express his or her intended meaning.
4   The questioner must understand the answer in the same way as the respondent does. Even if the previous three conditions have been met, the questioner may misunderstand the respondent's answer.

To obtain valid answers to questions it is necessary (but not sufficient) that both the questioner and the questioned must understand the questions and answers in the same way. This is the Principle of Invariance of Meaning. What matters is not that the same words are used, or that questions are presented in the same order, but that the questioner and questioned share the same frame of reference and understand the meanings of their communication in the same ways. The implications for questioning procedures are as follows:

1   If a question is to have the same meaning for the questioner and respondent, the questioner may need to word it in different ways for different respondents. To achieve invariance of meaning, questions must be formulated in language

that is familiar to the respondent. The use of self-completion questionnaires will therefore be limited to simple topics that are well understood by both parties.

2   The order in which questions are asked may need to be varied for different respondents if the information the questioner seeks is to be given. No fixed sequence of questions is satisfactory in all circumstances. The most effective sequence is one that reflects the respondent's willingness and ability to talk. Only interviewing permits this and so will often be preferable to using questionnaires.

3   The conditions in which interviews take place cannot be 'held constant' and are significant only when they are likely to interfere with the exchange of invariant meanings. Interviewers can never fully 'standardize' their behaviour, and in any case, inflexible behaviour is likely to be unhelpful rather than helpful to promoting mutual understanding.

A theory of error detection and its failure

It seems that there are plenty of opportunities for things to go wrong during the process of questioning. Indeed, it may seem rather remarkable that we succeed in communicating with even a moderate degree of success. What is especially difficult to deal with from a researcher's point of view is that misunderstanding may go completely undetected. Obvious misunderstandings may be able to be corrected or excluded from the final dataset where correction is not possible. An interviewer, for example, might ask the question again to indicate that it has been misunderstood or may rephrase it in order to make its meaning clear. Or in the case of a self-completion questionnaire, the answer to a question or the answers to the entire questionnaire may be excluded from the dataset. However, undetected misunderstandings will, by definition, be treated as if they were valid answers.

How do invalid answers go undetected? We need a little theory of question understanding and misunderstanding. The process seems to operate in the following way. When a question is asked, the questioner expects an answer that is at least feasible. If the answer is adjudged to be a feasible answer to the question, then it will be assumed that the question has been understood. If it seems infeasible, then it will be concluded that there has been a misunderstanding. The questioner compares each answer given to the question with the feasible set of answers that could accompany the question if it had been correctly understood.

For example, suppose the question is 'In which country were you born?' An answer referring to any one of dozens of countries is feasible, and so long as the questioner detects one of these responses, the question will be assumed to have been understood. Suppose, however, that the respondent replies by saying '1980'. The questioner will not recognize this as a feasible answer and therefore may, given the opportunity, point out to the respondent that there has been a misunderstanding. In this way misunderstandings may be detected. So far, so good.

According to this theory of question understanding, questioners rely heavily on the answers respondents give in order to decide whether their questions have or have not been understood correctly. This much seems obvious. Unfortunately, some answers give no such information. For example, where questions require Yes/No answers, whichever alternative is given yields no confirmation that the question has been understood. 'Does your company use the Inter-Max production scheduling system?' Whether the respondent answers 'Yes' or 'No', both are feasible answers and the questioner records the answer and moves to the next question. This yields no information on whether the respondent knows what is meant by 'the Inter-Max production scheduling system' – in this case they can know nothing, because it is completely fictional.

There are many ways in which respondents may appear to be answering the question they have been asked when in fact they are answering a *different* question. These misunderstandings may never be detected. For example, respondents, as Belson (1981) shows, may:

- Rephrase a question they cannot answer into a form that they can answer. For example, if asked 'How many hours a week do you usually spend doing X?' they may respond as if the question were 'How many hours did you spend last week doing X?'
- Interpret broad questions more narrowly. If asked 'What is the company policy on this?' they may respond as if the question was 'What is your department's policy on this?'
- Ignore part of a question once enough has been understood to enable an answer to be given. If asked 'How many meetings did you attend last week, excluding meetings with your boss?' they may answer as if they had been asked 'How many meetings did you attend last week?'

Similarly, respondents rely heavily on their understanding of what *kinds* of answers are required in order to judge whether they have understood a question as the researcher intends it to be understood. They need to understand the context of the questions and the perspective from which they should interpret them. For example, a question such as 'How did you first hear about this company?' could receive the response 'A colleague mentioned it' (indicating a source), 'I was at a business conference in Tokyo at the time' (indicating a location), or 'It was when we needed a new supplier' (indicating a problematic circumstance). So, respondents will try to judge whether they have understood a question as intended by seeking a feasible set from which to select an answer. This answer set may or may not be that which the questioner had in mind when formulating the question.

Questionnaire design

We may think of social research as a scientific enterprise, but the methods we use to generate data are more like the products of art and craft. This is nowhere truer than in the case of questionnaire design. Although a considerable body of knowledge based on custom and practice has developed over the years since social surveys were first undertaken in the mid-nineteenth century (Tonkiss, 1998), there is still no one best way to design a questionnaire.

Questionnaire design involves both the formulation of individual questions and the layout and organization of those questions and related material such as completion instructions, return addresses, and so on. Layout was covered in Chapter 7, so here we concentrate on the questions themselves.

Question design

Many of the difficulties in securing valid and meaningful answers to survey questions stem from the design of the questions themselves. Difficulties often arise from:

- language;
- question phrasing;
- question length;
- question order;
- response formats.

These and other problems have been identified by methodological research as well as through working experience with surveys. There have been two main research approaches. One has involved interviewing respondents after they have completed a questionnaire or been involved in an interview to discover how they have interpreted the questions. The other has used dual random samples in which one group has been given questions phrased in one way and the other the same questions but phrased differently. In the latter studies, any differences in results can be attributed to the differences in the questionnaires rather than between the groups.

Language

Terms can be introduced into questions that are imprecise, ambiguous or incomprehensible to respondents. It is very difficult to know in advance whether particular words will prove problematic. Even everyday words such as 'you' or 'weekday' may have different meanings for different people. In one survey on birth control some respondents thought that 'family planning' meant the process of organizing the family's activities.

Question phrasing

Seemingly minor differences in the wording of questions can significantly influence survey results. For example, the question 'Are you in favour of the democratic right to withhold one's labour in an industrial dispute?' is much more likely to secure agreement from respondents than the question 'Are you in favour of the right to strike?' (Marsh, 1979). Even factual questions, as opposed to attitudinal ones, can be affected. Peterson (1984) found that the question 'What is your age?' was likely to be answered, rather than ignored, by a much higher percentage of respondents than the question 'How old are you?'

Question length

Questions containing many words are more likely to be misunderstood than those containing few. If your question contains more than 20 words, it should be considered suspect. Rewording can often produce a shorter, simpler way of expressing the same idea. It is often the case, however, that overly long questions need breaking down into several shorter ones. This increases the number of questions to be asked but increases the chance of obtaining meaningful answers.

Question order

The position in which a question appears in a sequence of questions can affect respondents' answers to it. Where respondents are presented with a list of alternative answer categories, they will be more likely to select those towards the top of the list. However, if the list is read out to them by an interviewer they are more likely to choose those towards the end of the list.

Response formats

Open questions (where no answer categories are given) often get different results as compared with closed questions (where a set of alternative answers are given) even when the question wording is identical in each case. If two identical samples are asked a question such as 'Which business magazines do you read?' the results from the sample presented with a set of periodical names to tick is likely to differ from that from the sample presented with the question but no list – hence the concern that the researcher might be 'putting words in the mouths' of respondents.

Unfortunately, it is impossible to know in advance precisely which aspects of questions are likely to prove problematic, but there are six types of questions that are often used in questionnaires and that are known to frequently cause problems (Belson, 1981):

1   *Two or more questions are presented as if they are one.* For example, 'Do you like seminars and lectures? Yes ☐ No ☐ Don't know ☐.' If the respondent feels differently about the two experiences they have no way of indicating this.
2   *Questions with many words that define the scope of the question*: 'How many hours do you usually watch cable television on weekday evenings in summer?' Respondents tend to miss key words.

Box 9.1 Some examples of terms misunderstood in questions

Question A: 'Do you think that the television news programmes are impartial about politics?'
Interpretations of 'impartial':

Unbiased, fair, treating all parties alike	25
Biased, unfair	5
Spend too much time on	9
Spend too little time on	2
Term ignored/not understood at all	15
Total respondents	56

Question B: 'When the advertisements come on between two television programmes on a weekday evening, do you usually watch them?'
Interpretations of 'weekday':

Monday to Friday	116
Saturday to Sunday	72
Monday to Saturday	2
All days except Saturday	2
Term ignored or unclear interpretation	24
Total respondents	216

Source: Belson (1981)

---

3   *Questions using a qualifying phrase*: 'Have you attended any meetings this week, not counting today?' Respondents tend not to take into account the qualifying phrase.
4   *Questions containing several ideas or subjects*: 'Can you give me an estimate of the types and makes of electrical equipment you own or have owned during the last 12 months?' Complex questions tend to be simplified to make them answerable, or parts of the question may be ignored.
5   *Questions containing difficult or unfamiliar words.* Almost any word could be difficult or unfamiliar depending on the nature of the respondent group. It may be ignored or misinterpreted.
6   *Questions accompanied by one or more instructions*: 'Which of the following words apply to this product? Please look at the list and tick all those that apply. Add other words of your own in the space provided.' Parts of the instructions may be overlooked.

Activity 9.1 Does one word mean one thing?

Design a question intended to discover which days of the week a person considers to be 'weekdays'. Then ask a sample of your friends and colleagues this question. Are there differences in the answers you receive?

Dealing with question design

The main aim of question design is to try to ensure that respondents will understand the researcher's questions in the way that they are intended. Unless we can be reasonably confident that this will be so, the chances of obtaining valid responses are reduced. As mentioned earlier, this does not mean that even the most poorly designed questions will fail to be answered. On the contrary, the evidence from experience with surveys shows that most respondents will try to answer questions, if only by translating them into terms they can deal with. And very often there may be no immediate way of distinguishing answers that reflect a correct understanding of a question from those that do not.

Unfortunately, there is no way of guaranteeing that questions will be understood as intended. However, there are several steps that researchers can take to improve the chances that this will be so.

Editing the questions

Foddy (1993) recommends three principles that researchers should keep in mind when they are constructing questions for interviews and questionnaires:

1   The topic should be properly defined so that each respondent clearly understands what is being talked about.
2   The applicability of the question to each respondent should be established: respondents should not be asked to give information that they do not have.
3   The perspective that respondents should adopt, when answering the question, should be specified so that each respondent gives the same kind of answer.

More specifically, the first draft of the questionnaire or interview schedule should be edited according to the rules listed in Box 9.2. It should be obvious from these that a considerable degree of language awareness is required if this is to be done successfully. Students who are working in a language other than their own are strongly recommended to secure the help of a native language speaker if they are designing a survey instrument.

Box 9.2 Rules for constructing survey questions

1   Make sure that the topic has been clearly defined.
2   Be clear both about the information that is required about the topic and the reason for wanting this information.
3   Make sure that the topic has been defined properly for the respondents by:
  • avoiding the use of 'blab' words (i.e. words that are so abstract or general that they lack empirical referents);
  • avoiding words that are unlikely to be understood by all respondents either because they are rarely used in everyday life, or because they are specialist (i.e. jargon) words.
4   Make sure that the question is relevant to respondents by:
  • using an appropriate filter;
  • avoiding asking for information respondents are likely to have forgotten;
  • avoiding hypothetical issues.
5   Make sure that the question is not biased, by:
  • ensuring balance in the introduction to the question (e.g. 'Some people like X, and some people dislike X. Do you like or dislike X?');
  • ensuring that sets of response options are complete;
  • ensuring that sets of response options are balanced;
  • avoiding using words that are likely to invoke stereotypical reactions.
6   Eliminate complexities that prevent respondents from easily assimilating the meaning of the question, by:
  • avoiding asking two or more questions at once;
  • avoiding the use of words that have several meanings;
  • checking whether the question has been worded as simply as possible;
  • avoiding the use of too many 'meaningful' words in one question;
  • avoiding the use of qualifying clauses and phrases and the addition of complicating instructions which cause respondents to start to answer before they have been exposed to the whole question – if qualifying clauses and phrases have to be used, they should be placed at the beginning rather than at the end of the question;
  • making sure that the question is as short as possible;
  • avoiding the use of both negatives and double negatives.
7   Ensure that respondents understand what *kind* of answer is required by:
  • setting the question in context;
  • informing respondents why the question is being asked;
  • informing respondents what will be done with the information they give;
  • specifying the perspective that respondents should adopt.

Source: Foddy (1993, pp. 184–5)

Piloting the questionnaire

As I indicated during our discussion of the survey in Chapter 7, testing out the questionnaire on a small sample of respondents is an essential step in the design process. Although this can reveal some problems with the questions and in the workability of an interview schedule, it may not be especially helpful unless it is followed up by detailed question-testing.

Activity 9.2 Testing questions for adequacy

Examine the following questionnaire item. Is this a well-designed or a poorly designed question? What, if anything, is wrong with it?

Question: *'When the holiday advertisements come on between two television programmes on a weekday evening, do you usually watch them or not?'*

Question-testing involves taking individual questions and working with a pilot sample of respondents in order to discover how those questions are being understood. Specific procedures that can be adopted are:

• *Comprehension tests.* Respondents can be asked to put the question in their own words in order to see if they have understood it as intended.
• *Double interview.* Respondents are presented with the question in the way envisaged in the survey. Each respondent is then interviewed to discover what meanings have been attached to it.
• *Think aloud.* Respondents are asked to talk through the processes they are using to interpret and answer questions as they are doing so.

Question-testing should continue until a question form has been constructed that does convey its intended meaning to, if not all, then at least the vast majority of the members of the pilot samples. There are practical limits to how far this process can be taken, but some degree of question-testing is almost always to be recommended.

Other factors to take into account when designing the questionnaire are:

1   *Research relevance.* To avoid overloading respondents it is important to be fairly ruthless in including only questions that are relevant to your research objectives.
2   *Respondent ability.* It is important to consider whether your respondents are likely to be able to answer your questions. Are they likely to be in possession of the information you seek? Are you making unreasonable informational demands upon them?

3   *Respondent willingness?* Will the respondents have time to answer all your questions? Are they likely to be embarrassed or offended by any of them? Will they be interested enough to participate and to do so with sufficient commitment to make their response worthwhile?

A useful source of survey questions is the CASS (Centre for Applied Social Surveys) Question Bank. This can be accessed via the National Centre for Social Research at www.scpr.ac.uk. Miller's (1991) *Handbook of Research Design and Social Measurement* gives details of numerous rating scales. In general, experience suggests that if you intend to use questionnaires in your research, you should take care with question design, avoid unnecessary complexity, and always pilot your questionnaire to test its adequacy.

In this section I have emphasized the difficulties associated with questioning procedures because they are both important and frequently underestimated. The design of survey questions is of crucial importance for obtaining both high response rates and high-quality responses. It is especially important in postal surveys because then the respondent is entirely dependent on the written word in the questionnaire for an understanding of the researcher's intentions.

Questionnaire design may look simple – anyone can simply write down a list of questions on a sheet of paper. But vast amounts of time and effort are wasted each year producing survey findings of doubtful validity. At best this is an inefficient use of resources. At worst it gives researchers and those who read their reports the dangerously misleading impression that they know what respondents think when they almost certainly do not. In reality it is a difficult and time-consuming process to design and develop a questionnaire that 'works', but that is the price that has to be paid to achieve good-quality data.

Research interviewing

Interviews take many forms and are used for a wide variety of purposes. Here we concentrate on research interviews. Unlike other types of interview, such as those used in therapy or during employee selection, these are concerned exclusively with obtaining data from respondents for research purposes. However, interview formats vary widely ranging from the highly structured survey interview to the informal conversational interview used in ethnographic research.

Box 9.3 What do survey interviewers do?

Interviewers spend their days approaching strangers, asking them for answers to questions in which they may have no special interest, for a purpose they may find obscure on behalf of an organization they may not have heard of.

(Wood, 1978, p. 91)

Interview formats vary widely according to the nature of the research, but in survey research there are two main types: the structured and the semi-structured. Some writers refer to the latter as 'unstructured' interviews but I prefer to avoid this usage. Each type of interview makes different assumptions about the data construction process and requires different behaviour from the interviewer, but all research interviews are structured in the sense of being thoughtfully conducted and purposeful.

Interview schedules

The design of interview schedules raises much the same issues as that of the self-completion questionnaire and requires just as much care. However, some additional considerations apply because the schedule is intended for use by an interviewer.

Structured schedules

Structured schedules generally assume that to avoid biasing respondents' answers, every respondent in a survey must be asked exactly the same questions, in the same order and, ideally, by the same interviewer, whose behaviour should never vary from interview to interview. The aim is to standardize the interviewer's behaviour so that the only things influencing the respondents' answers are the questions and differences among the respondents themselves. This assumes that it is possible to design questions that have the same meaning for all respondents. It also assumes that it is possible for interviewers' behaviour to be invariant across interviews. Both assumptions are problematic.

The structured schedule therefore includes:

- *Questions* written in a form that can be delivered word for word by the interviewer.
- *Standard phrases* that are to be used to guide the respondent, such as 'Can you please explain your reasons?' and 'In what way?'
- *Instructions* to the interviewer on question sequencing and the recording of answers.

Visually, a structured interview schedule bears a close resemblance to a self-completion questionnaire, as you will see if you compare the examples of an interview schedule and a postal questionnaire reproduced in the appendix to Hoinville *et al.* (1978). Everything is pre-specified and the interviewer's task is to *stick to the schedule*.

Standard phrases used in structured schedules include prompts and probes.

PROMPTS

A prompt is any implicit or explicit suggestion of a possible answer to a question (Atkinson, 1968). Prompts are used to define the meaning of a question more precisely and to make it easier for the respondent to answer. Where a lengthy set of alternatives are involved, a prompt list may be printed on a card which is handed to the respondent and from which a response is selected. However, one problem with prompts is that they may suggest answers to the respondent that might otherwise not have been given.

Example prompt: 'Do you travel to work by *car, bus, train* or in *some other way?*' Without the prompt, the question might have been phrased 'How do you travel to work?' This might lead some respondents to describe their route to work rather than the means of transport used.

PROBES

A probe is any stimulus which is not a prompt applied in order to obtain a more explicit or extensive response (Atkinson, 1968). Probes can be clarificatory or exploratory:

Clarificatory: 'Can you explain a little more fully what you mean by that?'
               'In what way?'
               'How do you mean?' [quoting interviewee's unclear phrase]
Exploratory: 'Is there anything else?'
               'Are there any other reasons?'

Box 9.4 Probing interviews: persistence pays off

This interchange took place between a government interviewer and an American farmer during a survey on problems of farm production:

INTERVIEWER: How many bushels of wheat did you harvest last year?
FARMER: My gosh, we had a *terrible* year! When we'd thought to be planting last spring, it rained all the time and then it got dry and everything burned up. We didn't get more than 300 bushels.
INTERVIEWER: I see. Well, you said you didn't get more than 300 bushels. Can you give me a little closer estimate?
FARMER: Well, like I said, it was an awful year around here, but I guess we got a little more than 300 bushels – between 350 and 400 I guess actually.
INTERVIEWER: 350 to 400 you say. Which would be closest?
FARMER: Oh, I think we estimated it at right around 400 bushels.

Source: Cannell and Kahn (1965, p. 360)

Semi-structured schedules

The assumptions underlying semi-structured interview schedules are that questions may need to be worded differently for different respondents if they are to have the same meaning for all respondents, and that the order in which questions are presented should depend on the specific context of each interviewer–respondent interaction. The schedule therefore consists of the set of topics and sub-topics about which information is sought. It is up to the interviewer to word specific questions and to manage the order of introduction of topics during the interview itself. A good example of a semi-structured schedule is given by Hoinville *et al.* (1978, pp. 200–3).

Conversational interviews

Formalized interviews are typically associated with survey research but interviewing also takes place in other research contexts. In some styles of research, such as ethnography, information may be sought by the researcher through informal interaction with informants. As Burgess (1984) has pointed out, in survey research the relationship between researcher and researched is fleeting and it is assumed that the role of the respondent is simply to answer questions that the researcher has formulated in advance of the interview. In ethnographic field studies, by contrast, the researcher is likely to be in a long-term relationship with those being studied. The researcher learns about the culture and setting of the field site through informal, conversational interviews with informants. Burgess (1984, p. 102) refers to this approach as a 'style of interviewing which employs a set of themes and topics to form questions in the course of conversation'.

Spradley (1979) refers to three types of question used in this style of research: descriptive questions, structural questions and contrast questions. Descriptive questions ask informants to describe their activities. Structural questions are intended to discover how informants organize their knowledge. Finally, contrast questions encourage informants to compare and contrast various situations and events in their environment. For example, a manager might be asked to describe the job she does and the types of problems she faces, and to compare the pattern of activities and problems she encounters in her unit with the situation in other parts of the organization that she is familiar with.

As Burgess (1984) points out, conversational interviews are liable to some of the same problems as more structured forms, such as the effects of question wording and interviewer bias. They also present problems of their own.

- *Time.* The length of the interviews needs to be controlled to avoid fatigue for both parties. One and a half to two hours is likely to be the maximum.
- *Coverage.* The interviewer needs to allocate blocks of time to the topics to be covered to ensure that none is ignored or squeezed out.
- *Recording.* Unlike structured and semi-structured interviews, which are usually conducted in a formal setting such as an office or interview room, conversational interviews may take place in the field, close to the activities that are being researched. Recording these interviews is likely to be by means of field notes written after the conversation has taken place rather than on an interview schedule as the interview takes place. Accuracy of recall may be

threatened. Where a formal space is used, tape-recording of the interview is widely advocated. However, as with other forms of tape-recorded interview, the transcription process can be very time-consuming and laborious.

Informal interviews may seem less demanding to conduct than the structured forms but this is misleading. Considerable skill is required to manage the fluid social situation characteristic of the conversational interview and to emerge with more than a rambling set of notes. As Fontana and Frey (1994) indicate, interviewing is an aspect of the 'art of science'.

Interviewer bias

Interviewer bias refers to distortions introduced into the respondents' answers and behaviour as a result of the interviewer's characteristics, attitudes and behaviour. Characteristics such as the interviewer's age, sex, ethnicity and social status interact with those of respondents and influence the interview process. For example, male interviewers receive more refusals than female interviewers, especially from male respondents.

The interviewer's attitudes, as perceived by the respondents, may also influence the respondents' behaviour. For example, when presented with opinion or attitude questions, respondents may conform to what they believe to be the interviewer's views about the topic. Inappropriate interviewer behaviour, such as inaccurately recording respondents' answers or failing to ask the questions as written (in a structured schedule), also introduces bias.

A major concern in interview surveys is the control of interviewer effects, which can operate in ways that are subtle and difficult to detect. Interviewer training is one way of attempting to achieve control, together with the use of structured schedules.

Choosing an interview format

The structured schedule reduces the problem of interviewer bias and facilitates the categorization and comparison of responses. However, the standardized format may weaken validity. It is best suited when factual data are sought from homogeneous samples.

The semi-structured schedule gives the interviewer considerable discretion over the conduct of the interview. Interviewer bias is more likely to arise but the potential for meaningful communication is also strong. Categorization and comparison of responses is more difficult and the recording of responses is also more problematic. The semi-structured interview is suited to exploratory studies where the issues of interest are ill-defined, sensitive or highly personal and where the sample is heterogeneous.

Conversational interviews are likely to be appropriate in field settings where the researcher is present long enough to develop informal relationships with participants. Recording may be more problematic than with the more formalized structured and semi-structured interview. Considerable flexibility is required of the investigator in the absence of a preconceived plan.

> ## Activity 9.3 Design a semi-structured interview schedule
>
> How much do you know about your friends' backgrounds and biographies? Prepare a list of topics that you would like to ask them about, for example their family, education and work experience. Approach one of them for an interview using this as an aide-memoire.

The structured interview process

Interviews may be conducted in a wide variety of settings: in offices, on factory floors, and so on. Control of the setting by the interviewer is desirable but is possible only if the respondent can be interviewed on the interviewer's territory. A quiet, comfortable, private setting free from intrusions is the ideal for interviews of any length.

A structured interview moves through three main phases: the opening phase, the question–answer phase and the closing phase, as depicted in Figure 9.2.

The opening phase

The opening phase begins at the moment the interviewer and respondent meet in the setting and may take no more than a few minutes. However, this stage is

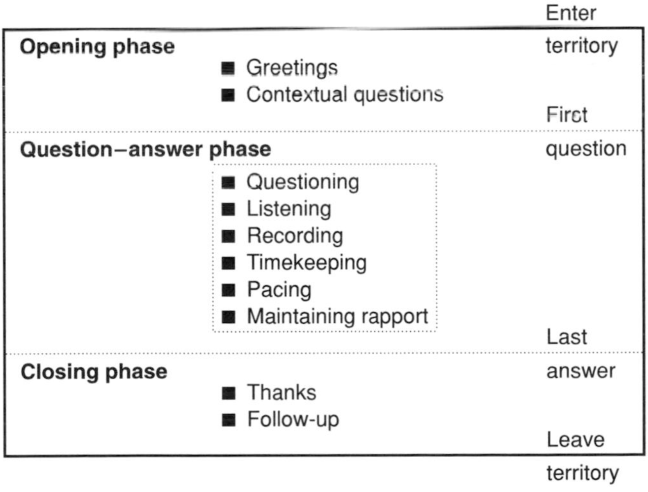

	Enter
Opening phase	territory
■ Greetings	
■ Contextual questions	
	First
Question–answer phase	question
■ Questioning	
■ Listening	
■ Recording	
■ Timekeeping	
■ Pacing	
■ Maintaining rapport	
	Last
Closing phase	answer
■ Thanks	
■ Follow-up	
	Leave
	territory

Figure 9.2 The structured interview process.

vitally important for setting the tone of the interview. It is likely to be mildly stressful for both parties.

At this stage of the interview, respondents will typically be concerned with various matters to do with the context of the interview, such as:

- the purpose of the research;
- what will be done with the results;
- the status of the interviewer and his or her organization;
- how the respondent was chosen;
- how long the interview will take;
- whether the interviewer is competent and trustworthy.

Respondents may or may not raise these issues during the opening stage but the interviewer should be prepared to deal with them.

Since anxiety is likely to be present, an important aim of the interviewer at this stage is to encourage the respondent to relax. It is essential to spend a little time on the pleasantries of introductions and greetings. Avoid rushing ahead by starting immediately with first question on the interview schedule.

The question–answer phase

The question–answer phase is the core of the interview, the meat in the interview sandwich. The phase begins as the interviewer asks the first question and ends when the respondent finishes answering the last question. During this phase the interviewer has to pay *simultaneous* attention to a number of tasks:

- *Question delivery*. It is necessary to follow the schedule and keep track of the topics that have been covered.
- *Listening*. Concentrated, active listening is required throughout to enable accurate recording of answers and smooth movement from question to question.
- *Recording*. Rapid writing skills are needed, particularly if there are many open questions. In structured interviews, interviewers are normally expected to record answers to open questions verbatim. Tape recorders can be used but subsequent transcription and analysis is extremely time-consuming and laborious unless the interview is very brief. Ratios of 8:1 transcribing to recording time are to be expected.
- *Timekeeping*. The respondent may be able to give only limited time and the interviewer may have other interviews arranged. The interviewer is under pressure to complete the schedule in the time available.
- *Pacing*. The interviewer must maintain the momentum of the interview, avoiding lengthy silences and dealing with respondents who speak too rapidly or too slowly.
- *Maintaining effort*. He or she must keep the respondent 'in play' by establishing a positive climate and maintaining it throughout.

One reason why interviewing is a tiring activity is that the interviewer has to pay continuous attention to all these activities during the question–answer phase.

Closing phase

The interview should be closed in a businesslike manner, the respondent duly thanked and any requests for further cooperation (such as a further interview) mentioned. Some of the respondent's concerns about the research, such as its purpose and the use of results, may be raised at this point if they have not been dealt with during the opening. Occasionally, respondents see this phase as their opportunity to interview the interviewer!

Box 9.5 The interviewer's attitude

In the interview I use a number of simple rules or ideas; I listen. I do not interrupt. I do not give advice. I avoid leading questions. I refrain from making moral judgments about the opinions expressed. I do not express my own opinions, beliefs or sentiments. I avoid argument at all cost.

(Roethlisberger, 1941, p. 93)

Interviewing hints

- *Construct a well-designed schedule.* A reliable schedule is a major source of confidence for the interviewer and this will communicate itself to the respondent.
- *Don't go too fast.* Rushing the interview is one of the commonest problems for inexperienced interviewers. Give yourself and especially the respondent time to think. They may well have never been asked the questions you are putting to them and need time to formulate well-considered answers. Try to establish a calm, timeless atmosphere even if you feel under pressure.

Activity 9.4 Design your own structured interview schedule

Using the same questions that you created for your questionnaire in Activity 7.2, redesign it as a structured interview schedule. Interview one or two friends. Write a short account of your experience of each interview. How do the results compare with those obtained from the questionnaire?

- *Spread the interview load.* Interviewing is mentally exhausting, requiring high degrees of concentration. Three one-hour interviews in a single day may be as much as can be managed without loss of efficiency.
- *Develop a professional attitude.* The task is to obtain the data needed for your research project but you are also relating to another human being. Try to combine the approach of the businesslike technician with that of the humane diplomat.

Key points

1   It is essential to take questioning procedures seriously and to give as much and probably more thought to the design of questionnaires and interview schedules as to sampling issues and methods of analysis.
2   Questions in surveys may be answered as if they have been understood when in fact they have not been, and this may be impossible to detect without further investigation. Question-testing should therefore be a part of any survey design process.
3   There is little point in building elaborate statistical analyses on top of data that are of doubtful validity.
4   Although ethnographic interviewing takes place in a different context, many of the issues concerning question design and the interview process are still relevant.

Key reading

Arksey, H. and Knight, P. (1999) *Interviewing for Social Scientists*, London: Sage.
Foddy, W. (1993) *Constructing Questions for Interviews and Questionnaires: Theory and Practice in Social Research*, Cambridge: Cambridge University Press.

Further reading

Belson, W.A. (1981) *The Design and Understanding of Survey Questions*, Aldershot, UK: Gower.
Converse, J.M. and Presser, S. (1987) *Survey Questions: Handcrafting the Standardised Questionnaire*, Beverly Hills, CA: Sage.
Fowler, F.J. and Mangione, T.W. (1990) *Standardized Survey Interviewing*, Beverly Hills, CA: Sage.
Hart, S.J. (1991) 'A First-Time User's Guide to the Collection and Analysis of Interview Data from Senior Managers', in N.C. Smith and P. Dainty (eds) *The Management Research Handbook*, London: Routledge, pp. 190–204.
Healey, M.J. and Rawlinson, M.B. (1994) 'Interviewing Techniques in Business and Management Research', in V.J. Wass and P.E Wells (eds) *Principles and Practice in Business and Management Research*, Aldershot, UK: Dartmouth, pp. 123–46.

Mishler, E.G. (1986) *Research Interviewing: Context and Narrative*, London: Harvard University Press.
Morton-Williams, J. (1993) *Interviewer Approaches*, Aldershot, UK: Dartmouth.
Scheurich, J.J. (1997) 'A Postmodernist Critique of Research Interviewing', in *Research Method in the Postmodern*, London: Falmer Press, pp. 61–79.
Spradley, J.P. (1979) *The Ethnographic Interview*, New York: Holt, Rinehart and Winston.

Interviews by telephone

Frey, J.H. (1989) *Survey Research by Telephone*, London: Sage.
Frey, J.H. and Oishi, S.M. (1995) *How to Conduct Interviews by Telephone and in Person*, London: Sage.
Groves, R. and Kahn, R. (1980) *Comparing Telephone and Personal Interview Surveys*, New York: Academic Press.

The interviewer's perspective

Converse, J.M. and Schuman, H. (1973) *Conversations at Random: Survey Research as Interviewers See It*, New York: Wiley.
Pahl, R.E. and Pahl, J. (1965) *Managers and Their Wives*, Harmondsworth, UK: Penguin – see the appendix in which the interviewer describes her work.

The interviewee's perspective

Gilbert, G.N. (1980) 'Being Interviewed: A Role Analysis', *Social Science Information*, 19, pp. 227–36.

10 Data construction by making observations

Observing as a method of gaining knowledge about the world plays an important role in the natural sciences. Indeed, science is widely thought of as a method of inquiry based on observation and experiment. In management studies observation is also an important means of obtaining data. Seeing or witnessing what people do might even be thought to take precedence as a source of evidence over being told by them what they do. If 'actions speak louder than words', then it seems that 'observations speak louder than self-reports'. Questionnaires and interviews can only take us so far. Observation can take us further.

In management research, observational methods have been applied within widely differing research designs ranging from highly structured experimental studies of group behaviour carried out in artificial laboratory settings to field studies of working life carried out in natural settings such as offices, factories and other workplaces. I have described some examples of these types of study in earlier chapters. In this chapter we will be examining the main issues and activities associated with observation as a method of data construction.

What is observation?

The term 'observation' is ambiguous. One dictionary definition is 'to keep in view, to watch, to subject to systematic watching, to regard attentively, to direct watchful and critical attention with a view to ascertaining a fact' (Garmonsway, 1970). The emphasis on watching implies that observation is to be equated with visual processes, rather as if research using observational methods is like that of a naturalist observing animal behaviour from the safety of a hide, or an astronomer peering through a telescope at distant planets.

In social research, observation usually involves more than simply watching. To be an observer almost certainly involves listening, and sometimes the researcher will be engaged in active participation in the settings that are being studied. On the other hand, methods that we do not normally associate with observation, such as face-to-face interviewing, require the researcher to engage in 'observation': looking at the interviewee for visual cues as the interaction progresses. There is, then, no clear-cut dividing line between observational and other methods of obtaining data.

Box 10.1 Observation – not as easy as it looks

This is the most classical and natural of techniques. It simply involves looking at what is going on – watching and listening. We all do it, most of us badly because we do not know what to look for or how to record it.

(Bennett, 1991, p. 100)

The great detective Sherlock Holmes once teased Dr Watson by asking him how many steps it took to climb the staircase to their first-floor rooms at 221B, Baker Street. Watson did not know, despite the fact that he went up and down that staircase every day. Holmes commented that while Watson had 'seen' he had not 'observed'. Observing is, then, not a straightforward process. We notice only some of the things we see, we remember only some of the things we notice, and different people notice and remember different aspects of the same experiences. This is very clear from witnesses who have been asked to give systematic accounts of some dramatic event such as a street crime or urban disaster. Their descriptions often differ substantially.

These psychological limitations on our capacity to observe influence all researchers whatever their style of research, although they can be mitigated by training and experience. But observation is also problematic in a more fundamental sense. Thus epistemologists have debated whether it is possible in principle to make straightforward and unequivocal 'observations' at all. Positivism assumes that there is a bedrock of observables that provide the starting point for investigation. These are the data, a term that is derived from the Latin *datum* meaning 'something given'. Constructionism rejects this view, arguing that all observations

Activity 10.1 What do you see in it?

Look at the material below from Sanger (1996, p. 7). How many Fs and fs are present in this piece of text? Allow yourself 10–20 seconds to produce your answer. Then ask some friends or colleagues to try. Do you all agree? If not, what do you think is the reason for this? The correct number can be found at the end of this chapter.

Count the Fs

The significance that we attach from today to Friday's Great Education Reform Bill is a matter of great concern to the scientific community of physicists, chemists and all students of the inside of the atom.

are 'theory laden'; observing is at one and the same time a process of sense-making, or interpretation. Interpretation always takes place within some framework of concepts and in that sense presupposes 'theory'. We will examine these issues a little further in the section below on the 'observer inference problem' but for further discussion of the philosophical status of observation see Chalmers (1978, chapter 3) and Sayer (1992, chapter 2).

Why observation?

If we are interested in describing and explaining patterns of human behaviour, we have three broad choices. We can:

- ask people what they are doing and why;
- consult written and other records of what people have done;
- observe what they do.

Of these three, only observation gives direct access to people's behaviour. It could therefore be claimed that observation is the best and perhaps the only way to obtain valid data about human activities. Such a claim arises in part from an awareness of the difficulties in obtaining valid data using alternative methods.

Scepticism about self-reports

Many researchers doubt whether what people say they have done, are doing or will do in the future bears much relation to their actual behaviour (Deutscher, 1973). Relying on answers to questions in postal surveys or interviews is seen to be naïve because of such factors as:

- *Memory errors.* As we saw in Chapter 9, people often give inaccurate accounts of events when asked to recall them at a later time (Foddy, 1993). Observation of events at first hand by the researcher overcomes the need to rely on the reports of others.
- *Prestige bias.* People tend to give 'respectable' accounts based less on what they actually do and more on what they feel they are supposed to do. This is especially the case where 'deviant' or socially reprehensible behaviour is concerned. An observer may be able to gain access to aspects of behaviour that are normally hidden.
- *Situational bias.* Someone's response to a hypothetical question about how they would behave is likely to be different from their response to the actual situation. A symbolic situation as portrayed in a questionnaire or as an interview question is 'cold' and unreal. For example, consider the difference between being asked the question 'What would you do if you were visiting your bank and an armed robber rushed in?' and actually facing the situation. Could you be certain how you would react? Observation of actual behaviour in real situations avoids having to rely on hypothetical answers to hypothetical questions.

Box 10.2 What we say and what we do

Salaman and Thompson (1978) observed the British army officer selection process at first hand. The overt and stated intention of selectors was to be fair and unbiased. But when the selection and decision-making process was observed, the same behaviour was interpreted by the selectors in different ways according to how they perceived the candidates. For example, an upper-class candidate who hesitated over a decision was described as 'remarkably cool' whereas a working-class candidate who hesitated was described as 'lacking in natural authority'. Despite the selectors' stated intentions, their decisions favoured upper-middle-class candidates. See Salaman and Thompson (1978, pp. 283–304).

Observation is one way of obtaining more valid data than self-reports provide, although problems with self-reports can be dealt with in other ways too (Podsakoff and Organ, 1986).

You can't tell what you don't know

Observation enables patterns to be detected in people's behaviour of which the actors themselves are unaware. For example, in order to identify the daily patterns of movement of shoppers around the floor of a hypermarket, it is necessary to observe them rather than simply to ask customers what they do. Similarly, observations of behaviour in small groups reveal patterns of interaction among the group members that they do not notice (Bion, 1961). These are aspects of life that can only be detected by an outside observer.

Is what you see what you get?

Observation may be able to offset some of the disadvantages of alternative methods of data construction but it is itself far from problem free. Two of the most significant issues are the observer-inference problem and the reactivity problem.

The observer-inference problem

As Box 10.1 indicates, observation may seem like a straightforward process but it is both practically and epistemologically problematic. The issues are philosophically complex and disputed, so only a brief sketch of the problem will be given here. It concerns the relationship between what we observe and the meaning we attribute to those observations, or what Kerlinger (1964, p. 505) calls the 'observer-inference' problem.

A traditional view of science places considerable emphasis on the importance of objective observation. Implicit in this view is that there is a real and stable external reality that has properties which can be observed by anyone. Positivists tend to assume that reality can be observed directly and that, in practice, objective observation has been accomplished when multiple observers offer identical reports of that reality. These observers are taken to represent 'everyman': if the world looks the same to everyone, then whatever it looks like must be real rather than, say, a figment of someone's imagination. Moreover, human behaviour is governed by external stimuli to which individuals react, much in the way in which pool balls ricochet around in response to being struck. Explanations can be obtained by observing and relating external factors and behaviour.

Constructionists, in contrast, argue that we have no direct access to reality. Our sense experience is mediated by both our perceptual equipment and the interpretations we place upon that experience. Since people's actions are largely derived from their intentions and goals and we are all immersed in a world of meaningful interpretations, behaviour cannot be understood purely from the outside: a meaningful understanding of the inner meaning of a person's actions is necessary even to be able to describe those actions validly, let alone explain them. Observation without reference to the actors' meanings and intentions can only yield interpretations based on the observer's own frame of reference. Although we may not notice this when dealing with social situations in our own society, where observers and observed tend to share the same interpretative schemes, when culturally unfamiliar settings are observed, the observer is likely to impose interpretations that are meaningless to the participants.

Behaviourists tend to respond to this problem by assuming that interpretation is mainly an issue once the 'basic facts' have been ascertained. Kerlinger and Lee, for example, argue that observers should record 'pure behaviour as nearly as possible' whenever appropriate (2000, pp. 732–3). Such occasions are, they say, rare, but on other occasions reliability can be promoted by training observers how to interpret their observations in terms of a pre-established labelling scheme.

Constructionists, on the other hand, deny that there can be any 'pure' observations (Spinelli, 1989): the world is inherently meaningless and is comprehensible only in terms of the interpretations put upon it through language. Whether someone is 'waving' or 'drowning' cannot be determined from observations of an arm moving to and fro, but only by reference to the meaning which the actor intends to convey. Observer interpretations and categorizations made without reference to the actor's intentions are, from this point of view, always suspect and of doubtful validity.

The reactivity problem

An important methodological prescription is that observers must not disturb or change the reality they are attempting to observe in the act of trying to observe it. To do so is to contaminate that reality and so generate biased observations of it. Methods of observation must therefore be designed that avoid provoking a reaction from whatever is being observed. Such methods must be *non-reactive*.

Box 10.3 Mass Observation

In the 1930s Tom Harrisson created an independent research organization called Mass Observation. Through the use of a panel of thousands of volunteer observers who watched and recorded the behaviour of those around them, Harrisson created the world's largest social observation study. The idea for the research came from his hobby, which he pursued with a passionate interest – bird-watching.

The problem when studying human behaviour is in some ways much the same as that faced by the naturalist who wishes to study an animal's behaviour in its natural habitat. For the naturalist, if the animal is disturbed there may be a risk of its fleeing, attacking the observer or behaving in an abnormal way. Both behaviourists and constructionists have been aware of the problem that observation can influence the activities that are being observed. One response to this has been to adopt covert observational methods, on the assumption that if people do not know they are being observed, they will behave naturally. Under these conditions the chances of a study's findings being methodological artefacts, largely created by the researchers themselves, are much reduced. However, they also introduce other problems of both a practical and an ethical kind.

Methods of observation

To speak of observational 'methods' implies clear, well-structured and unambiguous procedures. Although these may be evident in laboratory-type research, in field research and particularly in ethnography, it is only relatively recently that research procedures have become more codified. In an influential text, McCall and Simmons (1969, pp. i, ii) noted that field research was 'the least systematised and codified' of research methods and even went on to say that their own book could not claim 'to have made any substantial progress towards codification of participant observation procedures'.

Although there has been considerable change since then as ethnography has become more popular, there has not been and probably cannot be anything like the proceduralization found in survey research. Bate (1997) suggests that while qualitative researchers tend to favour this trend towards proceduralization (the creation of how-to guides), ethnographers retain a more relaxed attitude to methods. They prefer to follow the anthropological tradition of pitching one's tent in the jungle and then going out to record whatever is to be seen, or, as Bate (1997, p. 1152) puts it, 'many ethnographers believe there are no rules as such, and the only way to do ethnography is to just get out and do it'. This makes it difficult to train researchers in ethnography other than through experience and by immersion in the classic reports of ethnographic studies.

A researcher contemplating using observation as a method of obtaining data has to answer the following questions in the course of designing the study:

Where to observe?

The answer to the question of where to carry out observations is likely to depend on both the nature of the research problem and the resources available. The key choice is between artificial and natural settings.

Some topics may require the use of specialized observation suites equipped with audio and visual recording facilities, observation windows, and one-way mirrors which enable researchers to watch research subjects' behaviour without being seen themselves. Less elaborate facilities may, however, be appropriate. For example, all that may be required is a room set aside to accommodate the researcher and those to be observed. Teaching rooms or meeting rooms may well suffice.

Where the style of the research requires naturalistic fieldwork, sites for observation must be identified and selected. These sites will be chosen partly in the light of the substantive nature of the project, and, where necessary, access to the sites must be secured. If the research involves observation in public spaces, access is likely to be unproblematic. If, on the other hand, it is planned to observe behaviour in organizations, as is often the case in management studies, then careful and possibly time-consuming negotiations may need to be entered into to obtain access to the people and places needed. They must also, of course, be practically accessible, which may mean choosing locations within easy travelling distance of the researcher's base.

Researchers intending to carry out observational fieldwork in organizations need to be realistic about the likelihood of gaining access to every part of an organization. One way of thinking about access is in terms of the map presented in Figure 10.1. This depicts an organization as a series of concentric zones that are progressively more difficult to access as we near the centre. Thus:

- The outermost *public zone* is one that is open to anyone. Most organizations present a public face which can be observed without any special permission or negotiation: its Web pages, annual reports, advertising, the exterior of its buildings, its products, and so on.
- Depending on the nature of the organization, it may also possess a *semi-public zone*. This area is open to the public although it remains a privately controlled space. Shops, railway stations, cinemas, restaurants and sports stadiums are examples of organizations with semi-public zones.
- The *private zone* is one that is open only to the organization's members or employees, and outsiders must obtain permission to enter it. In a bank or building society, for example, this is represented by the office areas that are open only to staff.
- Finally, at the heart of the organization is the *inner sanctum*, a place where the organization's most precious assets are stored and where its secrets

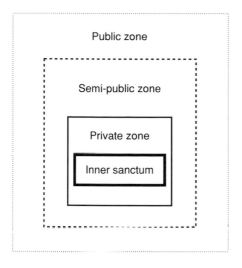

Figure 10.1 Organizational access zones.

are hidden. Special permission is required to enter this zone, even by the vast majority of the organization's own personnel. Most members of the organization will never have access to the inner sanctum: many may not even know of its existence.

In his study of a police station, Holdaway (1980) found zoning of this kind. There were public and private areas within the station that were used by the police officers in distinctive ways. In the public areas, such as the foyer, the officers behaved in strict accordance with the law, but in the private areas, such as the charge room and cells, they were less careful to behave within the prescribed limits. Similarly, it seems to be a common feature of life in service organizations that customers or the public are spoken of in humorous and sometimes derogatory terms when staff are in the private zone.

Gaining access to those parts of the organization that are normally off limits to outsiders usually requires negotiation with gatekeepers which may or may not be successful. The boardroom and those who occupy it represent the inner sanctum of most large companies. It is not surprising, therefore, to find that access to study boardroom behaviour has often proved problematic. For example, Pahl and Winkler (1974) succeeded in obtaining access to the directors of 19 British companies and observed each executive director for one full working day. Even so, over 80 per cent of the 130 companies they approached refused to participate in the research.

Where permission to enter a site for observation has been refused or where it is thought unwise to request it, the researcher may try to enter the organization covertly. This is not a decision to be taken lightly and we will return to the matter of covert observation below.

What to observe?

Decisions about what to observe are unavoidable since it is impossible to observe everything. As Bechhofer and Paterson (2000, p. 5) point out:

> No social situation or behaviour can be described exhaustively. We must always select from a potentially infinite wealth of possible observations, and in making them we implicitly compare what we see with something else. Good research design requires social scientists to make those selections in a conceptually informed way and their comparisons explicit.

Highly structured approaches are those in which the investigator begins the study with a specific and clearly stated set of items to be observed. Categorization schemes or observational checklists, such as that developed by Bales (1950) for his studies of small groups (see p. 185), enable observed instances of these items to be recorded systematically. Typically, highly structured approaches are associated with laboratory settings although they may also be used in the field by non-participant observers.

The diary method is a version of the structured approach in which observations are made not by the researcher but by those being researched, who record details of their own behaviour. It therefore involves self-observation. In management research this technique has been used in several studies of managerial work such as those by Carlson (1951), Mintzberg (1973) and Stewart (1965). In part, use of the diary technique helps to overcome the problem of the researcher being unable to observe the behaviour of all subjects in all places and at all relevant times. Mintzberg has discussed the use of diaries and other aspects of structured observation in several articles (Mintzberg, 1970, 1971) as well as in appendix C of the book reporting the study (Mintzberg, 1973).

Semi-structured approaches tend to be favoured by ethnographers. Given that the aim of ethnography is to produce a rich description of the way of life of those observed, rather than to test predefined hypotheses, many ethnographers try to enter the field with as few presuppositions as possible. Even so, the fact that not everything can be observed still applies, and ethnographers are faced with problems of selecting both what to observe and what to record (see Burgess, 1984, chapter 3).

How to observe?

The observer's relationship with those observed is heavily dependent on whether he or she acts as a participant or non-participant and by whether observation is to be conducted openly or covertly. Decisions on these matters have significant methodological, personal and ethical implications.

Participant and non-participant observation

To act as a participant observer means that the researcher takes on a role within the organization or group being observed. The advantage of participation is that the observer gains first-hand exposure to the setting and is able to experience the events, processes and demands which arise there from the same perspective as those being studied. Furthermore, in some circumstances it may only be by becoming a participant that the researcher can gain access to the setting.

But participation also has disadvantages. One is the risk that objectivity will be impaired by too close an identification with members. Another is that the observer may influence the behaviour of those studied in artificial ways. However, some see the capacity to influence events directly as an advantage. Reactions to the presence of an observer can themselves be taken as data (Hammersley and Atkinson, 1995) and observers may be in a position to invoke the events they wish to study (Emerson, 1981). But such interventions raise ethical questions since the observers' actions may have negative consequences for the members.

Overt and covert observation

The choice between open and covert methods of observation causes much more soul-searching than that of whether to act as a participant or not. While the ornithologist need have no qualms about observing the birds from the obscurity of a hide, management researchers may well feel themselves to be caught in a classic dilemma: covert observation seems desirable in order to avoid the reactivity which threatens the validity of observations made openly, yet covert methods are widely regarded as unethical. The unenviable choice seems to be between poor-quality data or a bad conscience.

However, some methodologists believe that the problem of reactivity has been overstated. Kerlinger and Lee (2000, p. 729) claim that it 'is not a severe problem' and that observers seem generally to have little effect on the behaviour of those they observe. 'Individuals and groups', they say, 'seem to adapt rather quickly to an observer's presence and to act as they would usually act', although they are probably thinking mainly of laboratory-type studies where participants have relatively little to gain from acting abnormally. In field settings, and especially where illicit or illegal behaviour is concerned, open observation may simply be impractical; access to the field is likely to be denied or, if it is obtained, observers may only be allowed to see what the participants wish them to see.

Researchers interested in observation may thus face a difficult methodological choice. If they do decide to adopt a covert role, they are likely to pay a significant personal price, for experience indicates that the role is stressful and difficult to maintain.

How to record observations?

In principle, observations may be recorded in a variety of ways ranging from video recordings to field notes. As with interviewing, it may be tempting to record everything by mechanical means, where these are available, but the same risk of accumulating vast quantities of raw material is likely to be encountered. For laboratory-type work, it may be both possible and desirable to record observation sessions from start to finish for subsequent analysis. In field settings this is impossible and so simpler, more selective methods are appropriate.

Field notes are written records of the researcher's observations and play a crucial role in ethnography. Burgess (1984) suggests that the researcher should keep both methodological and substantive field notes. Substantive field notes are predominantly a descriptive record of the events and conversations witnessed by the observer for each period of observation. The structure of the substantive notes has partly to be improvised in the light of the specific nature of the project, but they should always be kept systematically and record details of where and when the notes were made, the nature of the events observed, who was involved in them, and where they took place.

Methodological field notes serve chiefly to stimulate researchers to reflect on their experiences and their methods. They therefore record such matters as the investigators' impressions, problems and reflections on their own role as observers. An element of self-analysis, Burgess notes (1984, p. 173), 'is to be recommended to all who engage in field research'.

How long to observe?

Practical constraints are likely to dictate for how long observation can be maintained. In laboratory studies, subjects can rarely be expected to make themselves available for more than a few hours or, at most, a few days. In addition, systematic observation requires intense concentration so that the observer risks fatigue if observation is maintained over extensive periods. Field studies are typically of longer duration than those based in the laboratory.

Mintzberg's (1973) study of managerial work was based on his doctoral research in which he observed the work of five chief executives for one week each. In two doctoral research projects, Al-Maskati (1995) observed five bank training groups for periods of between 4 and 12 days, while Hyde spent over 400 hours as an observer in four mental health units (2002). In her study of group development, Gersick (1988) observed the meetings of eight project groups, the number of meetings varying between 4 and 25. Watson (2001) spent a year as an observer at a telecommunications factory, ZTC Ryland. Observations of the Relay Assembly Test Room during the Hawthorne studies were maintained for five years (Madge, 1963).

Observer roles

The roles available to the observer can be categorized in a variety of ways (see, for example, Adler and Adler, 1994; Bailey, 1994) but one useful approach is to combine the decision on participation with that on openness versus concealment in much the way that Gold (1958) has done. The choices open to the researcher are thus defined by the answers to two key questions:

1   Will those to be observed know they are being observed?
2   Will the observer participate as a member of the observed group?

This yields four roles: covert participant observer, open participant observer, covert non-participant observer and open non-participant observer. We will briefly review each of these roles, bearing in mind that in practice the differences are not necessarily as clear-cut as they might appear. For example, observers may be open about the fact that they are engaging in research and are recording what they observe, but they may conceal or only partially reveal their research objectives. Similarly, they may act as a participant during some parts of a study but as a non-participant in others.

Covert participant observer

The covert observer takes up a role in the setting to be observed but does so without the knowledge of others located there. The role is inherently stressful but enables close engagement with the setting and its members.

Dalton's (1959) classic research into managerial behaviour involved lengthy periods of covert participant observation, and Ditton's (1979) study of worker behaviour in a bread-baking plant entailed three months' covert observation as a bakery operative. In the study of a police station mentioned earlier, Holdaway (1980) adopted the role of a covert participant observer. As a serving police officer at the time of his research, he was, in effect, studying his own workplace but without the knowledge of his co-workers. He experienced considerable personal difficulty and stress in this role but felt that his approach was justified; secrecy, he argued, was necessary in order to study the police, an organization that has great power but which is highly sensitive to investigation by outsiders.

Open participant observer

The open participant observer takes a role within the organization being studied but is known by everyone to be doing so as a researcher. Lupton adopted this role when carrying out his doctoral research into shop-floor behaviour in two workshops (Lupton, 1959, 1963). He decided to act as an open participant observer partly because he felt covert observation would be unethical but also because he knew that certain documentary data he required could not be obtained without the disclosure of his purposes. Watson also acted as an open participant observer during his study of managerial work (Watson, 2001).

Covert non-participant observer

The role of covert non-participant observer is the one that comes closest to that of the bird-watcher in the hide; the observer is literally hidden from view. Because hiding in this way is problematic in natural settings, covert non-participant observation is usually confined to the laboratory setting, where concealed cameras and one-way mirrors enable researchers to observe and record behaviour undetected. Although reactivity may be reduced, covert observation remains problematic from an ethical point of view. Bales's well-known group study method is reviewed on p. 185 as an example of research using covert non-participant observation.

Box 10.4 Settling in as a participant observer

When I entered the workshop at Wye Garments I experienced the period of awkwardness in relationships which I had anticipated. Although the chargehands and the workers' representatives had told the workers who I was and what I was doing in the shop, many of them found difficulty in understanding; others did not care who I was or what I was doing. I decided that my best policy for the first month or so would be to concentrate entirely upon my work as a producer, not to ask questions of anyone, and to speak only when spoken to, except for exchanging pleasantries: in this way I hoped the workers would assign me a role in the workshop. I answered questions which people put to me as fully as possible, but I did not make a point of going around telling everyone who I was and what I was doing. During this whole period and throughout my stay in the shop I kept full notes of what I had observed each day. I did not make notes publicly but left the job whenever possible to jot headings in my notebook. I then wrote my notes up in full at home each evening.

(Lupton, 1959)

Open non-participant observer

Many field studies are carried out in which the researcher openly enacts the role of observer. The investigator works in the field purely as a researcher and does not act as a participant. For example, during Mintzberg's (1973) study of managerial work he openly observed and recorded the chief executives' activities. Hochschild (1983) researched the experiences of airline flight attendants partly by openly observing the recruitment and training process at Delta Airlines and Pan Am. In his study of the culture of night nurses, Brooks (1999) openly observed behaviour on the wards of a general hospital during both night and day shifts. Finally, Belbin's (1981) influential work on the characteristics of successful and unsuccessful management teams entailed open non-participant observation of groups of managers undertaking management development courses at a business college.

Styles of observation

Although there are many choices open to the researcher who intends to deploy observational methods of obtaining data, two broad styles of observational study can be identified (Table 10.1). Which of these is to be preferred depends on factors such as the nature of the research topic, the resources available for the project, and the skills and inclinations of the researcher. To illustrate these styles, I will briefly summarize an example of each type of study.

Table 10.1 Styles of observational research.

Laboratory style	Field style
Artificial setting	Natural setting
Pre-structured recording	Emergent recording
Non-participant observer	Participant observer
Short duration	Long duration

Laboratory observation in management

One important strand of management research has been that which examines behaviour in groups. Managerial issues such as leadership, communication, decision-making, creative problem-solving and other group processes have been studied in laboratory settings. Here groups are given tasks to perform and the group members' behaviour is observed and recorded as they attempt to deal with them.

One of the best examples of research on group behaviour using laboratory observation is that of Robert Bales. He devised a method of observation known as Interaction Process Analysis (Bales, 1950) which was used to record patterns of behaviour in problem-solving groups. Group members were observed in a group relations laboratory, an artificial setting on university premises.

The observer was not a group participant and observed the group from behind a one-way mirror. Behaviour was recorded according to a categorization scheme that was derived from a theoretical framework for understanding groups that remains influential today. According to this theory, work groups have to deal with two interrelated sets of problems: the group's overt task and the social and emotional responses of group members as they attempt to achieve it. The categorization scheme was designed to highlight and record behaviour related to these problems.

Each group member's actions were classified by the observer into one of 12 categories, such as 'Gives opinion', 'Shows disagreement', 'Shows solidarity', according to what they said and their gestures on each occasion they spoke. The observers were told to classify what they saw in the way that 'other people in general' would do. They also recorded who acted, towards whom they acted, and the time of their action. The data obtained from a group session could then be analysed to reveal the frequency of different types of behaviour, the influence of group characteristics such as size and composition on those frequencies, and sequences and patterns of interaction over time.

For a fuller account of Bales's methods see Bales (1950, 1970) and Bales and Slater (1955). Bailey (1994) provides a valuable overview of the methodological strengths and weaknesses of Bales's approach.

Field observation in management

Field studies in management have typically been set in a single organization where a lone researcher has spent relatively lengthy periods observing organizational life. Examples include the American studies by Jackall (1988) at Covenant

Corporation and by Kanter (1977) at Industrial Supply Corporation, and Watson's (2001) British study at ZTC Ryland.

The style of research adopted by Watson could hardly be further away from that of Bales. As was mentioned in Chapter 8, Watson conducted his study in a telecommunications company over a one-year period. The basis for access was that he would carry out a study of management competencies for the firm and, in return, would be able to pursue his own interest in managers and their work.

Watson was based in one of the company's manufacturing plants. He chose this plant partly for convenience (it was close to his home) but mainly because it had experienced a wide range of cultural and organizational change initiatives and programmes. The aim of his research was to discover how the managers had responded to these, and how these practical responses could be understood in terms of more academic management frameworks and theories.

Bales's observational studies were guided by a detailed observing scheme derived from behavioural theory, but Watson's approach was much broader. His methods of obtaining data were threefold. They consisted of an interview programme with a sample of 60 managers, informal observation during the course of his daily work at the plant, and personal conversations with managers, including those who were not involved with his interviewing programme. However, he did not treat his interviews in the manner of a survey researcher, mechanically recording 'responses'. Rather, he tried to interpret what was said to him according to the understanding of the company that he was building up during his work there, the specific context of the interchange, and his awareness of where the speakers were located in the organization's social and political processes.

Bales's research strategy was intended to minimize reactivity and maximize the objectivity of his data. Watson also strives for objectivity but by attempting to make explicit how his own actions were likely to have influenced the managers around him. He was not, he says, 'collecting' data, as if he had no hand in constructing those data, and he reports his materials accordingly.

Activity 10.2 Field observation

Select a 'public' space in your college or workplace, such as an entrance lobby or cafeteria. Spend 20–30 minutes during a reasonably busy period observing and recording what you see there. What does this experience tell you about:

1   the need for research objectives to guide observation;
2   structured (checklists) versus unstructured (field notes) recording methods;
3   the role of the observer and its effect on those observed;
4   your own feelings when acting as an observer?

Key points

1   Observing people and processes at first hand has a strong common-sense appeal as an approach to securing valid data.
2   Observation is a problematic process epistemologically and psychologically.
3   The potential reactivity of open observation can reduce its potential to yield valid data.
4   Covert observation is ethically questionable and in natural settings can place the investigator under considerable strain.

Key reading

Burgess, R.G. (1991) *In the Field: An Introduction to Field Research*, London: Allen and Unwin.
Weick, K.E. (1985) 'Systematic Observational Methods', in G. Lindzey and E. Aronson (eds) *The Handbook of Social Psychology*, vol. 1, *Theory and Methods*, New York: Random House, pp. 567–634.

Further reading

Adler, P.A. and Adler, P. (1994) 'Observational Techniques', in N.K. Denzin and Y.S. Lincoln (eds) *Handbook of Qualitative Research*, Thousand Oaks, CA: Sage, pp. 377–92.
Emerson, R.M. (1981) 'Observational Fieldwork', *Annual Review of Sociology*, 7, pp. 351–78.
Nandhakumar, J. (1997) 'Issues in Participant Observation: A Study of the Practice of Information Systems Development', in G. McKenzie, J. Powell and R. Usher (eds) *Understanding Social Research: Perspectives on Methodology and Practice*, London: Falmer Press, pp. 210–20.
Stewart, R. (1965) 'The Use of Diaries to Study Managers' Jobs', *Journal of Management Studies*, 2, pp. 228–35.

Count the Fs. The number of Fs and fs in the passage is 10.

11 Data construction by using documents and records

In previous chapters we have considered questioning and observation as methods for generating data in management research. Here we examine 'artefacts', the products of human actions that have been created without the researcher's intervention, as sources of data. These sources are many and varied and include organizational and personal documents, statistical records and the physical outcomes of human activity. The latter, non-documentary artefacts include intentionally created items such as office layouts, machine technologies and manufactured goods, and unintentionally created physical traces of behaviour such as wear-marks on machine controls or on the floors of supermarkets. Researchers refer to such items in order to make inferences about the attributes and behaviour of those who created them.

Although less obviously relevant than documents as data sources, non-documentary artefacts have been used in some management studies. For example, interest in corporate culture has drawn attention to such physical aspects of organizations as the buildings they occupy, the settings in which they are located, and the products they make. These physical manifestations are taken to be akin to texts in that they can be 'read' in order to understand various aspects of an organization's functioning (Barley, 1983). I will briefly refer to examples towards the end of the chapter.

The role of documents and records in management research

Because of the organizational context of management, documentary sources, including statistical databases, are particularly significant in management research. Fields such as economics, finance and accounting, and areas within organizational studies such as organizational demography and organizational ecology, rely almost exclusively on such sources. In addition to government organizations and other publishers of business information, commercial organizations tend to produce large volumes of documentary material as part of their everyday activities. These range from relatively ephemeral office memoranda to semi-permanent statistical data archives recording the organization's financial history. Except perhaps in the laboratory experiment, documents and records can play an important role in all types of study. Documents thus offer a particularly rich potential to management researchers, and expertise in using them is an important element of the management researcher's skill.

Epistemological orientations to documentary sources

An important distinction in the way documents are treated in social research is whether they are seen as a *resource for* research or a *topic of* research. When they are treated as a *resource*, the analyst's main interest is in the contents of the document. The document simply 'carries' the data of interest. The researcher should pay attention to the characteristics of the document in so far as they impinge on the validity of the data. It is important to be assured that it is authentic, is free from errors, and meets other criteria of adequacy (see pp. 197–8), but the document itself is of no interest beyond that.

When treated as a *topic*, however, it is the document itself that is the focus of analysis. Documents can be analysed in terms of their textual properties using content analysis (see Chapter 12) to reveal their stylistic features, the rhetorical techniques used, the amounts of space devoted to different topics, and so on. In addition, questions can be asked about the social context of their production and the ways in which these influence their content. In the case of newspapers, for example, news content needs to be understood in terms of the conventions of journalistic reporting, editorial practices, established 'news values', proprietorial involvement, dominant sources of advertising revenue, and so on.

Ethnographers have become interested in the social organization of documents in terms both of how they are structured and of the organized social processes that surround their creation. Organizational ethnographers are likely to pay particular attention to them. As Silverman (1993, p. 61) has said of documents that are used to record information (rather than fiction or poetry), 'people who generate and use such documents are concerned with how accurately they *represent* reality. Conversely, ethnographers are concerned with the social *organization* of documents, irrespective of whether they are accurate or inaccurate, true or biased'. Hammersley and Atkinson (1995) say that ethnographers must examine how documents are produced and that 'a comprehensive ethnographic account must include reference to how organizational documents are read, interpreted and used' (p. 168). The questions ethnographers ask of documents include: How are they written and read? By whom and on what occasions? With what effects? What is recorded and what is left unrecorded? What assumptions do writers tend to make about readers? What do readers need to know in order to make sense of what is written?

The topic–resource distinction is thus in part a reflection of different epistemological orientations. Documents and records are likely to be treated differently depending on whether those working with them are governed by positivist or constructionist assumptions. Positivists have tended to treat official documents as relatively unproblematic sources of data, especially when those data are in numerical form (Morgenstern, 1963). Statistical records can be seen as depositories of facts which are ontologically independent of the records that represent them. Constructionists tend to treat documentary sources more circumspectly, seeing them as human products that cannot be fully understood unless attention is paid to how they are produced. The 'facts', they point out, are in part constructed in the processes of record-keeping and so are ontologically contingent on those processes. This does not mean that such records are useless for research purposes, but it does mean that analysts must take into account the social nature of officially produced data. Indeed, for some researchers the social construction of official records and statistics in organizational settings has itself been a significant topic for research (Cicourel and Kitsuse, 1963; Irvine *et al.*, 1981; Sudnow, 1968).

The use of existing datasets

A distinction is commonly made in social research between *primary* and *secondary* data. Primary data have been constructed by the researcher in the context of his or her own research project. Secondary data have been constructed by others, who may or may not be fellow researchers, for purposes which may or may not be research. Increasingly, such data are held in databases and databanks such as those shown in Box 11.1. These can contain both quantitative and qualitative data. Quantitative data may be held in raw, summary and aggregated forms.

Box 11.1 Example electronic databases and business directories

Amadeus – www.jordans.co.uk – financial data on European companies

CAROL (Company Annual Reports On Line) – www.carol.co.uk – financial information and annual reports for listed companies in Europe and the United States

Datastream – www.datastream.com – global company financial data and government economic data

Directory of Directors – www.directoryofdirectors.co.uk

FAME (Financial Analysis Made Easy) – contains financial details of British public and private companies

Fortune 500 – www.pathfinder.com/fortune/fortune500/

SCORE (Search Company Reports) – www.score.ac.uk – catalogue of collections of company reports held in UK libraries

Standard and Poor's – www.compustat.com

The Stock Exchange Yearbook – www.caritasdata.co.uk – data on companies on the London and Dublin stock exchanges

UK Data Archive – www.data-archive.ac.uk – holds the largest collection of digital data in the social sciences and humanities in the UK

Who Owns Whom – worldwide information on corporate parents and their subsidiaries

---

As Hakim (1982) has pointed out, most social scientists tend to assume that their research objectives can be met only by collecting primary data, perhaps believing that for their work to be considered original it must use original data. The term 'secondary' when applied to data may give the misleading impression that they are of lesser importance than primary data or even that they are second-rate. Yet it is often possible to carry out original and important research projects using 'old' data that have already been collected by others. Working with such secondary data is sometimes known as secondary analysis.

Box 11.2 What is secondary analysis?

Secondary analysis is any further analysis of an existing dataset which presents interpretations, conclusions, or knowledge additional to, or different from, those presented in the first report on the inquiry as a whole and its main results. Secondary analyses will thus include studies presenting more condensed reports . . . ; more detailed reports (offering additional detail on the same topic); reports which focus on a particular sub-topic . . . or social group . . . ; reports angled towards a particular policy issue or question; analyses based on a conceptual framework or theory not applied to the original analysis; and reanalyses which take advantage of more sophisticated analytical techniques to test hypotheses and answer questions in a more comprehensive and succinct manner than in the original report.

(Hakim, 1982, p. 1)

Punch (1998) mentions several advantages and disadvantages of using existing datasets. Expenditure on obtaining data can be significantly reduced (although access to some commercial databases can be costly) and data analysis can begin immediately, so saving time. Also, the quality of some datasets may be superior to anything the researcher could have created alone. However, data that have been gathered by others for their own purposes can be difficult to interpret when they are taken out of their original context. It is also much more difficult to appreciate the weak points in data that have been obtained by others. Finally, the data may be only partially relevant to the current research question.

Documentary sources

We tend to think of a document as 'words on paper' but the medium on which a text is recorded is irrelevant to its status as a document. Texts stored electronically as computer files are just as much documents as those recorded on paper and stored in the traditional filing cabinet. In addition, of course, documents can contain numerals as well as or instead of words.

Although paper documents are likely to continue to be important in management research, electronic means of recording and storing texts present new opportunities and problems. For example, e-mail exchanges, although taking the form of texts, are not necessarily stored, so their existence is transient and they are more akin to verbal conversations than to written correspondence. Research access to such routine organizational communications may therefore be becoming more difficult. On the other hand, electronic storage of financial and accounting records in electronic databases has greatly eased the problems of accessing and processing these kinds of data.

Advantages of documents and records

Documents and records offer a number of advantages as data sources.

Ready availability and low cost

Routine company documents are usually plentiful and are relatively inexpensive to acquire for research purposes. They are often also of good quality since commercial organizations usually devote considerable efforts to documenting their activities and often use highly qualified employees to carry out the documenting process.

Because they are relatively plentiful and cheap to obtain, it can be appropriate to collect organizational documents even when their specific relevance to the investigator's research is unclear. If they have been obtained while the researcher is on-site, they can be stockpiled and then at a later date searched for pertinent information. On the other hand, if the need to consult documents is not appreciated until some months after the researcher has left the field, it may be difficult or impossible by then to secure what is required. As a general rule it is worth bearing in mind that material that *has* been obtained does not *have* to be used; but material that *has not* been obtained *cannot* be used and may be impossible to retrieve.

Non-reactive nature

Documents and records are generally regarded as non-reactive, unobtrusive sources of data. When they have been produced before the research commences, their contents obviously cannot have been influenced by the researcher's presence or by the existence of a research investigation. This is a considerable advantage in comparison with questioning and open observation. However, where the production of documents is ongoing, as it often is in organizations, and where those producing them know that they will be scrutinized by a researcher, they may modify their behaviour to conform more closely with organizational expectations. In any event, documents cannot be assumed to be unbiased sources and should be treated with the same degree of critical scrutiny as any other data source. Organizational records may, for example, be falsified or distorted as a matter of course irrespective of whether a research study is under way (see Box 11.6, p. 201).

Possibility of using large samples

Large samples can be obtained relatively easily and cheaply. Funding constraints may mean that use of existing data is the only practical way of undertaking some projects. Where company records are held in archives or where information is available from directories, large samples can be studied without the costs involved in securing data directly from each firm.

Carroll *et al.* (1993) used industry directories to identify samples of breweries in Germany and the United States. The German sample, drawn from a five-volume directory for the period 1861–1988, consisted of 15,293 breweries. The American sample for the same period totalled 6,458 companies. Data on each brewery were then obtained, the entire study using published data sources. Similarly, Messallam's (1998) study of the founding rates of investment firms in Egypt used a variety of directories and published listings to identify and gather data on a sample of 1,040 companies.

Directories listing people, such as the *Directory of Directors* and *Who's Who in Industry* (Margetts, 1991), offer the same advantage as does using directories for studying firms: individuals do not have to be approached with a request to provide information. However, inclusions in these types of directory tend to be limited to those at the higher levels of organizations. Also, the range of information provided for each person may not be sufficient, depending on the objectives of the study. Nonetheless, they often enable data to be gathered on individuals and groups that are otherwise inaccessible. Stanworth and Giddens (1974) utilized directories as a source of data on the backgrounds and careers of 640 chairs of large corporations and banks in the UK who were active between 1900 and 1972.

Appropriateness for longitudinal research

As Stanworth and Giddens's study illustrates, documentary sources can facilitate studies over lengthy time periods. Using documents, studies can be undertaken using data that are beyond the memory of any living individual. Where databases stretch back over many years it is possible to obtain information that could not be obtained by questioning or from observation.

In an American study, Lieberson and O'Connor (1972) used corporate and other records to investigate the impact of CEOs on company financial performance over a 20-year period. Thomas (2001) obtained data on company board membership for a sample of the largest retail firms in Britain. Data for six sample years spanning a 42-year period were taken principally from the *Stock Exchange Yearbook* as well as from a number of business directories and other types of directory. In a further study (Thomas, 2002) the changing structure of membership linkages among Britain's largest retailers was charted for the years 1975, 1984 and 1997. In both these studies documents and records were the sole source of data.

Appropriateness for historical studies

Documents are the main source of data for research in business and management history. Where no living witnesses remain, documentary records provide the only access to past events apart from physical remains. The histories of individual companies can be reconstructed from corporate archives, which may contain qualitative as well as financial information. Examples of corporate histories include studies of Barclays Bank (Hannah and Ackrill, 2001), Glaxo (Jones, 2001) and Standard Life (Moss, 2000). See also Warren and Tweedale (2002).

User-friendliness

Finally, unlike interview-based and observational field studies, research based on documentary sources does not require extended encounters with research subjects. Many of the ethical issues that arise when dealing face to face with people in the context of research can therefore be avoided, and the need for highly developed interactional skills is minimal. Documents can often be consulted at the researcher's convenience, are stored or can be gathered together in one or a few locations so reducing travel demands, and can be readily subjected to electronic processing.

Types of document

The range of documentary sources available to the management researcher is potentially vast. Scott (1990) has proposed a very useful classification scheme for documents in social research which combines the nature of the document's authorship with its degree of accessibility.

Authorship is distinguished in terms of the 'personal' versus the 'official'. Personal documents are those that have been written by individuals in their personal capacity rather than as job-holders or officials. Personal diaries and letters are prime examples. Official documents are those produced by functionaries in organizations. These organizations can be divided into state organizations, such as government departments and agencies, and private organizations, such as firms and voluntary organizations. There are also, of course, some quasi-governmental organizations which straddle the state–private boundary but they are not considered separately in this scheme.

Accessibility refers to the degree to which a document is open to those other than its author. Where access is 'closed', only the author or a few confidants are permitted access. In effect they are not available to researchers. 'Restricted access' means that the documents are open to outsiders but under specific conditions; special permission is likely to be required from the documents' holders and conditions of use may be imposed. 'Open-archival' access means that the documents are housed in a publicly accessible archive. 'Open-published' access means they are available as printed publications obtainable commercially or through libraries.

Box 11.3 Examples of document-based management studies

Bettman, J.R. and Weitz, B.A. (1983) 'Attributions in the Boardroom: Causal Reasoning in Corporate Annual Reports', *Administrative Science Quarterly*, 28, pp. 165–83.

Dobrev, S.D. (2001) 'Revisiting Organizational Legitimation: Cognitive Diffusion and Sociopolitical Factors in the Evolution of Bulgarian Newspaper Enterprises, 1846–1992', *Organization Studies*, 22, pp. 419–44.

Fiol, C.M. (1990) 'Explaining Strategic Alliance in the Chemical Industry', in A.S. Huff (ed.) *Mapping Strategic Thought*, New York: John Wiley, pp. 227–49.

Hellgren, B., Lowstedt, J., Puttonen, L., Tienari, J., Vaara, E. and Werr, A. (2002) 'How Issues Become (Re)constructed in the Media: Discursive Practices in the Astra–Zeneca Merger', *British Journal of Management*, 13, pp. 123–40.

Lieberson, S. and O'Connor, J.F. (1972) 'Leadership and Organizational Performance: A Study of Large Corporations', *American Sociological Review*, 37, pp. 117–30.

Mazza, C. and Alvarez, J.L. (2000) 'Haute Couture and Pret-a-Porter: The Popular Press and the Diffusion of Management Practices', *Organization Studies*, 21, pp. 567–88.

McEvoy, G.M. and Cascio, W.F. (1987) 'Do Good or Poor Performers Leave? A Meta-analysis of the Relationship between Performance and Turnover', *Academy of Management Journal*, 30, pp. 744–62.

Osborne, J.D., Stubbart, C.I. and Ramprasad, A. (2001) 'Strategic Groups and Competitive Enactment: A Study of Dynamic Relationships between Mental Models and Performance', *Strategic Management Journal*, 22, pp. 435–54.

Rondinelli, D.A. and Berry, M.A. (2000) 'Environmental Citizenship in Multinational Corporations: Social Responsibility and Sustainable Development', *European Management Journal*, 18, pp. 70–84.

Salancik, G.R. and Meindl, J.R. (1984) 'Corporate Attributions as Illusions of Management Control', *Administrative Science Quarterly*, 29, pp. 238–54.

Thomas, A.B. (1988) 'Does Leadership Make a Difference to Organizational Performance?', *Administrative Science Quarterly*, 33, pp. 388–400.

Thomas, A.B. (2001) 'Women at the Top in British Retailing: A Longitudinal Analysis', *Service Industries Journal*, 21 (3), pp. 1–12.

Thomas, A.B. (2002) 'The Changing Structure of Inter-corporate Relations among Britain's Largest Retail Firms, 1975–97', *Service Industries Journal*, 22 (4), pp. 22–40.

The combination of three categories of authorship – 'personal', 'official: state organizations' and 'official: private organizations' – and the four categories of access listed above yields a 12-fold classification of documents (see Scott, 1990, p. 14, figure 1.2). Here we will look briefly at documents according to their authorship and their uses in management research.

Personal documents have played a relatively limited role in management research to date, partly because relevant examples are relatively scarce. Managers normally produce documents about management as an integral part of their jobs rather than in a personal capacity. The exception has been the autobiographies of 'celebrity managers', which have been used as empirical data by some leadership researchers such as Kets de Vries (1996). Accounts by 'ordinary' managers of their experience of managing have, however, been largely absent, invaluable though they might be for improving our understanding of managerial work.

Personal documents have been used by entrepreneurial and business historians in the construction of business biographies (Jeremy and Tweedale, 1994). Some organizational researchers have drawn on textual ephemera produced by organizational members as data for the study of corporate cultures. In general, though, personal documents have been much less prominent in management research than official documents produced by organizations and especially firms.

Official documents produced by private organizations rather than the state include those created by companies and other types of private organization. These organizations produce a wide variety of documents and records as a part of their routine functioning. Organizational documents thus include such items as office memoranda, business letters, records of meetings, reports and policy proposals, operating and procedure manuals, staff lists, accounting and financial records, employee and customer records, PR materials, corporate presentations and speeches, sales brochures, advertisements, company annual reports, and so on. 'Minor' documents, such as labels, tickets, stationery and forms, have also become the focus of study in the emerging discipline of ephemera studies (see Box 11.4 and Matthews, 1993).

These documents differ in their accessibility to investigators. Commercially or politically sensitive information is likely to be closed to researchers, particularly students. Less sensitive company records and contemporary documents may be available on restricted access. Sometimes company records have been deposited in a public archive so that access is fairly straightforward. Finally, some forms of document, such as the annual report and accounts, must be published by law, and copies can readily be obtained either direct from the company or through business or commercial libraries.

While all organizations produce documentation as part of their everyday operations, most or all of which may not be openly accessible, some organizations also produce published documents as their primary function. Newspapers such as the *Financial Times* and publishers of business and commercial directories and yearbooks provide information about other companies and their management which can contribute importantly to management research.

Box 11.4 Permanent home for ephemera studies

The world's first Centre for Ephemera Studies was established at the University of Reading, UK, in 1993. The centre defines ephemera as 'the minor transient documents of everyday life', and tens of thousands of items are held in its collections. The Centre aims to promote the serious study of ephemera, develop research methods for ephemerists, and teach courses on ephemera. See Rickards (2000).

Official documents produced by the state that may provide data for management research include official statistics relating to such matters as employment, production and investment; departmental reports on various aspects of business; reports of official inquiries into such matters as competition, corporate governance and trading practices; and parliamentary records.

Evaluating documentary sources

Like other sources of data, documents and records should not be treated as unproblematic. Four criteria have been proposed by Scott (1990) for the evaluation of documents:

Authenticity

The analyst must be satisfied that the document is genuine. If, for example, it is a copy, has anything been omitted that appeared in the original? And can the authorship of the document be authenticated?

For example, it might be tempting to analyse the statements of company chairs that appear in annual reports in order to infer something about the psychology or the communication styles of corporate leaders. But can it be safely assumed that such a statement has actually been written by the chairman or woman? It seems more probable that the paragraphs that appear above the chair's name in the annual report will have been polished and perhaps even drafted by members of the company's press office. Whether this is an important consideration depends on the objectives of the research. For example, Salancik and Meindl (1984) argue that in the case of their research into the explanations given for poor corporate performance by company presidents in annual reports, it is not particularly significant that public relations staff may well have assisted with the production of the text.

Credibility

It is necessary to assess the nature and extent of biases the author has brought to the document. The analyst needs to know why the author produced the document and what interest she or he had in producing it. If the document is a report of events the author claims to have witnessed, how near to those events was the author both in time and in space? And what were the author's state of mind and physical condition at the time?

Think again of the example of company chairs' statements. Should optimistic-sounding statements be taken to mean that the company is in good health? Or should it be the reverse, on the grounds that when a company is performing badly, the chair's statement will tend to play this down in an attempt to 'talk up' the situation?

Representativeness

If the analyst is trying to generalize from documentary data, the question arises of how representative the documents are. Webb *et al.* (1999) identify two sources of sampling bias that can affect documents: selective deposit and selective survival. Selective deposit refers to the process whereby only an unrepresentative subset of the events of interest are recorded in documentary form. For example, the autobiography of a top business leader giving insights into corporate leadership is much more likely to be written and published than is that of the chief executive of a small firm. Similarly, the stories of successful firms are more likely to be documented than those of firms which fail.

Selective survival refers to the process whereby only an unrepresentative subset of documented materials survive over time. Minutes of board meetings seem more likely to survive than those of low-level committees. Some documents may be deliberately destroyed in order to prevent evidence emerging on embarrassing or illegal corporate actions. The now-defunct accounting firm Andersen was accused of destroying incriminating documents in the wake of the Enron collapse in the United States. In such ways, the records that do survive may give a slanted view of events.

Meaning

The essence of a document is the text which it contains. The analyst has to ensure that the meaning of the text has been understood. This involves two processes: the understanding of the text's literal meaning and that of its interpretative meaning. Comprehension of what the words in the text mean is a first step to understanding. Technical terms, for example, need to be translated into familiar language. Beyond this, it is necessary to grasp what the message conveyed by the words means and this requires an understanding of the context in which the text was produced. How such interpretations can be achieved and the question of how the validity of competing interpretations can be established are contentious issues. We will return to them in the next chapter when we discuss the analysis of qualitative data.

Box 11.5 Taking documentary sources seriously

The assessment of evidence derived from documents requires the same basic questions to be answered as with all forms of research. The test of reliability is still whether another researcher would extract the same information from the available documents. There is still a need to assess whether enough care has been taken to ensure that superfluous information has not been taken as central. Finally the extent to which the information that has been extracted can be generalised has to be determined. Reliability and validity are still central issues.

(Shipman, 1988, p. 109)

Problems with documents and records

As with other types of data source, the use of documents and records presents the researcher with certain difficulties.

Retention

Documents may be retained by companies for only a relatively brief period depending on the nature of the information they hold. Where electronic communications have become dominant, information that might once have been committed to paper may now be held only briefly in electronic form. In general, companies do not have much incentive to retain records other than to conform to legal obligations and to protect their commercial interests. On the contrary, retaining records beyond minimum requirements is likely to entail a company in costs that it may find hard to justify.

Inconsistent recording

The content and organization of official records may have changed over time and different organizations and units or departments within them may have implemented recording procedures in different ways. This makes aggregation and comparison problematic. For example, definitions of company size categories can differ significantly. Not only may different variables be chosen as measures of size, such as sales, capital employed, or number of employees, but boundaries between categories may be located differently for the same variable. In one study in Norway a firm was defined as medium-sized if it had between 200 and 499 employees, whereas in the United States a firm with fewer than 500 employees was regarded as small (Ghauri *et al.*, 1995). Care must always be taken when aggregating data from different sources that like is being combined with like.

Availability

Even where they exist, some records may be withheld, especially where issues of commercial security are concerned. When they are not withheld, restrictions on their use and especially on publication of their contents may be problematic from a research point of view. A thesis that contains information so sensitive that it cannot be divulged even to examiners is clearly far from ideal!

Validity

Where documents contain reports of activities and events, the validity of the material cannot simply be assumed. Mistakes and misrepresentations, whether accidental or deliberate, can occur. In the case of reports by witnesses to events, Gottschalk *et al.* (1945) have approached the problem in much the same way as lawyers do when trying to establish the credibility of evidence. These authors suggest the application of the following tests to assess validity:

1   Was the ultimate source of the information (the primary witness) *able* to tell the truth?
2   Was the primary witness *willing* to tell the truth?
3   Has the primary witness been *accurately reported*?
4   Is there any *external corroboration* of the information?

Organizational records and reports can also be problematic. Whatever the stated intentions of record systems, some matters may be routinely over- or under-recorded, especially where external monitoring systems are used to assess the achievement of performance targets. In Britain, accusations of 'massaging' of performance records have been levelled at the police service, health service and elsewhere. Falsification of corporate accounts has given rise to some well-publicized scandals. Similarly, minutes of meetings may exclude sensitive 'off-the-record' discussions, and reports may omit potentially embarrassing information or even falsify key data (see Box 11.6). Personal documents such as business biographies should also be treated critically. Business leaders can rarely be considered as disinterested reporters of their careers and their organizational experiences. The analyst must assess the likelihood of their having overdramatized their role in the events they recount and must be sensitive to the social and political perspective from which they view the world.

Non-documentary artefacts

The records we have considered so far have been in textual form, whether stored in hard-copy form or as electronic records. While these are likely to predominate in management research, non-textual records have also been used in some studies. Two areas in which non-documentary artefacts have found a place have been in the study of corporate culture and in consumer research.

Box 11.6 Setting the record straight

Extract from the record of the hearing before the Subcommittee on Economy in Government of the Joint Economic Committee of the Congress of the United States, 91st Congress, 13 August 1969:

> MR. VANDIVIER: In the early part of 1967, the B.F. Goodrich Wheel & Brake Plant at Troy, Ohio, received an order from the Ling-Temco-Vought Co. of Dallas, Texas, to supply wheels and brakes for the A-7D aircraft, built by LTV for the Air Force. . . . Generally speaking, the brake passed all the static brake tests, but the brake could not and did not pass any of the dynamic tests. . . .
>
> CHAIRMAN PROXMIRE: How long did you work as a technical writer?
>
> MR. VANDIVIER: Approximately three years . . .
>
> CHAIRMAN PROXMIRE: In your statement you say 'Accordingly I wrote the report but in the conclusion I stated that the brake had "not" met either the intent or the requirement of the specification and therefore was "not" qualified.' Then you add 'When the final report was typewritten and ready for publication the two "nots" in the conclusion had been eliminated, thereby changing the entire meaning of the conclusion' . . .
>
> Was this the only time in the three years you worked as a technical writer with Goodrich, the only time that you made false entries into a report of manufacture?
>
> MR. VANDIVIER: Yes it was.
>
> (Quoted by Daft, 1992, pp. 418, 423)

Artefacts in corporate culture research

The precise definition of corporate culture has been a matter of some debate but physical artefacts are usually seen to constitute one aspect of an organization's culture. Brown (1995) refers to a number of examples of these physical artefacts: the organization's products; its production technologies, such as manufacturing equipment; its office technologies, such as computers, photocopiers, fax machines, telephones; its buildings, their decoration and decor and their attendant landscapes; the uniforms and dress codes adopted by staff; and organizational documents such as annual reports, advertising brochures, and so on.

Various documents have been included in this list of cultural artefacts. Documents can, then, be treated both as physical objects (an aspect of their being used as topics) and as repositories of meaning expressed in text. As objects their cultural meanings can be 'read' and sometimes these readings may run counter to those available from the text. For example, the size, shape, quality of paper, use of colour and visual imagery in a company annual report may be read as indicating wealth, security and quality whereas the text may report substantial losses!

Artefacts in the study of consumer behaviour

In their discussion of non-reactive research, Webb *et al.* (1999) refer to 'trace records', which consist of physical traces of human activity that can be used to infer types or patterns of behaviour. They cite the example of a study that attempted to estimate whisky consumption in the city of Wellesley, Massachusetts, where store sales records were not available. The investigator overcame this problem by counting the number of empty whisky bottles discarded in domestic waste bins (Sawyer, 1961).

The use of refuse or garbage as a data source has been adopted in some other studies of consumer behaviour and has been dignified with the delightful name 'garbology' (see Box 11.7). Rathje *et al.* (1977) used an elaborate and detailed recording system to measure and classify refuse items gathered from domestic households and public landfill sites. Important information on both the

---

Box 11.7 Garbology: the science of rubbish

Refuse dumps have been important sources of evidence for archaeologists trying to reconstruct the ways of life of ancient peoples. But Dr William Rathje has spent the past 30 years analysing the contents of modern waste tips to learn more about contemporary patterns of household consumption and disposal, an increasingly important topic in a resource-conscious world. Himself an archaeologist and anthropologist, he is Director of the University of Arizona's Garbage Project and has published numerous articles and books on garbology including *Rubbish! The Archaeology of Garbage* (Rathje and Murphy, 2001). See also Rathje *et al.* (1977).

Activity 11.1 Who's who at the top?

Select five to ten prominent companies. Produce a 100-word profile of each of the chairmen or chairwomen of these firms including such items as their education, qualifications, social background and career experience. Use only published sources as the basis for your research. Which sources did you consult? How much confidence do you have in these sources? To what extent were you able to corroborate your findings? Could all the data you required be obtained from these sources? Were there items that could *not* be found in the records?

composition and decomposition of refuse has been created from these efforts. For example, 20 per cent of landfill consists of food-related waste, and hot dogs decompose at a very slow rate, often lasting 15 years. No doubt we can all look forward to seeing the first professorial chair established in this relatively new research area!

Key points

1 High-quality, low-cost studies in management research can be undertaken using only documents and records as a data source.
2 Much management research takes place in organizations where documents and records are produced as part of the organization's routine functioning. They can often be obtained cheaply and may be worth stockpiling for later examination.
3 The validity of documents and records should not be taken for granted. Documentary sources should be rigorously evaluated.

Key reading

Scott, J. (1990) *A Matter of Record: Documentary Sources in Social Research*, Cambridge: Polity Press.
Webb, E.J., Campbell, D.T., Schwartz, R.D. and Sechrest, L. (1999) *Unobtrusive Measures*, Thousand Oaks, CA: Sage.

Further reading

Dunkerley, D. (1988) 'Historical Methods and Organization Analysis: The Case of a Naval Dockyard', in A. Bryman (ed.) *Doing Research in Organizations*, London: Routledge, pp. 82–95.
Macdonald, K. (2001) 'Using Documents', in N. Gilbert (ed.) *Researching Social Life*, London: Sage, pp. 194–210.
Silverman, D. (1993) *Interpreting Qualitative Data: Methods for Analysing Talk, Text and Interaction*, London: Sage.
Webb, E. and Weick, K.E. (1979) 'Unobtrusive Measures in Organizational Theory: A Reminder', *Administrative Science Quarterly*, 24, pp. 650–9.

12 Data analysis and interpretation

The range of techniques available for the analysis and interpretation of both quantitative and qualitative data is enormous. A full account of statistical methods alone would fill many volumes. The purpose of this chapter is therefore to provide an overview of the main methods of analysis and to indicate their potential applications rather than to give detailed instruction in how particular statistics are calculated or how to undertake textual interpretation. Guidance to sources dealing with these topics in depth is given at the end of the chapter.

Basic processes: describing and explaining

Once the dataset has been constructed, its contents must be analysed and interpreted. The accumulated body of data does not speak for itself. At this stage the researcher has to confront two key problems:

1   How can the data be transformed from an extensive assortment of raw materials into a concise and meaningful description of what has been observed?
2   Once a valid and coherent descriptive account has been constructed, how can it be connected with the problem field? Have new descriptive materials been created? Have theoretical expectations been tested? Has a new theory or causal model been constructed?

These questions must, of course, be tackled in relation to the overall objectives of the study, but the general aim of analysis and interpretation is to enable the analyst to 'see the wood for the trees'. The analyst seeks *structure* in the data: generalities and commonalities within all the variety and the differences that are displayed in the dataset, and linkages, patterns and connections among elements, variables, categories and types.

Data can mount up alarmingly as a study progresses: datasets may swell and field notes bulge to the point where it may seem impossible to make any sense out of the material. The data must undergo data reduction in order to condense and summarize them so that they are meaningful in terms of the study's objectives.

Whether quantitative in the form of numbers or qualitative in the form of words, 'raw data' are reduced in various ways. Quantitative data are subjected to statistical analysis. Qualitative data are reduced by textual interpretation. For both, the data are condensed into more manageable and intelligible forms. The results of these compressions can be displayed in a variety of ways, such as in textual narratives, numerical tables, diagrams and charts. The processes of describing and explaining that we discussed in Chapter 2 are the focus of these analytical efforts.

Data reduction has two broad aims irrespective of whether the data are quantitative or qualitative: summarization, and the identification of relations. With quantitative data, summarization involves reducing a whole set of numbers to one or a few statistics that express something in general about the set. Similarly, with qualitative data, summarization condenses a larger volume of text into a category label, a type name or a few sentences. In both cases the aim is to make the data more intelligible but with as little loss of information as possible.

With quantitative data, the identification of relations involves establishing the existence and strength of links between the variables in a study. In effect the analyst explores the elements of the variable net for which data have been obtained and the net's structure. With qualitative data the analyst seeks patterns in the textual materials that comprise the data. A historian, for example, seeks to make sense of the events that have been recorded in historical documents by emplotting them in a recognizable narrative form.

In summarizing the data and depicting relationships and patterns within it, the analyst is engaging in the task of description. Explaining these descriptions or findings is the next task. However, as I emphasized at the start of the book, the boundaries between many research concepts are fluid and fuzzy so that rigid distinctions cannot be sustained. Summarizing and relating, describing and explaining, are not completely separable processes but rather interpenetrate and overlap. And there are many ways of interpreting data.

Box 12.1 Is there only one way to interpret your data?

There is no use looking for perfect interpretations of data: it would be terribly hard to find perfection if it were available, and it isn't. You never look for *the* interpretation of a complex data set, or *the* way of analyzing it, because there are always lots of interpretations and lots of approaches depending on what you are interested in. There are many good answers to different questions, not one right answer as in the detective story.
(Erickson and Nosanchuk, 1979, p. 5)

Interpreting quantitative data

The widespread availability of personal computers and the development of software packages for the analysis of both quantitative and qualitative data have placed complex analytical techniques within reach of every researcher. Calculations that once took teams of clerks literally weeks to process by hand can now be generated instantaneously from your PC or laptop in the comfort of your own home and displayed in all manner of graphical and tabular forms. Yet this easier accessibility has proved both a boon and a bane. Although advanced analyses can now be produced by even inexperienced researchers, the temptation to print reams of statistics without much appreciation of what they signify is sometimes overwhelming. Needless to say, this temptation should be resisted.

Time spent understanding the computational and theoretical bases of the statistics you use will be a very worthwhile investment. In part, such understanding can be achieved by studying some of the statistical texts such as those recommended here as Further Reading. Working with small datasets, preferably by hand, can also be indispensable for acquiring an intimate knowledge of what is happening to data when they are processed to produce statistics such as correlation coefficients. Hand-tallying of some data into frequency distributions is also recommended. These methods can help to keep the analyst in close touch with the dataset and the methods used to manipulate and transform it.

Quantitative summarization

The summarization of quantitative data can be simultaneously an important outcome of the research and a prelude to further analysis. Because the more advanced statistical procedures often make assumptions about the data to which they are applied, it is usually necessary to begin by producing summary statistics.

Levels of measurement

Quantitative data are likely to be organized in the form of a data matrix as discussed in Chapter 7. Each row in the matrix will contain the data for a single case, with each column representing a variable. The cells of the matrix will contain the values recorded for each variable for each case.

Box 12.2 What is measurement?

In its broadest sense measurement is the assignment of numerals to objects or events according to rules.

(Stevens, 1951, p. 1)

The possibilities for quantitative summarization depend on the nature of the variables we wish to summarize. With some variables, cases can only be distinguished from each other quite crudely. With others, more information is potentially available. The more information a variable can yield, the higher that variable's level of measurement. Four levels can be distinguished, each higher level encompassing the properties of those below:

- *Nominal-level variables.* These variables only permit *differences* between cases to be identified. For example, with the variable 'head office location', we may find that three different companies have their headquarters in London, New York and Rome respectively. The companies differ from each other in this respect but it does not make sense to ask how much they differ.
- *Ordinal-level variables.* These variables enable us to rank cases, to place them in a rank order. A list of the best business schools might be of this kind. For any school we can tell how it stands in relation to the others listed, but we cannot tell exactly how much better or worse it is.
- *Interval-level variables.* The variable has equally spaced categories that fall into a natural order but there is no true zero point. The Fahrenheit temperature scale is an interval measure with no true zero point. Temperatures can fall 'below zero'.
- *Ratio-level variables.* The variable has equally spaced categories that fall into a natural order and that have a true zero point. Weight and age are examples. It is impossible to weigh less than nothing or to be younger than at the moment of birth.

The distinction between interval and ratio levels is not too important in social research. Both are metric scales in which the interval or distance between each category is the same. This means that mathematical operations such as addition and subtraction can be performed with them and this allows the calculation of various statistics. In general, higher levels of measurement are to be preferred to lower because they contain more information.

Frequency distribution

The frequency distribution (Table 12.1) is one of the simplest ways of organizing and summarizing data. For each variable, the number of cases falling into each category is tallied. Where only a few or none of the cases appear in some categories it can be convenient to group the categories together into ranges.

Table 12.1 Example frequency distribution.

V3 Job title	Frequency	Percentage	Cumulative percentage
Director	2	28.6	28.6
Manager	3	42.8	71.4
Supervisor	2	28.6	100.0
Total	7	100.0	
Missing cases	0		

Note: Data from Table 7.2.

Hand-tallying using check marks can be an especially useful way of constructing frequency distributions since it gives an immediate visual representation of the shape and spread of the distribution. For this and other methods of creating frequency distributions see Erickson and Nosanchuk (1979, chapter 2).

Measures of central tendency

Measures of central tendency indicate where the 'centre of gravity' of a distribution lies. They attempt to show what a 'typical' or 'usual' case looks like. The three commonly used measures are the mean, median and mode, each being more or less appropriate depending on the specific features of the frequency distribution.

- The *mean*, or 'average', is the sum total of the values recorded for all the cases divided by the number of cases. The mean can be misleading when a few exceptionally high or low values occur in the distribution. These 'outliers' have a disproportionate impact on the magnitude of the mean.
- The *median* is the mid-point of a distribution so that an equal number of cases lie above and below this value. It is largely unaffected by outliers.
- The *mode* is the value that occurs most frequently in the distribution. It is completely unaffected by outliers.

Despite its sensitivity to outliers, the mean is the most important measure of central tendency for statistical purposes. Its interpretation depends, however, on a knowledge of how much variability there is among the values from which it has been calculated.

Measures of variability

Measures of variability are sometimes known as measures of dispersion because they express the extent to which the values of a distribution are dispersed or spread out around the distribution's mean. A simple measure of this is the range, which indicates the lowest and highest values present. But a more important measure is the variance.

Variance

Variance is one of the key concepts in quantitative research analysis. From the point of view of variable analysis the aim of research is to explain or account for the variance in dependent variables. Indeed, for variable analysis the existence of variance is crucial, for without it there is nothing to explain!

The variability among a set of values is summarized in a statistic called the standard deviation. This indicates how much 'on average' the cases differ from the mean value for the distribution and so how much variability or variance they display. The standard deviation summarizes the degree to which a set of measures are bunched up or spread out around the mean value. Where they are widely spread, the standard deviation will be larger than when they are tightly grouped together. If, for example, a sample of firms were selected of identical size, then they would exhibit no variance. Every case would have the same value as the mean, and the standard deviation would equal zero. Mostly, of course, samples contain members that differ from each other and so exhibit variance.

Researchers are particularly interested in variance that is shared by variables because this gives grounds for claiming that they are causally related. Shared variance means that for the same set of cases, each case tends to lie at the same distance from the mean of each variable. For example, Child (1984) noted that the larger a firm, the larger the number of management levels in its organization chart. So the largest firms would tend to have the most levels, the smallest firms the fewest levels, and average-size firms average levels. The variables 'firm size' and 'management levels' tend to vary together.

A number of important analytical techniques are based on the analysis of variances. The extent to which variables are related to each other is expressed in terms of their shared variance. The analysis of variances (of which the technique called the 'analysis of variance' is one application – see p. 214) is therefore central to the process of identifying connections and patterns among the variables that comprise the data.

Quantitative relations: making patterns

As well as describing the sample in terms of summary statistics for each measured variable, we can also explore the relationships between variables. This process is at the heart of explanatory analysis: the strength of relationships between variables is assessed using measures of association and correlation. Full details of these measures can be found in de Vaus (2002, chapter 36).

The more complex procedures are able to incorporate large numbers of variables as part of an analysis but as the degree of complexity increases, so do the difficulties in interpreting the results. When using procedures which involve many transformations of the original data it is possible to experience a disconcerting sense that the numbers have taken on a life of their own. If your sense of closeness to the data is reduced to the point of discomfort, it may be time to take stock. A return to basic, simpler analyses may well help to restore your control over the data – which, of course, it is vital to retain throughout your study.

Cross-tabulation

The relatively simple device of the cross-tabulation (Table 12.2) can be used to great effect. The frequency distribution displays the distribution of the cases across the categories of a single variable. When we juxtapose two or more variables we produce a cross-tabulation (also known as a cross-break, cross-classification or contingency table). Typically, a cross-tabulation is used when at least one of the measures is a nominal variable. At its simplest, two variables

Table 12.2 Example cross-tabulation, job title against sex.

	Supervisor	Manager	Director	Total
Female	1	2	1	4
Male	1	1	1	3
Total	2	3	2	7
Missing cases 0				

Note: Data from Table 7.2.

each with two categories are brought together to form the rows and columns of a 2 × 2 table. Larger numbers of variables can be used but the tables become more difficult to interpret and the cases become scattered thinly over larger and larger numbers of cells.

The strength of the association of the variables can be assessed using a variety of statistics. Complex cross-tabulations are analysed using log-linear methods.

Two-variable correlation

The correlation between variables is the extent to which they vary in unison. When two variables are correlated, their values move together. Positive or direct correlation means that as the value of one variable increases, so does that of the other. Among companies, for example, the amount of capital employed and the number of people employed tend to be positively correlated. Negative or inverse correlation means that as the value of one variable increases, the value of the other decreases.

Correlation coefficients can range between −1.00 and +1.00. These extreme values (never found in practice) indicate perfect correlation. A value of 0.00 shows that the variables are completely unrelated or independent. Conventionally, a correlation of around 0.60 (−0.60 or +0.60) and above is regarded as indicating a 'strong' relationship between the variables (Salkind, 2000, p. 96). However, a more meaningful indicator is the coefficient of determination, which is the square of the correlation coefficient. This shows what percentage of the variance in the dependent variable is accounted for or explained by the independent variable. A 'strong' correlation of even 0.70 between variable X and variable Y explains only 49 per cent of the variance in Y; most of the variance is still unaccounted for. In management research correlations as high as even 0.70 are likely to be very rare. A scan of the correlation matrices that regularly appear in articles in management journals such as the *Academy of Management Journal* and *Administrative Science Quarterly* is likely to show typical values of a much more modest magnitude.

Correlations may be spurious as indicators of causal links between variables. It cannot be assumed that even a very strong statistical correlation means that there is a real connection between the variables. Spurious correlations can arise by chance and the probabilities of this can be estimated through significance

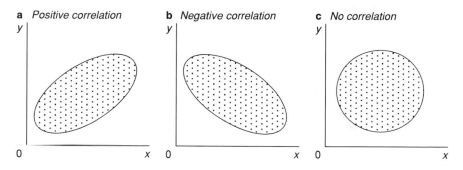

Figure 12.1 Example scatter plots showing different relationships between two variables, *x* and *y*.

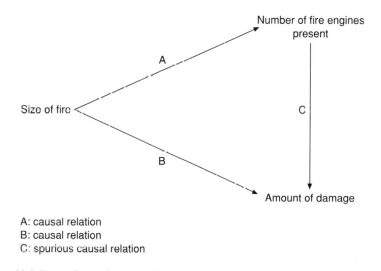

A: causal relation
B: causal relation
C: spurious causal relation

Figure 12.2 Example spurious correlation.

testing (see pp. 213–16). They can also occur when two variables are themselves unconnected but both are influenced by a third. A well-known example is the correlation between the number of fire engines attending a fire and the amount of damage caused. There is a relationship but this is not causal: the fire engines do not cause the damage. Rather, both the number of fire engines attending and the amount of damage done are caused by a third variable, the magnitude of the fire.

Many-variable correlation and regression

Techniques of multiple correlation enable the researcher to extend simple two-variable correlation analysis to large variable sets. The underlying logic is the same as for two-variable correlation. The aim is to identify the amount of variance that is shared by the independent variables and the dependent variable. This is achieved by calculating the coefficient of multiple correlation, R. The square of R is the coefficient of multiple determination, R^2, which indicates the proportion of the variance in the dependent variable that is accounted for by the independent variables.

In addition, the technique of multiple regression can show how influential each independent variable is. Regression analysis enables us to assess which variables are most important in accounting for the variance of the dependent variable. Statistics called regression coefficients, or beta weights, can be calculated for each independent variable. These indicate by how much the dependent variable would change following a one-unit change in the independent variable when all the other independent variables are held constant.

Multiple regression and its variants have become standard analytical techniques in some areas of management research. They have been widely applied to data obtained from surveys and from documentary and statistical records, and to financial datasets. Some examples of studies making use of multiple correlation and regression include those of Carpenter *et al.* (2001), Parasuraman and Simmers (2001), Randall *et al.* (1999), Simonton (1998), and Slater and Olson (2000).

Path analysis

As the name suggests, path analysis seeks to identify interconnected pathways through a set of variables. Whereas multiple correlation and regression envisages variables as an interconnected net, with no assumption about the temporal sequence of variables, path analysis requires the analyst to construct an explicit causal model. This model depicts the linkage between variables over time. Path analysis then estimates the degree to which the data fit this causal model. Example studies include those of Boshoff and Mels (2000), Chiu *et al.* (1998), Cohen (1999), Raymond *et al.* (1998), and Yan and Gray (2001).

Factor analysis

Factor analysis is a technique that can be used to identify the underlying structure within a set of variables. It serves to reduce a large set of variables to a smaller number of 'super-variables' or 'factors' by exploring the inter-correlations among them. It has been used particularly for the analysis of attitudinal measures where the responses to large numbers of individual questions may all point in the same direction, indicating a common attitudinal factor. For example, Ticehurst and Ross-Smith (1992) explored the factors comprising 'communication satisfaction' in Australian organizations. See also Lewis and Harvey's (2001) work on perceptions of environmental uncertainty.

Factor analysis has acquired something of a mystique by virtue of the terminology associated with its procedures: 'orthogonal rotation', 'varimax rotation', 'eigenvalues', and so on. However, in common with much quantitative analysis in research, its underlying basis is the analysis of variances. Interval-level variables that are normally distributed are required for this analysis. Some authorities recommend that a minimum of at least 300 cases are necessary before this procedure can be applied (Comrey and Lee, 1992).

One difficulty with factor analysis is the possibility of its generating factors that make no clear substantive sense. Another is the extent to which the analysis is arbitrary in nature. Different analysts can produce different factors from the same data depending on the decisions they take during the various stages of the procedure. The technique therefore remains somewhat controversial.

Cluster analysis

Cluster analysis is a technique for systematically grouping together cases according to the degree to which they share common characteristics. It operates by calculating distances between the cases in terms of the variables measured. It then groups together those cases which are closest to each other and furthest away from the rest. In effect, the cases are located in specific regions within the multidimensional space bounded by the variables. The resulting clusters may be sufficiently distinct to constitute a typology of the entities being analysed. As with factor analysis, the outcomes of this procedure are partly dependent on decisions made on such matters as how to define 'similarity' and the order in which the clusters are formed: top-down analysis progressively divides the entire set of cases into smaller clusters whereas bottom-up analysis aggregates the cases into larger clusters.

Cluster analysis has been used in marketing to identify distinct market segments and in the analysis of brands. It has also been applied to such topics as the identification of leadership types, groupings of national cultures, industry clustering and strategy typologies. Example studies using cluster analysis are those of Chenhall and Langfield-Smith (1998), Gupta *et al.* (2002), Mumford *et al.* (2000), Pandit *et al.* (2001), and Slater and Olson (2001).

Statistical inference

The techniques I have introduced so far have been concerned with describing data. Statistical tests are also available which enable us to assess how likely our results are to have arisen by chance. A test of statistical significance is a way of estimating the probability that results obtained from sample observations are due to chance variations (sampling error) rather than indicating actual differences. Where a test shows that the obtained results are very unlikely to have occurred by chance, they are regarded as statistically significant. A statistical value that would occur by chance five times or less in a hundred (the 5 per cent level) is likely to be regarded as 'significant'. One that would occur once or less in a hundred (the 1 per cent level) may be regarded as 'very significant' (Kerlinger, 1964, p. 180).

The analysis of variance

As we noted in Chapter 7, the experimental strategy entails a quantitative analytical procedure known as 'the analysis of variance'. The phrase is rather misleading because correlational analyses are also analyses of variance but by different methods. However, the analysis of variance applies to the analysis of group differences rather than individual differences. The measures to be compared are the average values of the dependent variable of the experimental and control groups. The aim of the analysis is to establish whether the magnitude of observed differences between experimental and control groups on the dependent variable is large enough to indicate that they are unlikely to have occurred by chance. If that is the case, it is assumed that the independent variables really did have an effect.

To assess this, a test of statistical significance is applied to the observed difference between the mean values of the dependent variable. Analysis of variance uses the data on all the members of the groups (called the 'within-groups variance') to calculate the range within which values of the difference between the means could occur by chance. The actual difference between the means (the 'between-groups' variance) is compared with this range. If it exceeds it, then the difference is statistically significant.

Full understanding of the analysis of variance requires a detailed consideration of the calculative procedures involved. An excellent account is given by Kerlinger and Lee (2000, part 5).

Assessing significance

In the analysis of variance a statistical test is applied to assess the significance of differences between means, but other statistics, such as correlation coefficients and other measures of association, can also be assessed for significance. Kanji (1993) describes an extensive collection of significance tests, and clear guidance on which tests are appropriate in which conditions is given by de Vaus (2002). The role that significance tests should play in social research has, however, been a matter of debate.

Researchers are often preoccupied with the 'significance' of their findings. This is perfectly proper and understandable. But what is less understandable is that many researchers, even experienced ones, mistakenly equate *statistical* significance with *substantive* significance. Statistically significant findings are ones that are unlikely to have arisen by chance. Substantively significant findings, on the other hand, are ones that are important in the light of the objectives of a study and the current state of knowledge or theory about the topic.

There is no necessary relation between substantive and statistical significance. For example, very low levels of correlation between two variables in a sample may be highly 'statistically significant'. All this means is that this degree of correlation would be very unlikely to occur in a sample of this size by chance. A weak correlation remains nonetheless a weak correlation and may be regarded as 'substantively insignificant' or even trivial.

An important influence on the levels of statistical significance a statistic reaches is the sample size. The larger the sample, the greater the likelihood that a given statistic will reach high levels of significance. This can be readily appreciated from the scrutiny of statistical inference tables which show what values a statistic must reach in order to be regarded as statistically significant. For example, the table for the correlation coefficient Pearson's *r* shows that for a sample size of 20, *r* has to reach 0.38 before the 5 per cent level is reached and 0.52 to reach the 1 per cent level. For a sample of 200 it must reach only 0.11 and 0.16 respectively. For a sample of 2,000 the thresholds are lower still at 0.04 and 0.06. If the sample is large enough, correlation coefficients, however small, will nearly always be statistically significant.

On the other hand, a finding may be statistically insignificant but substantively significant. For example, where little is known about a phenomenon, almost any information about it could be substantively significant, if only by providing a starting point for further research. It should also be remembered that whatever is observed in a sample holds for that sample even if there are no statistical grounds for distinguishing it from a chance outcome.

Box 12.3 How significant are statistical significance tests?

Tests of significance provide an estimate of the probability that a pattern in a sample is due to sampling error. They tell us *nothing* more than this, and certainly indicate nothing about the nature of relationships.

(de Vaus, 2002, p. 178)

Statistical significance tests have been widely misapplied and misinterpreted. For this reason, they have become controversial (see Carver, 1978, 1993; Morrison and Henkel, 1970a). Some critics have called for their abandonment in social science (Morrison and Henkel, 1970b). Babbie (1990) argues that they should not be used because the required sampling assumptions can seldom be met in social research and because they are frequently interpreted as if they are indicators of substantive significance. Others have advocated their continued use but in a more informed manner (de Vaus, 2002). At the very least, management researchers need to be aware of the arguments surrounding significance testing

Activity 12.1 Try your hand at number-crunching

Using the data you obtained from Activity 7.2, produce some statistical analyses. Be playful with the numbers – see what happens when you enter the data into different statistical routines.

and to be prudent in the way they use and report statistical tests. Like other methods, they should not be allowed to become a fetish. The rule of thumb expressed by the IOT test of significance is worth keeping in mind. According to this Inter-Ocular Trauma test there's only one thing that really counts: if it hits you between the eyes, it's significant!

Interpreting qualitative data

In this section I briefly introduce some of the main approaches to the analysis of qualitative data. The raw data take the form of texts: interview transcripts or notes, responses to open items on questionnaires, field notes, documents, textual records, and so on. Techniques for interpreting textual materials are more varied than those applied to quantitative data. Unlike statistical methods, for which there is a standard set of well-understood procedures, there is less agreement on how texts can and should be analysed. Textual interpretation is a more subtle process than statistical analysis, natural language being so much more complex than the formal languages of logic and mathematics (see Box 12.4). Textual analyses generally involve interpretation rather than calculation, although statistical methods may be used in some forms of content analysis. Moreover, it is much more difficult to separate the construction of data from its analysis when dealing with qualitative data. In survey research a good deal of analysis takes place in the process of designing a questionnaire and before it ever reaches the hands of the respondents. In ethnographic field studies, data are analysed as part of an ongoing iterative process of data construction.

Interpreting qualitative materials is not an easy task. A large volume of items may need to be dealt with: for example, in their study of the culture of medical school students, Becker *et al.* (1961) produced 5,000 pages of field notes. But it is important that it is undertaken systematically so that it can be seen how conclusions have been arrived at.

Box 12.4 Putting computer power in perspective

Some analysts believe that we should be in awe of the growing power of computers. Instances such as the series of chess duals between the world's leading grandmasters and the most advanced chess computers have shown 'mere' humans struggling against the might of the machine. Yet chess games play to the machine's strengths and the humans' weakness; the machine can calculate the outcomes for millions of alternative moves and go on doing so without fatigue. With fuzzier interpretive tasks the computer is much less impressive. If the day comes when a machine is able to solve the cryptic clues of the *Times* crossword faster than a human, or indeed at all, we might really have to worry. But I shouldn't lose any sleep over it.

Qualitative summarization

The techniques I introduce below are intended to condense textual materials by reducing them to summary statements or by identifying their structural properties. Depending on the approach, the focus may be on surface meanings and structures or deeper, underlying ones.

Summarization techniques

Making a précis

The ability to précis or summarize texts concisely and accurately is an important skill in the researcher's repertoire. It is important not only during the analysis of textual data such as interview transcripts or field notes, but also when undertaking a literature review and during the writing of the research report.

The aim of a précis is to express the content of a passage of text in a shorter, simpler way than in the original but with minimum loss of information. Depending on the length of the original and the difficulty of the material, this can be a challenging task. Paradoxically, it often requires more effort to compress a text than to write at length – hence the saying 'I would have written something shorter but I didn't have time!'

Three techniques for summarization are suggested by Hossack (1982):

- *Generalization.* This involves finding common elements in the text and using a single word or phrase to express them.
- *Fact rejection.* Elements that are irrelevant or unimportant to what is being stated in the text are omitted from the précis.
- *Word compression.* This means substituting short word structures in the place of longer ones, e.g. 'This method is the best available' instead of 'This method is ranked first in terms of quality of all those that are currently available.'

The précis, a basic form of textual summarization, underlies many of the other techniques of qualitative analysis, such as coding.

Coding textual data

Coding is the name given to the process of categorizing qualitative data. Methods of coding differ somewhat according to the research strategy adopted but the aim of reducing the data by summarizing it under a category label remains the same. It is often given a rather insignificant place in accounts of research methods, but is actually a crucial stage in the construction of data.

We have already looked at the use of codes in survey research in Chapter 9. Their summarizing function is most apparent in the coding of responses to open-ended questions. One or more sentences are represented by a category label that is intended to express the respondent's meaning in the context of the study's objectives. In laboratory observation studies the construction and application of a recording scheme such as that devised by Bales (1950) works in much the same way. A series of speech acts, physical gestures and expressions are labelled according to the coding scheme as they are being observed.

In field research, coding is typically undertaken on the basis of field notes. In addition, some field researchers recommend the keeping of analytic notes or memos in which preliminary questions, hypotheses and models can be recorded (Burgess, 1984). Field notes are indexed so that similar material can be brought together, compared and summarized. Data construction and analysis tend to be closely intertwined. Coding categories may be introduced from existing theories and models of the processes being researched or may emerge as the fieldwork progresses.

In the strategy of grounded theory, coding plays a central role that goes well beyond summarization. By means of successive coding processes the analyst moves from the raw data to the generation of theory. Three types of coding are involved: open coding, axial coding and selective coding. Open coding entails the categorization of the raw data. Axial coding identifies concepts that link the main categories obtained from open coding. Selective coding identifies a few core categories around which the theoretical analysis is built. For further details see Strauss and Corbin (1990) and Locke (2001).

Content analysis

Content analysis has been defined as 'a research technique for the objective, systematic, and quantitative description of the manifest content of communication' (Berelson, 1954, p. 489) and as 'any technique for making inferences by object-ively and systematically identifying specified characteristics of messages' (Holsti, 1969, p. 15). It has been used for many purposes, especially in communications research. For example, different newspapers have been profiled to see what they typically contain and how they differ.

Typically, content analysis deals with the surface or 'manifest' features of a text and involves classifying and quantifying its content. Content is classified according to units of classification defined in terms of the purpose of the study. Content is quantified in units of enumeration such as words, sentences, paragraphs and items. So, for example, in the chairman's statement of a company annual report we might measure the emphasis given to environmental concerns by the number of sentences mentioning them as a proportion of the total sentences in the statement. Clearly constructed and unambiguous classification schemes that are well fitted to the particular subject matter are essential to any rigorous scheme for content analysis.

The manifest features of a document include such things as space usage, style of expression and content emphasis. In the analysis of a newspaper, for example, the amount of space devoted to images in comparison with that allocated to words can be measured, its 'readability' can be assessed (for more on readability see Chapter 13), and the amount of space devoted to news *vis-à-vis* sport, and so on, can be calculated. The analysis focuses on manifest content in order to say something about the characteristics of the medium itself. In addition, the analysis of manifest content can be undertaken in order to draw conclusions about matters outside the text, its 'latent' content. For example, texts have been analysed in order to distinguish different writing styles so that the likely authors of unattributed documents can be identified (Yule, 1944). Content analysis has also been used to determine the interests, attitudes and current concerns of individuals, groups or organizations, particularly when they are otherwise inaccessible. In one ingenious study Chai (1977/78) analysed the contents of the obituary notices issued by 40 key bodies in China following the death of Chairman Mao in order to assess the political orientations of different factions.

Examples of the use of content analysis in management research include the work of Breton and Taffler (2001), Farrell and Cobbin (1996), Harris (2001), Osborne *et al.* (2001), and Rondinelli and Berry (2000).

The internal validity of a content analysis is relatively unproblematic when it simply describes manifest content. The assessment of latent content is more troublesome, because the same text can be interpreted in different and even opposite ways. Berelson (1954) gives the example of analysing an enemy's pronouncements during wartime: if the enemy profess to be ready for war, does this mean they are indeed ready? Or should such a pronouncement be taken to indicate lack of war readiness, an empty threat uttered in the hope of buying time? Such problems point to a more general issue in textual analysis: what statements can validly be made about a text that go beyond reference to its manifest attributes? How, in other words, are we to set about interpreting texts?

The interpretation of texts

In this section I introduce two of the main analytical streams of thought concerning the interpretation of texts: hermeneutics and semiotics.

Hermeneutics

Hermeneutics has been defined as 'the science of correct understanding or interpretation' (Polkinghorne, 1983, p. 218), with specific reference to the understanding of the meaning of texts. In modern form it originated in the sixteenth century as a response to the demand for authoritative interpretation of the Bible and other ancient texts, but was developed as a methodology in the social sciences by Wilhelm Dilthey (1833–1911). Its scope has since been expanded by Paul Ricoeur from textual interpretation to the more general under-standing of social action. On this view, all human behaviour can be 'read' as if it were a text.

Hermeneutics sought to establish a reliable means of obtaining the objective interpretation of a text. Hirsch (1967) argued that although certainty cannot be achieved in interpretation, an objective interpretation is possible. Even so, there is no method that can guarantee the best possible interpretation. Interpretation involves probabilities of correctness rather than certainties. The aim of interpretation is to elucidate what the author meant to convey by means of the text. To do this it is important to know about the context in which the text was produced: its author, when it was written, the tradition in which it was written, related texts by the same author, and so on. The process of interpretation entails a 'hermeneutic circle', as Dilthey had called it, in which preconceptions of the overall meaning of a text are the initial basis for understanding its parts. As the reading progresses, however, the understanding of the parts may lead to a reinterpretation of the whole. Understanding is thus established by moving backwards and forwards between the text's whole and its parts and between the context in which it was written and the text itself. In this way the analyst, says Hirsch, moves towards the interpretation that is most probably correct in the light of all the evidence.

This objectivist conception of hermeneutics gave way to the view that several legitimate readings may be made of the same text. The interpretation of a text involves the interaction of the reader's frame of reference and prior understandings with the meanings in the text itself. To the extent that readers differ in their preconceptions and accumulated understandings, so will their interpretations. Interpretations are therefore relative to the standpoints from which they are made.

Whether and how correct interpretation or understanding of texts can be achieved continue to be matters of considerable debate. Post-structuralist writers such as Jacques Derrida argue that there are no grounds for asserting that any particular interpretation is authoritative, for texts remain indefinitely open to redefinition and reinterpretation. The author's interpretation or intended meaning is of no greater significance than any reader's. For post-structuralists, the search for criteria of validity in interpretation is a pointless exercise, for none can exist.

Others, such as Scott (1990), adopt a position that accepts the possibility of if not an 'objective' then at least an 'anchored' understanding of a text. Scott argues that the meaning of a text has three aspects: the author's intended meaning, the meaning constructed by its readers, and the text's 'internal' meaning (or perhaps meanings). The latter is a meaning that an analyst such as a semiotician (see p. 221) might discern without reference to the author's intentions. However, he points out that analysts are in the same position as any reader: they interpret texts according to their own frames of reference. If no one correct interpretation of a text can be established, it is still possible to produce interpretations that are justifiable in terms of evidence of the intentions of the author and the frames of reference or perspectives of readers. Thus

> the reading of a text is validated by relating it to the intentions of the author, and by taking account of the fact that its 'objective meaning' goes beyond those intentions, and also by relating the text to its audience.
>
> (Scott, 1990, p. 35)

Rickman (1990) proposes three tests that can be applied to assess the adequacy of interpretation:

- *Consensus*. Agreement by others that meaning has been correctly grasped is one ground for asserting the validity of an interpretation.
- *Coherence*. If the interpretation of one expression is consistent with other expressions made by the same person, then that interpretation is more likely to be valid than if it is inconsistent.
- *Pragmatic consequences*. If we act on the basis of an interpretation and it 'works', then that interpretation is more likely to be valid.

In general, though, the issue of validating the interpretation of texts continues to be problematic in social research.

Examples of management research informed by a hermeneutic approach include work by Arnold and Fischer (1994), Francis (1994), Heracleous and Barrett (2001), and Prasad and Mir (2002).

Semiotics

Semiotics is the study of language conceived in terms of signs and sign systems. It is closely associated with the work of the Swiss linguist Ferdinand de Saussure (1857–1913). He distinguished between language as a system (*la langue*) and the words and sentences actually spoken in daily life (*la parole*). The latter, which are readily observable, are the products of the hidden language system that governs the forms that sentences can take. Semiotics studies the structure of this language system. This is rather like studying a computer's program in order to understand how it processes data rather than being concerned with the output produced by any particular use of it.

Just as language structures lie concealed beneath everyday usage, semiotics assumes that texts exhibit both readily accessible surface features and deeper underlying structures or patterns of elements that can be accessed by applying various analytical techniques. These techniques include semiotic chains, semiotic clustering and semiotic squares (Feldman, 1995). The purpose of semiotic analysis is to reveal these underlying structures and so give a more comprehensive and possibly an unexpected interpretation of a text. So, for example, in the study of folk tales Propp (1968) isolated a small number of plot forms which underlie the enormous variety of actual stories.

Texts can be analysed in terms of three structural levels. The surface structure is akin to the manifest content examined in content analysis. The deep structure consists of 'oppositions': pairs of mutually exclusive properties such as 'opportunity/threat', 'growth/decline' and 'success/failure' upon which themes are organized. Linking the surface and deep structures is the narrative structure. This consists of a specific pattern of elements determined by the interrelation of the deep and surface structures. In the course of analysis the researcher proceeds from the surface level of words through the narrative structure to the deep structure of meanings.

Fiol's (1990a) work on strategic alliances in the chemical industry can be used to illustrate the application of semiotic analysis. Fiol wished to explore the nature of chief executives' beliefs about choice and constraint in their industry environment and their relation to the firms' propensity to engage in joint ventures. The texts she analysed were 30 examples of CEOs' letters to shareholders published in company annual reports. Her analysis entailed three main steps. In Step 1: Decomposition, sections of each letter were identified as expressing certain themes, together with instances of the 'narrative forces' that Greimas (1966) suggested exist in any text (such as subjects, environments, mode, tone and time). In Step 2: Interactions of Textual Narrative Forces, she plotted the interactions of the narrative forces within each theme. By the end of this stage the letters were represented as abstracted structures which displayed common and contrasting patterns, the structures having been derived from the surface text but lying 'below' it. Finally, in Step 3: Reconstruction of Texts, the themes of each company's text were positioned in a semiotic square which defined the main oppositions that underlay the texts' organization. The square designated the oppositions of 'opportunity/non-opportunity' and 'threat/non-threat'. The locations of the firms in the cells of the square closely reflected their actual behaviour in respect of engagement or otherwise in joint ventures.

Other authors who have used semiotic analysis in management research include Arnold *et al.* (2001), Barley (1983), I. Clarke *et al.* (1998), Grayson and Shulman (2000), and Harvey and Evans (2001).

Qualitative relations: making maps and telling stories

As we have seen, the search for patterns in quantitative data involves the application of statistical methods which express relationships and patterns of connectedness in predominantly numerical form. These patterns can also often be displayed graphically by means of charts and diagrams. Patterns in qualitative data have, by contrast, traditionally been presented in narrative form. The organization of research reports into sections in which detailed descriptive accounts are given of events and processes has played a large part in the presentation of qualitative analyses. Recently, however, alternative means of mapping the relations within qualitative data have been developed. We will briefly introduce some of these techniques before turning to the use of narrative methods.

Making maps

Maps are abstract representations of some structure which depict key relations between its elements for a given purpose. Street maps, for example, depict the positional relationships between roads and some other landscape features so that road users can find their way from A to B. The kinds of maps that researchers are interested in are those that depict the links between observed phenomena.

With quantitative data a statistical table such as a correlation matrix is such a map and there are explicit formulae that can be applied to numerical data in order to construct one. But the problem with qualitative data, as writers such as Miles and Huberman (1984) have seen it, is that it is difficult to assess the value of the maps built on them because there have been few explicit and agreed methods of constructing them. The maps may look convincing, but how do we know they are a good representation of the territory they profess to depict?

Miles and Huberman see the analysis of qualitative data as involving three interrelated activities: data reduction, data display and conclusion drawing. Of particular interest here is data display. A data display is 'an organized assembly of information that permits conclusion drawing and action taking' (1984, p. 21). It may take the form of a matrix, scatter plot, summary table, network, and so on. Whatever its form, the purpose of a data display is to help the analyst to 'see what is happening' in the data. It should also help the analyst to see what he or she is doing to the data as well as with the data.

Box 12.5 You know what you display

In the course of our work we have become convinced that better displays are a major avenue to valid qualitative analysis. The displays discussed in this book include many types of matrices, graphs, networks, and charts. All are designed to assemble organized information in an immediately accessible, compact form, so that the analyst can see what is happening and either draw justified conclusions or move on to the next-step analysis the display suggests may be useful . . . the dictum 'You are what you eat' might be transposed to 'You know what you display.'

(Miles and Huberman, 1984, pp. 21–2)

Yin (1984) distinguishes between two general approaches to the analysis of case evidence. One is to use any theoretical propositions that have been stated prior to designing the fieldwork as a basis for organizing and guiding the analysis process. Where these are absent, an alternative is to create a descriptive framework within which the case materials can be presented in an orderly and comprehensive manner. He also proposes three major techniques for analysing case study evidence: pattern-matching, explanation-building and time series analysis.

Pattern-matching

Pattern-matching entails comparing patterns in the data with those that have been predicted from theory. With this approach, theory guides the analyst by suggesting the types of pattern that should be present in the data. Observed patterns may or may not support the guiding theory and, depending on the design of the study, it may also be possible to test for alternative explanations. It is worth noting that it is sometimes the absence of an element in the data, some event that did not happen or a condition that was not present, that forms an important part of a pattern.

Time series analysis

Time series analysis is a particular application of pattern-matching where the data are in the form of time series, or can be arranged as such. The tracking of sequences of events over time is key to historical modes of explanation. Case studies, and especially ethnographies, offer the possibility of being able to record processes over relatively lengthy time periods. The material may be analysed by comparing the observed sequence with theoretical expectations.

Complex analyses involving many variables observed over time are possible. One example of this approach is that adopted by Pettigrew (1985) to analyse the materials gathered for his study of ICI. He used a 'contextual framework' using three levels – the process, the inner context and the outer context – in order to study organizational change. His account was organized within this framework and traced the development of the firm over a 23-year period.

Explanation-building

The aim of explanation-building is to build an explanation of the case. To do this requires the analyst to repeat the following steps until a 'final' explanation is reached:

*   State a proposition or hypothesis about the topic being studied.
*   Use an initial case and assess the fit between the evidence and the proposition.
*   If there is no close fit, amend the proposition and match this to the evidence.
*   Test the proposition on further cases.
*   Continue the process until a satisfactory explanation has been developed.

This may sound like a straightforward process, but Yin warns that it is 'fraught with dangers' (1984, p. 115). Further guidance on theory-building from case studies can be found in Eisenhardt (1989).

Telling stories

Analysts such as Miles and Huberman (1994) and Yin (1984) have been critical of reliance on narrative as a means of analysing and presenting qualitative data. However, some other writers have asserted the importance of narrative as a way of organizing qualitative data and making them intelligible.

One dictionary definition of 'narrative' is that it is 'a spoken or written account of connected events: a story' (Pearsall, 1999). Polkinghorne (1988) argues that narratives are the principal means whereby humans make their experience meaningful both to themselves and to others. Locating events within a meaningful story is one way of explaining them. In particular, they are used to account for sequences of specific events over time; historians typically rely on narratives to convey their historical explanations.

Narratives function as explanatory devices for human behaviour and its outcomes. Stories organize events and actions into a coherent whole by showing the connections between them and the ways in which these linkages combine to produce end results or consequences. The outcomes to be explained range from individual conduct to large-scale collective events. For example, answers to questions such as 'Why did the chief executive resign?', 'Why did the company fail?' or 'Why did the strike take place?' involve linking specific events and actions in a sequence that leads to the outcome to be explained.

Box 12.6 The importance of plots in history

It can be argued that interpretation in history consists of the provision of a plot structure for a sequence of events so that their nature as a comprehensible process is revealed by their figuration as a *story of a particular kind.* . . . One can argue, in fact, that just as there can be no explanation in history without a story, so too there can be no story without a plot by which to make of it a story of a particular kind.

(White, 1978, pp. 58, 62)

A key element of a narrative is its plot or organizing theme. The plot is the story line that endows the reported events and actions with significance. Research narratives share a reliance on plots with fictional stories. The difference between research narratives and fictional ones is that research narratives have to incorporate real events in the story whereas in fiction the events can be made up. However, the plot is not part of the events: it is the organizing principle for the *account* of the events. It gives meaning and significance to the events by showing how they are related to each other. The same events will have different significance (as opposed to literal meaning) according to which plot they figure in. Thomas (2003c), for example, showed how an account of the development of business history could be emplotted in several ways, each of which implied a different understanding of the events. Hence the plot supplies the context within which the events are understood. At the same time, understanding of the events reinforces understanding of the plot. Interpretation takes place according to the hermeneutic circle mentioned earlier.

Because plots are not themselves part of the data but are introduced by the analyst, their status is akin to that of theories. They can be said to be 'theories of the particular' in that they attempt to account for specific outcomes. They do this by producing chains of evidence and reasoning in support of an explanation while also showing why alternative explanations are unsatisfactory. Such explanations are evaluated in terms of their plausibility, their capacity to account comprehensively for the events in question, and the extent to which there is consensus among fellow researchers that the explanation does account for the events. Narrative explanations can never be final because new information may emerge that changes understanding of the events. Novel story lines may also appear. They are therefore always probable or likely explanations – a characteristic that distinguishes them little if at all from explanations couched in terms of correlations or laws.

Understanding the importance of narrative is something that is relevant to researchers working with quantitative data as well as those using qualitative data. There is a sense in which all research is story-telling (R. Usher, 1997). Writing your own research story is the subject of the next chapter.

Activity 12.2 What the papers say

Obtain a copy of the executive appointments section of a national newspaper. Devise a categorization scheme that enables you to systematically assess variations in the content of each advertisement. How much information are readers usually given about (a) the job, (b) the company and (c) the experience and qualifications required? Compare your findings with those of Thomas and Partington (1981).

Key points

1   It is vital to appreciate the difference between statistical significance and substantive significance and not to equate the former with the latter.
2   Correlations between variables do not necessarily imply that those variables are causally related.
3   Even if variables are causally related, statistical explanation is not the same as substantive explanation.
4   The analysis of qualitative materials must be approached with the same rigorous attitude as that of quantitative data.
5   Techniques of qualitative analysis are more varied than those of quantitative analysis and because they are generally less proceduralized, they may be more difficult to learn.
6   Texts can be treated as topics and/or resources.
7   Content analysis is mainly used to quantify textual content.
8   Adequate textual interpretation depends on the analyst being competent in the language of the text and familiar with the cultural setting in which it has been produced.

Software for quantitative and qualitative analysis

Quantitative analysis

*   *MINITAB.* A general-purpose statistical package widely used in teaching and for research analysis. MINITAB 13 includes analysis of variance, regression analysis, multivariate analysis, time series and forecasting, and numerous other features. A student version is available. See Bryman and Cramer (1996), Morris (1993) and www.minitab.com.
*   *SPSS (Statistical Package for the Social Sciences).* Possibly the most widely used statistical package, it contains a comprehensive set of procedures for organizing, transforming and analysing quantitative data. Characterized by great flexibility and user-friendliness, it is accompanied by excellent manuals which provide concise overviews of the main statistical techniques. Bryman and Cramer (2001) provide detailed guidance to the package in a non-technical format, drawing on examples taken directly from SPSS output. See also Babbie and Halley (1995), Green *et al.* (1997) and www.spss.com.

Qualitative analysis

For general information on software for qualitative analysis, see caqdas.soc.surrey.ac.uk and Lewins (2001).

*   *ATLAS/ti.* A sophisticated package enabling extensive editing and analysis of textual materials. Well suited to grounded theory development, it is able to display conceptual diagrams showing the links between codes, with easy retrieval of the supporting data. See www.atlasti.de.
*   *Ethnograph.* Designed for the analysis of qualitative data in a variety of forms: interview transcripts, field notes, responses to open-ended survey questions, and other documents. Facilitates segmentation and coding, sorting, comparison and other kinds of analysis. See www.qualisresearch.com/.
*   *NUD.IST.* Widely used, it offers similar functions to the Ethnograph but includes the capacity to store and process analytic memos. Hierarchical trees of codes and categories can be displayed and edited. Available for both IBM PCs and Apple Macintosh machines. See www.qsr.com.au.
*   For information on content analysis software, see www.content-analysis.de/quantitative.html.

Key reading

de Vaus, D.A. (2002) *Analyzing Social Science Data: 50 Key Problems in Data Analysis*, London: Sage.
Seale, C. and Kelly, M. (1998) 'Coding and Analysing Data', in C. Seale (ed.) *Researching Society and Culture*, London: Sage, pp. 146–63.
Silverman, D. (1993) *Interpreting Qualitative Data: Methods for Analysing Talk, Text and Interaction*, London: Sage.

Further reading

Quantitative analysis and interpretation

Bryman, A. and Cramer, D. (2001) *Quantitative Data Analysis with SPSS Release 10 for Windows: A Guide for Social Scientists*, London: Routledge.

Byrne, D. (2002) *Interpreting Quantitative Data*, London: Sage.

Davis, J.A. (1971) *Elementary Survey Analysis*, New York: Prentice Hall.

Erickson, B.H. and Nosanchuk, T.A. (1979) *Understanding Data: An Introduction to Exploratory and Confirmatory Data Analysis for Students in the Social Sciences*, Milton Keynes, UK: Open University Press.

Keller, G. and Warrack, B. (2002) *Statistics for Management and Economics*, London: Thomson.

Morrison, D.E. and Henkel, R.E. (eds) (1970) *The Significance Test Controversy: A Reader*, London: Butterworths.

Salkind, N.J. (2000) *Statistics for People Who (Think They) Hate Statistics*, Thousand Oaks, CA: Sage.

Seale, C. (1998) 'Statistical Reasoning: From One to Two Variables', in C. Seale (ed.) *Researching Society and Culture*, London: Sage, pp. 164–79.

Seale, C. (1998) 'Statistical Reasoning: Causal Arguments and Multivariate Analysis', in C. Seale (ed.) *Researching Society and Culture*, London: Sage, pp. 180–91.

Qualitative analysis and interpretation

Bryman, A. and Burgess, R.G. (1994) *Analyzing Qualitative Data*, London: Routledge.

Dey, I. (1993) *Qualitative Data Analysis*, London: Routledge.

Feldman, M. (1995) *Strategies for Interpreting Qualitative Data*, Thousand Oaks, CA: Sage.

Fiol, C.M. (1990) 'Narrative Semiotics: Theory, Procedure and Illustration', in A.S. Huff (ed.) *Mapping Strategic Thought*, New York: Wiley, pp. 377–402.

Hossack, A. (1982) *Making a Summary*, London: Methuen.

Miles, M.B. and Huberman, A.M. (1994) *Qualitative Data Analysis*, Thousand Oaks, CA: Sage.

Silverman, D. (2000) *Doing Qualitative Research: A Practical Handbook*, London: Sage.

Slater, D. (1998) 'Analysing Cultural Objects: Content Analysis and Semiotics', in C. Seale (ed.) *Researching Society and Culture*, London: Sage, pp. 233–44.

Strauss, A. and Corbin, J. (1990) *Basics of Qualitative Research: Grounded Theory Procedures and Techniques*, Newbury Park, CA: Sage.

Weber, R.P. (1990) *Basic Content Analysis*, Newbury Park, CA: Sage.

Yin, R.K. (1984) *Case Study Research: Design and Methods*, Newbury Park, CA: Sage.

13 Writing and publication

> There is no more damaging myth than the idea that there is a mysterious 'gift', or that writing is a matter of 'inspiration'.
>
> (Hammersley and Atkinson, 1995, p. 239)

After months or possibly years of work, your study is nearing its conclusion. You have lived with it, got to know it and perhaps reached a point at which you are heartily sick of it. But as far as the rest of the world is concerned, it doesn't exist. Until your work has been recorded in written form it remains a mere gleam in the eye of its creator.

The written thesis, dissertation or article is the culmination of all the effort that has gone into carrying out the research. Writing comes easily to some people but for most of us it is hard work. A colleague of mine described his experience of book-writing as 'like chipping granite with a tooth-pick'! In part the difficulties are technical – to do with designing an appropriate structure, setting out references, keeping the text within set word limits, and so on. Fortunately, many of these obstacles can be overcome by following fairly straightforward guidelines. But perhaps the most significant problems researchers encounter are not so much technical as psychological – how to avoid or overcome writer's block, how to keep up motivation in the face of what may appear to be an impossible task, and how to deal with the emotions associated with having one's writing criticized. Dealing with these challenges is more problematic.

Full attention to writing tends to come in the final stage of a project, but in research, last most definitely does not mean least. The purpose of this final chapter is to provide guidance on how to organize and carry out a piece of academic writing and how to increase your chance of getting it published.

Getting round to writing

> A man may write at any time if he will set himself doggedly to it.
>
> (Dr Samuel Johnson)

As the model of research portrayed in Figure 2.3 shows, the research process is not linear but circular. As the project moves into its final stages, attention returns to its origins. The overall question in the researcher's mind should be 'To what extent have I achieved the aims I stated at the beginning of my project?' It is necessary to ask:

- whether the research questions have been answered;
- whether clear links have been made to the findings from previous research.

More generally, researchers have to return to the evaluative criteria that we discussed at the end of Chapter 2. By assessing the extent to which the study has been able to meet these criteria, you will be better prepared to deal with the two big problems that attend all research:

1   *The 'what-does-it-mean?' problem.* What does the material produced by the study tell us? To what extent are the claims made by the research true or valid? What is the story of this particular piece of research? What can be concluded from the evidence obtained in this research?
2   *The 'so-what?' problem.* How does the story told here relate to the wider story? If we consider the study as a chapter from a book, how does it fit with the other chapters that have been written by other people or that may be written in the future? How does it fit into the Big Picture? In what way is it significant?

It may seem unnecessary to mention that these matters must be dealt with at the conclusion of a project. But sometimes, after the long journey through the stages of designing and implementing a study, the starting point can be almost forgotten. By this time the conclusions may appear obvious to you and it may even seem that, despite all the hard work, there is nothing very much to report! This can be dispiriting or even alarming.

Fortunately, this sense of *déjà vu* is usually a psychological illusion that arises from the close familiarity of the investigator with the study and the interpretation of the data that goes on within one's head as the study progresses. This is one reason why it is advisable to begin writing early so that a running record is maintained of one's reflections and preliminary conclusions. If a start on writing is postponed until the data analysis and interpretation is complete, there is a risk that the project will never be written up. Having worked on the same project for an extended period of months or years, you may easily become bored to the point that the thought of having to put everything on paper becomes almost intolerable.

What should be included?

In writing the final document it is necessary to be selective about what to include. Initially the problem may seem to be how to produce enough words: 60,000–100,000 words certainly is a lot of words. As the writing progresses, however, the issue often becomes one of how to fit everything into the available space. Deciding what to leave out can be as important as deciding what to include.

One way of dealing with this problem is to use the 'must, should, could' framework for ordering content priorities:

- *Must*. Decide what *must* be included: key items of literature, essential information on methods, central findings, major conclusions, and so on.
- *Should*. Consider the remaining material. What *should* be included? What would it be highly desirable to include? Perhaps such things as supporting literature, additional findings, further conclusions, and so on.
- *Could*. Although not essential nor highly desirable, what further content *could* be included? This material must be relevant and support the main material. There is no point in stuffing the thesis with dozens of appendices that add nothing to the study.

When making these content decisions, a helpful principle to apply is: 'If in doubt, leave it out!' If you are not sure whether an item must be included, relegate it to the second stage. Perhaps this item should be included, but again if you are in doubt, relegate it to the third stage. If you are still doubtful about the need to include it, you probably need to leave it out altogether.

Overall, your aim should be to give a full account of the study, covering each of the stages and being as comprehensive as possible within the prescribed word limits. You should identify and explain the study's limitations and defects. There is no need to feel embarrassed about doing so. Every study has them and it is important to mention them in your report. For example, response rates for surveys must always be reported irrespective of how high or, more usually, low they are.

Detailed account should be given of the research methods used such as information on sampling frames, sampling methods, and methods of obtaining data. It may be desirable to include copies of questionnaires, interview schedules or observation checklists as appendices. Avoid including everything! Raw data, whether in the form of questionnaire responses, interview transcripts, field notes, and so on should seldom be included in full, although examples and extracts may be.

Structuring the text

> Tell 'em what you're going to tell 'em, then tell 'em, then tell 'em what you've told 'em.
>
> (Maxim for teachers)

The appropriate structure for a research report depends on a number of factors: the nature of the format (an article, a project report, an academic paper, a dissertation or a thesis); the types of research strategy and research methods that have been used (such as quantitative hypothesis-testing research or qualitative ethnography); and the type of audience (academic specialists, organizational practitioners). The simplest structure, however, generally has just three parts: a beginning, a middle and an end. If all else fails, this timeless structure should at least get you started.

- *Doctoral theses.* On the basis of a small sample of 20 theses successfully submitted at one university, it seems that there is no standard format (Box 13.1). For example, length varied between 180 and 500 pages with as few as 5 chapters or as many as 15. The 'heaviest' thesis literally weighed almost three times as much as the 'lightest'!

Box 13.1 Weighing up the thesis: does it have to be heavy to be heavyweight?

A thesis is an abstract claim to knowledge, but we also think of it as the bound volume that contains an account of a research student's work. What features does the 'typical' management thesis display? Remarkably, we have virtually no systematic evidence on this. The following statistics are based on a sample of 20 theses in Business and Management successfully submitted for the degree of PhD at the University of Manchester.

No. of pages:	mean 361	range 180–500
No. of chapters:	mean 9	range 5–15
No. of references:	mean 196	range 18–453
Thickness of spine:	mean 49 mm	range 28–69 mm
Weight:	mean 2.3 kg	range 1.25–3.25 kg

Source: Data constructed and analysed by Dr Paula Hyde

- *Research strategies.* Work produced in the positivist tradition has tended to be presented in the orthodox form common in the natural sciences. Typically, a paper begins with an introduction, followed by a literature review, a statement of the research hypotheses and methods, a presentation of the data, a discussion of the results and finally the conclusions. Qualitative work may follow a similar format but a wide variety of forms are available. Yin (1989), for example, lists six presentational structures for case studies that are akin to literary plots. In ethnography, writing is a major part of the research endeavour (Van Maanen, 1988).
- *Types of audience.* Kelemen and Bansal (2002) have argued that the style in which academic research is written tends to alienate managers. To communicate successfully with managers, the writer has to adopt a set of stylistic

conventions different from those that are normally applied in academic writing. Managers are more interested in immediately applicable findings than they are in academic theories or fine methodological subtleties. What academics think of as rigorous critical thinking may be perceived by managers as hair-splitting and as academics 'letting their hair down'.

Activity 13.1 Exploring presentational styles

Select an article from a recent issue of the academic journals *Academy of Management Journal* and *Administrative Science Quarterly*. Compare them with articles from the practitioner-orientated *Harvard Business Review* and *Organizational Dynamics*. What stylistic differences do you see? List the main points of difference. What do you think is the reason for any differences you notice?

The arts of scholarly writing

> A writer is a person who writes.
>
> (John Braine, novelist)

The comedian Peter Cook used to tell the story of how he would regularly go to cocktail parties where everyone, when asked what they were doing these days, would say, 'I'm writing a novel.' To which he would reply, 'I'm not either.' A lot of people, it seems, like the idea of being a writer but far fewer are able to translate the idea into a reality.

Researchers, however, have no choice in the matter; they *have* to write. And here, as in other ways, previous experience can sometimes be misleading. Most research students are experienced writers by virtue of their previous education and experience of examination writing. Even so, most of us are ill-equipped to write a long dissertation or thesis because:

1   Under examination conditions, writing answers requires the skills of getting a few thousand words right first time; there is no time to draft and revise. Speed is of the essence.
2   Essays and reports written in your own time are fairly short, and standards of accuracy and presentation, though often considerable, are less demanding than for a thesis.
3   Even an MBA dissertation may be no more than 10,000 words long. A dissertation or thesis may require anything from 60,000 to 100,000 words and rigorous standards of presentation, accuracy and referencing apply.

Box 13.2 Academic writing styles: plain ugly?

Plain English . . . was more difficult to write than ugly English, but was a flexible enough vehicle to communicate abstract ideas and concrete manifestations not only from specialist to specialist, but in a dialogue with the interested, ordinary, practical man and woman.

(Lupton, 1985b, p. 3)

In short, writing a thesis is a major undertaking in terms both of scale and of presentation, made even more challenging if your first language is not English.

The main differences as compared with writing projects you may have undertaken previously are the following:

- The scale of the work means that you must plan and organize your writing.
- The act of writing is now a means to finding out what you are trying to say. It is unwise to wait until you know exactly what you should write before starting because this can lead to blocking and an inability to write at all.
- You must not expect to get it right first time. Writing on this scale and to the required standard requires several drafts.

If you are fortunate, you may, like Lupton (see Box 13.2), be able to develop a writing style that makes your work accessible both to research specialists and to managers and other organizational practitioners. If that is not the case, you may have to adopt a different style for each audience.

Organizing the writing

Writing a thesis is a big task. One of the least helpful ways to start is by sitting down at the word processor, entering a heading and hitting the keyboard. If you do this, you may well get the uncomfortable feeling, as you write more and more, that there is no obvious place to stop! This is particularly troublesome with the Literature Review section, where, if there is a literature of any magnitude, you could probably write tens of thousands of words. After all, each book you mention is itself a book!

The principle for handling big tasks is always the same: break a big task down into a set of small tasks. If you start out thinking, 'I've got to write 100,000 words', you will naturally be daunted. But if you think, 'I have to write 500 words', the task looks much more manageable. Of course, you know that you've got to write 500 words 200 times over, but the point is to not think of that. Just concentrate on the next 500 words. It is, as they say, all in the mind.

Word budgets

To help solve this problem of breaking the big task into small tasks we can turn to the professionals who write for a living and who cannot afford to waste their time producing quantities of unnecessary words. One of the most valuable techniques I discovered from these professionals is the use of the word budget (Wells, 1981). It is simple yet powerful.

Suppose you start on a particular chapter. You must establish the total number of words you are going to devote to it. In this book, for example, I planned for ten chapters and the overall word limit, set by the publishers, was 100,000 words. So as a preliminary working figure I estimated 10,000 words per chapter. This is a starting figure and can be altered up or down later. As you can see, the finished product didn't turn out like that, but it is essential to have a definite number in mind as you start. You then divide the chapter into sections according to the main content you are going to include. Word limits are specified for each section. It is then immediately clear that for whatever you want to say about topic X or Y you have, say, about 1,000 words with which to say it. This is enormously helpful. You may see, for example, that there is simply no room, and probably no need, to provide that exhaustive summary of such and such study. All that is possible is perhaps one sentence. No need, then, to overwrite and then have to cut out precious and hard-won words.

Discovery through writing

How can I know what I think until I hear what I say?

When should you start writing your thesis? It is tempting to believe that you should not start writing until you know exactly what to write, but this is not necessarily helpful. Writing can be seen as simply putting down in print the words that are already in your head, and that is fine for some writing tasks. But when you are trying to wrestle with a complex body of material and express it in a coherent way it may be an unhelpful approach. What many writers know is that it is the act of writing itself that helps to clarify ideas. Indeed, Richardson (1994) considers writing to be itself a method of inquiry. Writing becomes a way of discovering what it is you are trying to say rather than simply one of setting down well-honed ideas. On this view you should start to write sooner rather than later.

Exactly when this point is reached is difficult to judge. If you start too soon, for example before you have done sufficient research on your topic or sub-topic, you may stall. Sometimes the anxiety to get at least something on the sheet can lead to false starts. If, on the other hand, you leave it too late, you may find that the ideas have gone cold. It is remarkable how quickly engagement with a project can go off the boil.

Box 13.3 Getting close to your data

'The important thing', an experienced researcher once told me, 'is to get close to your data.' At the time, I wasn't too sure what he meant by that. Indeed, it is difficult to explain. But after you have been working on a project for some months or years you get a 'feel' for the data: statistics, interview materials, observational records or whatever. There also comes a point when you start to lose that feel. So it's important to be writing while the feeling is strong!

Producing drafts

Most of us have been programmed to be critical of our own writing. This is, of course, essential. But the key is to know when to be critical and when to simply let yourself go. If you scrutinize every word and sentence as you write you may well find that you rapidly become stuck, more often than not on the very first sentence. Yet if you stop and struggle to get that one sentence right, you will lose the train of your thought and may well forget where you are going. As a colleague once described it, it is a bit like trying to walk down stairs watching your feet – you will probably trip yourself up.

The secret is to start off by suspending your critical faculties and simply get the words down, more or less any words. This does not come easily at first and can induce acute feelings of exposure and guilt. You imagine someone – a former teacher, your supervisor, the external examiner – reading your fumbling and incoherent sentences. The spectre of failure and shame looms! But you must dismiss these feelings as phantoms designed to distract you from your work, which they all too easily will. Many writers have well-rehearsed routines for avoiding writing – just going to tidy my desk, wash my hands, feed the cat before starting – until so much time has passed that, well . . . I might as well leave it until tomorrow.

The first attempt at writing produces what I call the 'zero draft'. This is the one *before* the first draft. By calling this initial pass the zero draft, the intention is to deliberately lower self-expectations. The main aim is to get whatever you can onto the screen or page. You are not expecting it to come out right first time.

The 'zero draft' concept is permissive. It gives you the freedom to make mistakes: typing mistakes, spelling mistakes, grammatical mistakes, clumsy sentences, pieces which don't seem to fit or follow. I have often found, for example, that after I have written a zero draft there are sentences or sections that belong somewhere else in the piece and sometimes in a different piece altogether. Perhaps it is just that I have an untidy mind. Another benefit of the zero draft is that it unburdens one's mind and memory and so frees up energy that will be needed when you come to review and to reflect on the work. It also has the morale-boosting effect of giving you a sense of achievement, of having put words down, of having filled blank pages, of having started.

The need for several drafts does not mean that you rewrite everything ad infinitum. I generally find that going through about four drafts gets the work close to a final draft, although some awkward or especially important sections may require more. The 'zero' draft is the initial attempt to get something down on paper. This will then undergo fairly extensive revision and extension to produce a more coherent second draft. The next draft will polish the expression. The fourth ties down all the missing details such as the missing or incomplete references, page layouts, addition of tables and diagrams, and completion of the reference list. Thereafter there are numerous readings and minor adjustments until a point is reached at which tinkering around further will probably make things worse rather than better. That is the point at which to leave the writing alone and rejoin the land of the living.

Two sections of the thesis are worthy of particular care: the Introduction and the Conclusion. It is not unknown for examiners to start evaluating a research report or thesis by studying the Introduction, to get an idea of what the study is about, and then going straight to the Conclusion to see if what comes in between is likely to be worth reading! This may sound harsh but it is realistic – examiners are usually overworked and underpaid people. So you cannot assume that the order in which you have written your thesis will necessarily be the order in which it is read. First impressions count, and these may well be gleaned from those two crucial chapters. Getting them into sparkling condition will repay your effort.

Pitfalls to avoid

- *Plagiarism*. Take care with the presentation of direct quotations from published work, making sure that these are used sparingly and are given full acknowledgement through referencing. A brief but valuable guide to citing references is a booklet by Fisher and Hanstock (1998) available from Blackwell's bookshops.
- *Poor presentation*. Probably the most frequent reason for a thesis being referred back to its author after examination is to enable 'minor corrections' to be made to the text. These corrections include such things as typing errors, missing diagrams and missing or poorly presented references. It is virtually impossible to eliminate all such errors before submitting the finished text, but care should be taken to reduce them to a minimum. It is always a good idea to get someone else to proof-read the text as well as doing so yourself. Examiners will probably notice the standard of presentation before they absorb the content, so it is important to create an impression of diligent effort and attention to detail. It may also be worth consulting or even buying a style manual, such as that by Turabian (1996), which shows how to deal with the vast number of textual details that must be considered when preparing a text.

Publish – and flourish!

It is hard for anyone outside academic life to appreciate how important publishing one's work is to a scholar. Who else, except perhaps the novelist or journalist, lives under the maxim of 'publish or perish'? Although the quality of an academic's teaching is becoming a more important criterion of excellence in academia, research reputation remains of key importance and that is judged to a large degree by publication record. Promotion or even continued employment depends on successful publication. No wonder that many academics are obsessed with getting published.

Box 13.4 How the academic journal publication system works

1 In every field there is a hierarchy of journals ranked in terms of prestige.
2 All high-quality journals use a refereeing system to evaluate submitted papers.
3 Papers are sent to anything from two to six or more referees, academics who are specialists in the field addressed by the paper.
4 Papers are 'blind'-refereed – the referees do not know the identity of the author and the authors do not know the identity of the referees.
5 Referees submit reports, following evaluation guidelines set by the journal's editors.
6 Unless papers are accepted without qualification (a fairly rare event), referees' comments and suggestions are sent to the authors, who are usually encouraged to revise and resubmit.
7 Authors may not submit their paper to more than one journal at the same time.
8 If a paper is accepted, it can take many months and sometimes several years before it actually appears in print.
9 Rejection rates for leading journals can be as high as 90 per cent, so don't be surprised if your paper is rejected by one, because that is statistically the most likely outcome.
10 Authors frequently display an ambivalent attitude towards referees – the whole system is almost bound to induce paranoid feelings!

Preparing to submit

However good student projects may be, they are seldom ready for publication as they stand. Some additional editorial work normally needs to be done to prepare them for submission to an editor. A good way of finding out what is required of publishable work is to read the guidelines for contributors produced by the journals. These are often published in issues of the journal or can be obtained on application to the editor. Box 13.5 contains an extract from one such set of guidelines. Details of the requirements of academic publishing houses are usually available at the company's Web site. It is also worth consulting experienced scholars for their views on what is normally required.

Box 13.5 Guidelines for journal contributors

The papers we wish to publish have the common characteristics of rigour and 'thought-throughness'. Rigour implies that authors are explicit about their assumptions, and open up those assumptions to challenge. This applies as much to the theoretical and normative stance taken in a paper as it does to the methodology or the data interpretation and analysis upon which a paper is grounded. 'Thought-throughness' implies that *Management Learning* is a vehicle for papers where the authors reveal care, commitment and excitement in their writing.

(Notes for Contributors, *Management Learning: The Journal for Managerial and Organizational Learning*)

The important points to keep in mind if you are preparing a paper for an academic journal are:

1   Do follow the journal submission guidelines to the letter. Irritating though it may be, each journal has its own house style and this must be followed. Unfortunately, no two editors seem to demand the same style of referencing!
2   Do not submit rough drafts. Your paper must be in final form. Editors are likely to become uncooperative if they believe that they and their (unpaid) referees are being used to do work that should have been done by the author.
3   Do not harass editors for a decision. Be patient. For no obvious reason, the refereeing of papers always seems to take far longer than any author could reasonably expect. A kind of Parkinson's law seems to operate whereby any paper received by a referee is ignored for at least two or three months.
4   Expose your paper to criticism before submitting. Present it at conferences and seminars and seek comments from friends and colleagues. Constructive criticism received before submitting your work to a journal can help you to make substantial improvements that increase the chances of publication.

Activity 13.2 What do editors want?

Select four or five journals in your field. Obtain copies of the Notes for Contributors or Guidelines for Authors for each of them. Studying these documents will tell you a good deal both about required writing and presentation standards and about the kinds of material and orientation journal editors seek.

If at first you don't succeed

Unfortunately, the road to publication is not always smooth. Somewhere along the way you are bound to experience having your work rejected. Fortunately, rejection does not necessarily mean that you have reached the end of the road. The more likely case is that the editors and referees wish to see your paper revised and improved. It is therefore wise not to over-react if your paper is not immediately accepted for publication.

If you do find yourself in this situation, it is probably a good idea to:

1   Remember that it happens to everyone.
2   If you must, get angry – and then get down to the work of revision. Many of us suffer from a disease known as 'revision aversion' but there is little to be gained by putting it off.

Activity 13.3 How readable is your writing?

Readability indices are not necessarily wholly reliable indicators of the intelligibility of someone's writing, but it can be instructive to see how one's style measures up. Your word-processing software may offer a readability assessment. If not, the delightfully named Fog Index may help. This index assumes that the longer the sentences a writer uses and the longer the words, the more difficult the writing will be to understand.

To calculate a Fog value for your writing:

1   Select a paragraph of about 100 words.
2   Calculate the average sentence length (ASL) = total words/total sentences.
3   Count the number of long words (NLW). These are words with three or more syllables. Exclude personal and place names, plural nouns in which the plural *es* is the third syllable, and verbs with *-ing*, *-es* or *-ed* as the third syllable.
4   The Fog Index is (ASL + NLW) × 0.4.
5   The Fog readability scale is 5 = easy, 10 = more difficult, 15 = difficult, 20 = very difficult. The average level suitable for university students is around 14–16.

The second paragraph at the beginning of this chapter has a Fog value of about 14. For more on readability see Seely (1998).

3   Do take referees' comments seriously; they usually make sound points, and even if you disagree with them, it will probably be necessary to comply with their requirements.

4   When you resubmit your paper, send a list of the referees' points explaining how you have responded to them. You do not necessarily have to accept all the points that have been made, but explain why you are rejecting those that you do reject.

5   Don't give up too easily. A writer is a person who writes, but a published writer is one who persists. If the editor encourages you to resubmit, then do so.

Key points

1   Begin writing drafts at an early stage in the project. Don't leave it all until the end.

2   Structure the text according to the nature of the content, the style of the publication and the characteristics of the readers.

3   Use word budgets to provide clear output targets for each section.

4   Encourage others to read your materials and provide constructive comment.

5   Study your markets. Do not send your material to journals or conference organizers without having studied their requirements.

6   To improve your writing style, find inspiration in examples of high-quality writing – and keep writing yourself!

7   'A writer is a person who writes.'

Key reading

Huff, A.S. (1999) *Writing for Scholarly Publication*, Thousand Oaks, CA: Sage.

Further reading

Barzun, J. and Graff, H.F. (1977) *The Modern Researcher*, New York: Harcourt Brace.

Becker, H.S. and Richards, P. (1986) *Writing for Social Scientists*, Chicago: University of Chicago Press.

Brown, R.B. (1994) 'You Can't Get There from Here: A Personal View of Management Research', *European Management Journal*, 12, pp. 71–5.

Germano, W. (2001) *Getting It Published: A Guide for Scholars and Anyone Else Serious about Serious Books*, Chicago: University of Chicago Press.

Harman, E. and Montagnes, I. (eds) (1976) *The Thesis and the Book*, Toronto: Toronto University Press.

Kelemen, M. and Bansal, P. (2002) 'The Conventions of Management Research and Their Relevance to Management Practice', *British Journal of Management*, 13, pp. 97–108.

Locker, K.O., Reinsch, N.L., Dulek, R. and Flatley, M. (1994) 'What Makes an Article Publishable?', *Bulletin of the Association for Business Communication*, 57 (2), pp. 59–66.

Moxley, J.M. (ed.) (1992) *Writing and Publishing for Academic Authors*, Lanham, MD: University Press of America.

Richardson, L. (1994) 'Writing: A Method of Inquiry', in N.K. Denzin and Y.S. Lincoln (eds) *Handbook of Qualitative Research*, Thousand Oaks, CA: Sage, pp. 516–29.

Seely, J. (1998) *The Oxford Guide to Writing and Speaking*, Oxford: Oxford University Press.

Van Maanen, J. (1988) *Tales of the Field: On Writing Ethnography*, Chicago: University of Chicago Press.

Wells, G. (1981) *The Successful Author's Handbook*, London: Macmillan.

Yin, R.K. (1989) 'Composing the Case Study "Report"', in *Case Study Research: Design and Methods*, Newbury Park, CA: Sage, pp. 127–52.

Bibliography

Abercrombie, N., Hill, S. and Turner, B.S. (2000) *The Penguin Dictionary of Sociology*, London: Penguin.

Academy of Management (2000) 'Code of Ethical Conduct', *Academy of Management Journal*, 43, pp. 1296–9.

Ackoff, R. (1979) 'The Future of Operational Research Is Past', *Journal of the Operational Research Society*, 30, pp. 93–104.

Ackoff, R. (1993) 'The Art and Science of Mess Management', in C. Mabey and B. Mayon-White (eds) *Managing Change*, London: Paul Chapman, pp. 47–54.

Ackroyd, S. and Fleetwood, S. (2000) *Realist Perspectives on Management and Organisations*, London: Routledge.

Adler, P.A. and Adler, P. (1994) 'Observational Techniques', in N.K. Denzin and Y.S. Lincoln (eds) *Handbook of Qualitative Research*, Thousand Oaks, CA: Sage, pp. 377–92.

Agar, M.H. (1986) *Speaking of Ethnography*, Beverly Hills, CA: Sage.

Ahmad, R. (1985) 'An Assessment of the Practice of Action Research as an Approach to Organizational Problem-Solving and Change', unpublished PhD thesis, University of Manchester.

Ahrens, T. (1997) 'Talking Accounting: An Ethnography of Management Knowledge in British and German Brewers', *Accounting, Organizations and Society*, 22, pp. 617–37.

Allen, D. (1981) *Research and Doctoral Training*, London: SSRC.

Al-Maskati, H.H. (1995) 'Participants' Strategies in Management Learning Events: An Ethnographic Study of Five Bank Training Programmes', unpublished PhD thesis, University of Manchester.

Alvesson, M. (1994) 'Talking in Organizations: Managing Identity and Impression in an Advertising Agency', *Organization Studies*, 15, pp. 535–63.

Alvesson, M. and Deetz, S. (2000) *Doing Critical Management Research*, London: Sage.

American Psychological Association Education and Training Board (1959) 'Education for Research in Psychology', *American Psychologist*, 14, pp. 167–79.

Anderson, R.J., Hughes, J.A. and Sharrock, W.W. (1985) *The Sociology Game: An Introduction to Sociological Reasoning*, London: Longman.

Arksey, H. and Knight, P. (1999) *Interviewing for Social Scientists*, London: Sage.

Arnold, S.J. and Fischer, E. (1994) 'Hermeneutics and Consumer Research', *Journal of Consumer Research*, 21, pp. 55–70.

Arnold, S.J., Kozinets, R.V. and Handelman, J.M. (2001) 'Hometown Ideology and Retailer Legitimation: The Institutional Semiotics of Wal-Mart Flyers', *Journal of Retailing*, 77, pp. 243–71.

Atkinson, J. (1968) *A Handbook for Interviewers*, London: HMSO.

Atkinson, P. and Hammersley, M. (1994) 'Ethnography and Participant Observation', in N.K. Denzin and Y.S. Lincoln (eds) *Handbook of Qualitative Research*, Thousand Oaks, CA: Sage, pp. 248–61.

Avison, D.E. (1997) 'Action Research in Information Systems', in G. McKenzie, J. Powell and R. Usher (eds) *Understanding Social Research: Perspectives on Methodology and Practice*, London: Falmer Press, pp. 196–209.

Babbie, E.R. (1990) *Survey Research Methods*, Belmont, CA: Wadsworth.

Babbie, E.R. and Halley, F. (1995) *Adventures in Social Research: Data Analysis Using SPSS for Windows*, Thousand Oaks, CA: Pine Forge Press.

Baburoglu, O.N. and Ravn, I. (1992) 'Normative Action Research', *Organization Studies*, 13, pp. 19–34.

Bailey, K.D. (1994) *Methods of Social Research*, New York: Free Press.

Bailey, V., Bemrose, G., Goddard, S., Impey, R., Joslyn, E. and Mackness, J. (1995) *Essential Research Skills*, London: HarperCollins.

Bales, R.F. (1950) *Interaction Process Analysis: A Method for the Study of Small Groups*, Cambridge, MA: Addison-Wesley.

Bales, R.F. (1970) *Personality and Interpersonal Behaviour*, New York: Holt, Rinehart and Winston.

Bales, R.F. and Slater, P.E. (1955) 'Role Differentiation in Small Decision-Making Groups', in T. Parsons and R.F. Bales (eds) *Family, Socialization and Interaction Process*, Glencoe, IL: Free Press, pp. 259–306.

Ball, S.B. (1998) 'Research, Teaching and Practice in Experimental Economics: A Progress Report and Review', *Southern Economic Journal*, 64, pp. 772–9.

Barker, J.D. (1966) *Power in Committees*, Chicago: Rand McNally.

Barker, S.B. and Barker, R.T. (1994) 'Managing Change in an Interdisciplinary Inpatient Unit: An Action Research Approach', *Journal of Mental Health Administration*, 21, pp. 80–91.

Barley, S.R. (1983) 'Semiotics and the Study of Occupational and Organizational Cultures', *Administrative Science Quarterly*, 28, pp. 393–413.

Barnes, J.A. (1979) *Who Should Know What? Social Science, Privacy and Ethics*, Harmondsworth, UK: Penguin.

Barzun, J. and Graff, H.F. (1977) *The Modern Researcher*, New York: Harcourt Brace.

Bate, S.P. (1997) 'Whatever Happened to Organizational Anthropology? A Review of the Field of Organizational Ethnography and Anthropological Studies', *Human Relations*, 30, pp. 1147–75.

Bateson, N. (1984) *Data Construction in Social Surveys*, London: George Allen and Unwin.

Batstone, E., Boraston, I. and Frenkel, S. (1977) *Shop Stewards in Action: The Organization of Workplace Conflict and Accommodation*, Oxford: Blackwell.

Baumrind, D. (1964) 'Some Thoughts on Ethics of Research: After Reading Milgram's "Behavioral Study of Obedience"', *American Psychologist*, 19, pp. 421–3.

Becher, T. (1989) *Academic Tribes and Territories: Intellectual Enquiry and the Cultures of Disciplines*, Buckingham, UK: SRHE and Open University Press.

Bechhofer, F. and Paterson, L. (2000) *Principles of Research Design in the Social Sciences*, London: Routledge.

Becker, H.S., Geer, B., Hughes, E.C. and Strauss, A.L. (1961) *Boys in White: Student Culture in Medical School*, Chicago: University of Chicago Press.

Becker, H.S. and Richards, P. (1986) *Writing for Social Scientists*, Chicago: University of Chicago Press.

Behling, O. (1991) 'The Case for the Natural Science Model for Research in Organizational Behaviour and Organization Theory', in N.C. Smith and P. Dainty (eds) *The Management Research Handbook*, London: Routledge, pp. 44–56.

Belbin, R.M. (1981) *Management Teams: Why They Succeed or Fail*, Oxford: Heinemann.

Bell, C. and Newby, H. (eds) (1977) *Doing Sociological Research*, London: George Allen and Unwin.

Belson, W.A. (1981) *The Design and Understanding of Survey Questions*, Aldershot, UK: Gower.

Bennett, R. (1991) 'How Is Management Research Carried Out?', in N.C. Smith and P. Dainty (eds) *The Management Research Handbook*, London: Routledge, pp. 85–103.

Berelson, B. (1954) 'Content Analysis', in G. Lindzey (ed.) *Handbook of Social Psychology*, Cambridge, MA: Addison-Wesley, pp. 488–522.

Berger, P. and Luckmann, T. (1967) *The Social Construction of Reality*, Harmondsworth, UK: Penguin.

Berry, M. (1995) 'Research and the Practice of Management: A French View', *Organization Science*, 6, pp. 104–16.

Bettman, J.R. and Weitz, B.A. (1983) 'Attributions in the Boardroom: Causal Reasoning in Corporate Annual Reports', *Administrative Science*.

Beynon, H. (1973) *Working for Ford*, Harmondsworth, UK: Penguin.

Bhaskar, R. (1989) *Reclaiming Reality: A Critical Introduction to Contemporary Philosophy*, London: Verso.

Biglan, A. (1973) 'The Characteristics of Subject Matter in Different Scientific Areas', *Journal of Applied Psychology*, 57, pp. 195–203.

Bion, W.R. (1961) *Experiences in Groups, and Other Papers*, London: Tavistock.

Blau, P.M. (1955) *The Dynamics of Bureaucracy*, Chicago: University of Chicago Press.

Bloomfield, R. and O'Hara, M. (1999) 'Market Transparency: Who Wins and Who Loses?', *Review of Financial Studies*, 12, pp. 5–35.

Bok, S. (1978) 'Deceptive Social Science Research', in *Lying: Moral Choice in Public and Private Life*, New York: Pantheon, pp. 182–202.

Boshoff, C. and Mels, G. (2000) 'The Impact of Multiple Commitments on Intentions to Resign: An Empirical Assessment', *British Journal of Management*, 11, pp. 255–72.

Bresnen, M. (1988) 'Insights on Site: Research into Construction Project Organizations', in A. Bryman (ed.) *Doing Research in Organizations*, London: Routledge, pp. 34–52.

Breton, G. and Taffler, R.J. (2001) 'Accounting Information and Analyst Stock Recommendation Decisions: A Content Analysis Approach', *Accounting and Business Research*, 31, pp. 91–103.

British Psychological Society (2000) *Code of Conduct, Ethical Principles and Guidelines*, Leicester: BPS.

British Sociological Association (2002) *Statement of Ethical Practice*, www.britsoc.org.uk/about/ethic.htm.

Bromley, D.B. (1986) *The Case Study Method in Psychology and Related Disciplines*, Chichester, UK: Wiley.

Brooks, A. and Watkins, K. (eds) (1994) *The Emerging Power of Action Inquiry Technologies*, San Francisco: Jossey-Bass.

Brooks, I. (1999) 'Managerialist Professionalism: The Destruction of a Non-conforming Subculture', *British Journal of Management*, 10, pp. 41–52.

Brooks, I. and Bate, P. (1994) 'The Problems of Effecting Change within the British Civil Service: A Cultural Perspective', *British Journal of Management*, 5, pp. 177–90.

Brown, A. (1995) *Organisational Culture*, London: Pitman.

Brown, R.B. (1994) 'You Can't Get There from Here: A Personal View of Management Research', *European Management Journal*, 12, pp. 71–5.

Brunskell, H. (1998) 'Feminist Methodology', in C. Seale (ed.) *Researching Society and Culture*, London: Sage, pp. 37–47.

Bryman, A. (1988a) *Quantity and Quality in Social Research*, London: Unwin Hyman.

Bryman, A. (ed.) (1988b) *Doing Research in Organizations*, London: Routledge.

Bryman, A. (1989) *Research Methods and Organization Studies*, London: Unwin Hyman.

Bryman, A. and Cramer, D. (1996) *Quantitative Data Analysis with Minitab: A Guide for Social Scientists*, London: Routledge.

Bryman, A. and Cramer, D. (2001) *Quantitative Data Analysis with SPSS Release 10 for Windows: A Guide for Social Scientists*, London: Routledge.

Burgess, R.G. (1984, 1991) *In the Field: An Introduction to Field Research*, London: Allen and Unwin.

Campbell, D.T. (1979) 'Reforms as Experiments', in J. Bynner and K.M. Stribley (eds) *Social Research: Principles and Procedures*, Harlow, UK: Longman, pp. 79–112.

Campbell, D.T. and Stanley, J.C. (1963) *Experimental and Quasi-experimental Designs for Research*, Chicago: Rand McNally.

Campbell, J.P., Daft, R.L. and Hulin, C.L. (1982), *What to Study? Generating and Developing Research Questions*, Beverly Hills, CA: Sage.

Cannell, C.F. and Kahn, R.L. (1965) 'The Collection of Data by Interviewing', in L. Festinger and D. Katz (eds) *Research Methods in the Behavioral Sciences*, New York: Holt, Rinehart and Winston, pp. 327–79.

Carey, A. (1967) 'The Hawthorne Studies: A Radical Criticism', *American Sociological Review*, 32, pp. 403–16.

Carlson, S. (1951) *Executive Behaviour: A Study of the Work Load and Working Methods of Managing Directors*, Stockholm: Strombergs.

Carpenter, M.A., Sanders, W.G. and Gregersen, H.B. (2001) 'Bundling Human Capital with Organizational Context: The Impact of International Assignment Experience on Multinational Firm Performance and CEO Pay', *Academy of Management Journal*, 44, pp. 493–511.

Carroll, G., Preisendoerfer, P., Swaminathan, A. and Wiedenmayer, G. (1993) 'Brewery and *Brauerei*: The Organizational Ecology of Brewing', *Organization Studies*, 14, pp. 155–88.

Carter, R.K. (1971) 'Clients' Resistance to Negative Findings and the Latent Conservative Function of Evaluation Studies', *The American Sociologist*, 6, pp. 118–24.

Carver, R.P. (1978) 'The Case against Statistical Significance Testing', *Harvard Educational Review*, 48, pp. 387–99.

Carver, R.P. (1993) 'The Case against Statistical Significance Testing, Revisited', *Journal of Experimental Education*, 61, pp. 287–92.

Chai, T.R. (1977/78) 'A Content Analysis of the Obituary Notices of Mao Tse-Tung', *Public Opinion Quarterly*, 41, pp. 475–87.

Chalmers, A.F. (1978, 1982, 1999) *What Is This Thing Called Science?*, Buckingham, UK: Open University Press.

Chaston, I., Badger, B. and Sadler-Smith, E. (2001) 'Organizational Learning: An Empirical Assessment of Process in Small U.K. Manufacturing Firms', *Journal of Small Business Management*, 39, pp. 139–51.

Chenhall, R.H. and Langfield-Smith, K. (1998) 'The Relationship between Strategic Priorities, Management Techniques and Management Accounting: An Empirical Investigation Using a Systems Approach', *Accounting, Organizations and Society*, 23, pp. 243–64.

Child, J. (1984) *Organisation: A Guide to Problems and Practice*, London: Harper and Row.

Chiu, R.K., Man, J.S.W. and Thayer, J. (1998) 'Effects of Role Conflicts and Role
Satisfactions on Stress of Three Professions in Hong Kong: A Path Analysis Approach',
Journal of Managerial Psychology, 13, pp. 318–33.

Cicourel, A. and Kitsuse, J. (1963) *The Educational Decision-Makers*, New York: Bobbs-
Merrill.

Clarke, I., Kell, I., Schmidt, R. and Vignali, C. (1998) 'Thinking the Thoughts They Do:
Symbolism and Meaning in the Consumer Experience of the "British Pub"', *Qualitative
Market Research*, 1, pp. 132–44.

Clarke, R.N., Conyon, M.J. and Peck, S.I. (1998) 'Corporate Governance and Directors'
Remuneration: Views from the Top', *Business Strategy Review*, 9 (4), pp. 21–30.

Cohen, A. (1999) 'Relationships among Five Forms of Commitment: An Empirical
Assessment', *Journal of Organizational Behavior*, 20, pp. 285–308.

Coleman, D.C. (1987) *History and the Economic Past: An Account of the Rise and
Decline of Economic History in Britain*, Oxford: Clarendon Press.

Colman, A.M. (1987) 'Obedience and Cruelty: Are Most People Potential Killers?',
in *Facts, Fallacies and Frauds in Psychology*, London: Hutchinson, pp. 81–108.

Comrey, A.L. and Lee, H.B. (1992) *A First Course in Factor Analysis*, Hillsdale, NJ:
Lawrence Erlbaum.

Converse, J.M. and Presser, S. (1987) *Survey Questions: Handcrafting the Standardised
Questionnaire*, Beverly Hills, CA: Sage.

Converse, J.M. and Schuman, H. (1973) *Conversations at Random: Survey Research as
Interviewers See It*, New York: Wiley.

Copeland, T.E. and Friedman, D. (1987) 'The Effect of Sequential Information Arrival
on Asset Prices: An Experimental Study', *Journal of Finance*, 42, pp. 763–97.

Crotty, M. (1998) *The Foundations of Social Research: Meaning and Perspective in the
Research Process*, London: Sage.

Crozier, M. (1964) *The Bureaucratic Phenomenon*, London: Tavistock.

Cryer, P. (1996) *The Research Student's Guide to Success*, Buckingham, UK: Open
University Press.

Cuff, E.C., Sharrock, W.W. and Francis, D.W. (1998) *Perspectives in Sociology*, London:
Routledge.

Cui, G. and Liu, Q. (2001) 'Executive Insights: Emerging Market Segments in a
Transitional Economy: A Study of Urban Consumers in China', *Journal of International
Marketing*, 9, pp. 84–106.

Cully, M., Woodland, S., O'Reilly, A. and Dix, G. (1999) *Britain at Work: As Depicted
by the 1998 Workplace Employee Relations Survey*, London: Routledge.

Cunnison, S. (1982) 'The Manchester Factory Studies: The Social Context, Bureaucratic
Organisation, Sexual Divisions and Their Influence on Patterns of Accommodation
between Workers and Management', in R. Frankenberg (ed.) *Custom and Conflict in
British Society*, Manchester: Manchester University Press, pp. 94–139.

Czaya, R. and Blair, J. (1995) *Designing Surveys*, London: Sage.

Daft, R.L. (1983) 'Learning the Craft of Organizational Research', *Academy of Management Review*, 8, pp. 539–46.

Daft, R.L. (1992) *Organization Theory and Design*, St Paul, MN: West Publishing.

Dalton, M. (1959) *Men Who Manage*, New York: Wiley.

Dalton, M. (1964) 'Preconceptions and Methods in *Men Who Manage*', in P. Hammond (ed.) *Sociologists at Work*, New York: Basic Books, pp. 50–95.

Danieli, A. and Thomas, A.B. (1999) 'What about the Workers? Studying the Work of Management Teachers and Their Orientations to Management Education', *Management Learning*, 30, pp. 449–71.

Davis, D. and Holt, C. (1993) *Experimental Economics*, Princeton, NJ: Princeton University Press.

Davis, M.S. (1971) 'That's Interesting! Towards a Phenomenology of Sociology and a Sociology of Phenomenology', *Philosophy of Social Science*, 1, pp. 309–44.

De Cock, C. (1994) 'Action Research: In Search of a New Epistemology?', *International Journal of Management*, 11, pp. 791–97.

de Vaus, D.A. (1990) *Surveys in Social Research*, London: Routledge.

de Vaus, D.A. (2001) *Research Design in Social Research*, London: Sage.

de Vaus, D.A. (2002) *Analyzing Social Science Data: 50 Key Problems in Data Analysis*, London: Sage.

Deal, T.E. and Kennedy, A.A. (1982) *Corporate Cultures*, Harmondsworth, UK: Penguin.

Denzin, N.K. (1978) *The Research Act*, New York: McGraw-Hill.

Denzin, N.K. and Lincoln, Y.S. (eds) (1994, 2000) *Handbook of Qualitative Research*, Thousand Oaks, CA: Sage.

Derrida, J. (1976) *Of Grammatology*, trans. G.C. Spivak, Baltimore: Johns Hopkins University Press.

Deutscher, I. (1973) *What We Say, What We Do: Sentiments and Acts*, Glenview, IL: Scott, Foresman.

Dickens, L. and Watkins, K. (1999) 'Action Research: Rethinking Lewin', *Management Learning*, 30, pp. 127–40.

D'Iribarne, P. (1996/97) 'The Usefulness of an Ethnographic Approach to the International Comparison of Organizations', *International Studies of Management and Organization*, 26 (4), pp. 30–47.

Ditton, J. (1979) 'Baking Time', *Sociological Review*, 27, pp. 157–67.

Dobrev, S.D. (2001) 'Revisiting Organizational Legitimation: Cognitive Diffusion and Sociopolitical Factors in the Evolution of Bulgarian Newspaper Enterprises, 1846–1992', *Organization Studies*, 22, pp. 419–44.

Dore, R. (1973) *British Factory–Japanese Factory*, London: Allen & Unwin.

Dubinskas, F. (ed.) (1988) *Making Time: Ethnographies of High-Technology Organizations*, Philadelphia, PA: Temple University Press.

Dunkerley, D. (1988) 'Historical Methods in Organization Analysis: The Case of a Naval Dockyard', in A. Bryman (ed.) *Doing Research in Organizations*, London: Routledge, pp. 82–95.

Dyer, W.G. and Wilkins, A.L. (1991) 'Better Stories, Not Better Constructs, to Generate Better Theory: A Rejoinder to Eisenhardt', *Academy of Management Review*, 16, pp. 613–19.

Easterby-Smith, M., Thorpe, R. and Lowe, A. (2002) *Management Research: An Introduction*, London: Sage.

Economic and Social Research Council (1993) *Commission on Management Research: Statements of Evidence*, Swindon, UK: ESRC.

Economic and Social Research Council (1994) *Building Partnerships: Enhancing the Quality of Management Research*, Report of the Commission on Management Research, Swindon, UK: ESRC.

Economic and Social Research Council (2001) *Postgraduate Training Guidelines 2001*, Swindon, UK: ESRC.

Eden, C. and Huxham, C. (1996) 'Action Research for Management Research', *British Journal of Management*, 7, pp. 75–86.

Eisenhardt, K.M. (1989) 'Building Theories from Case Study Research', *Academy of Management Review*, 14, pp. 532–50.

Eisenhardt, K.M. (1991) 'Better Stories and Better Constructs: The Case for Rigor and Comparative Logic', *Academy of Management Review*, 16, pp. 620–7.

Elden, M. and Chisholm, F. (1993) 'Emerging Varieties of Action Research', *Human Relations*, 46, pp. 121–42.

Emerson, R.M. (1981) 'Observational Fieldwork', *Annual Review of Sociology*, 7, pp. 351–78.

Emmett, I. and Morgan, D.H.J. (1982) 'Max Gluckman and the Manchester Shop-Floor Ethnographies', in R. Frankenberg (ed.) *Custom and Conflict in British Society*, Manchester: Manchester University Press, pp. 140–65.

Erickson, B.H. and Nosanchuk, T.A. (1979) *Understanding Data: An Introduction to Exploratory and Confirmatory Data Analysis for Students in the Social Sciences*, Milton Keynes, UK: Open University Press.

Evan, W.M. (1971) *Organizational Experiments: Laboratory and Field Research*, New York: Harper and Row.

Farran, D. (1990) 'Producing Statistical Information on Young People's Leisure', in L. Stanley (ed.) *Feminist Praxis: Research, Theory and Epistemology*, London: Routledge, pp. 91–102.

Farrell, B.J. and Cobbin, D.M. (1996) 'A Content Analysis of Codes of Ethics in Australian Enterprises', *Journal of Managerial Psychology*, 11, pp. 37–55.

Feldman, M. (1995) *Strategies for Interpreting Qualitative Data*, Thousand Oaks, CA: Sage.

Festinger, L. and Katz, D. (eds) (1965) *Research Methods in the Behavioral Sciences*, New York: Holt, Rinehart and Winston.

Fetterman, D.M. (1998) *Ethnography: Step by Step*, Thousand Oaks, CA: Sage.

Feyerabend, P.K. (1975) *Against Method: Outline of an Anarchistic Theory of Knowledge*, London: New Left Books.

Field, A. and Hole, G. (2002) *How to Design and Report Experiments*, London: Sage.

Filmer, P., Jenks, C., Seale, C. and Walsh, D. (1998) 'Developments in Social Theory', in C. Seale (ed.) *Researching Society and Culture*, London: Sage, pp. 23–36.

Fink, A. (1998) *Conducting Research Literature Reviews: From Paper to the Internet*, London: Sage.

Fink, A. and Kosecoff, J. (1998) *How to Conduct Surveys: A Step-by-Step Guide*, London: Sage.

Fiol, C.M. (1990a) 'Explaining Strategic Alliance in the Chemical Industry', in A.S. Huff (ed.) *Mapping Strategic Thought*, New York: Wiley, pp. 227–49.

Fiol, C.M. (1990b) 'Narrative Semiotics: Theory, Procedure and Illustration', in A.S. Huff (ed.) *Mapping Strategic Thought*, New York: Wiley, pp. 377–402.

Fisher, D. and Hanstock, T. (1998) *Citing References*, Nottingham: Nottingham Trent University.

Flood, M., Huisman, R., Koedjik, K. and Mahieu, R. (1999) 'Quote Disclosure and Price Discovery in Multiple-Dealer Financial Markets', *Review of Financial Studies*, 12, pp. 37–59.

Flyvbjerg, B. (2001) *Making Social Science Matter: Why Social Inquiry Fails and How It Can Succeed Again*, Cambridge: Cambridge University Press.

Foddy, W. (1993) *Constructing Questions for Interviews and Questionnaires: Theory and Practice in Social Research*, Cambridge: Cambridge University Press.

Fontana, A. and Frey, J.H. (1994) 'Interviewing: The Art of Science', in N.K. Denzin and Y.S. Lincoln (eds) *Handbook of Qualitative Research*, Thousand Oaks, CA: Sage, pp. 361–76.

Foster, M. (1972) 'An Introduction to the Theory and Practice of Action Research in Work Organizations', *Human Relations*, 25, pp. 529–56.

Fowler, F.J. and Mangione, T.W. (1990) *Standardized Survey Interviewing*, Beverly Hills, CA: Sage.

Fox, S. (1992) 'Self-Knowledge and Personal Change: The Reported Experience of Managers in Part-Time Management Education', unpublished PhD thesis, University of Manchester.

Francis, J.R. (1994) 'Auditing, Hermeneutics and Subjectivity', *Accounting, Organizations and Society*, 19, pp. 235–69.

Freeman, J. (1986) 'Data Quality and the Development of Organizational Social Science', *Administrative Science Quarterly*, 31, pp. 298–303.

Frey, J.H. (1989) *Survey Research by Telephone*, London: Sage.

Frey, J.H. and Oishi, S.M. (1995) *How to Conduct Interviews by Telephone and in Person*, London: Sage.

Gaffney, M.M. and Walton, R.E. (1989) 'Research, Action and Participation', *American Behavioral Scientist*, 32, pp. 582–611.

Garmonsway, G.N. (1970) *Penguin English Dictionary*, Harmondsworth, UK: Penguin.

Gash, S. (1989) *Effective Literature Searching for Students*, Aldershot, UK: Gower.

Gellner, E. (1987) 'The Scientific Status of the Social Sciences', *International Social Science Journal*, 114, pp. 567–86.

Germano, W. (2001) *Getting It Published: A Guide for Scholars and Anyone Else Serious about Serious Books*, Chicago: University of Chicago Press.

Gersick, C.J.G. (1988) 'Time and Transition in Work Teams: Toward a New Model of Group Development', *Academy of Management Journal*, 31, pp. 9–41.

Gersick, C.J.G., Bartunek, J.M. and Dutton, J.E. (2000) 'Learning from Academia: The Importance of Relationships in Professional Life', *Academy of Management Journal*, 43, pp. 1026–44.

Ghauri, P., Grønhaug, K. and Kristianslund, I. (1995) *Research Methods in Business Studies: A Practical Guide*, Hemel Hempstead, UK: Prentice Hall.

Gibbons, M., Limoges, C., Nowotny, H., Schwartzman, S., Scott, P. and Trow, M. (1994) *The New Production of Knowledge: The Dynamics of Science and Research in Contemporary Societies*, London: Sage.

Giddens, A. (1976) *New Rules of Sociological Method*, London: Hutchinson.

Gilbert, G.N. (1980) 'Being Interviewed: A Role Analysis', *Social Science Information*, 19, pp. 227–36.

Gilbert, N. (ed.) (2001) *Researching Social Life*, London: Sage.

Gill, J. and Johnson, P. (2000) *Research Methods for Managers*, London: Sage.

Glaser, B.G. and Strauss, A.L. (1967) *The Discovery of Grounded Theory*, Chicago: Aldine.

Gold, R. (1958) 'Roles in Sociological Field Observation', *Social Forces*, 36, pp. 217–23.

Golden-Biddle, K. and Locke, K. (1993) 'Appealing Work: An Investigation of How Ethnographic Texts Convince', *Organization Science*, 4, pp. 595–616.

Goode, W.J. and Hatt, P.K. (eds) (1952) *Methods of Social Research*, New York: McGraw-Hill.

Gottschalk, L., Kluckhohn, C. and Angell, R. (1945) *The Use of Personal Documents in History, Anthropology and Sociology*, New York: Social Science Research Council.

Goulding, C. (1998) 'Grounded Theory: The Missing Methodology on the Interpretivist Agenda', *Qualitative Market Research*, 1, pp. 50–7.

Gouldner, A.W. (1954) *Patterns of Industrial Bureaucracy*, Glencoe, IL: Free Press.

Gouldner, A.W. (1967) *Enter Plato*, London: Routledge and Kegan Paul.

Goyder, J.C. (1988) *The Silent Majority: Nonrespondents in Sample Surveys*, Oxford: Polity Press.

Grayson, K. and Shulman, D. (2000) 'Indexicality and the Verification Function of Irreplaceable Possessions: A Semiotic Analysis', *Journal of Consumer Research*, 27, pp. 17–30.

Green, S.B., Salkind, N.J. and Akey, T.M. (1997) *Using SPSS for Windows: Analyzing and Understanding Data*, Upper Saddle River, NJ: Prentice Hall.

Greenwood, D.J. and Levin, M. (1998) *Introduction to Action Research: Social Research for Social Change*, London: Sage.

Greimas, A.J. (1966) *Sémantique structurale*, Paris: Larousse.

Grey, C. and French, R. (1996) 'Rethinking Management Education: An Introduction', in R. French and C. Grey (eds) *Rethinking Management Education*, London: Sage, pp. 1 16.

Griffin, R. and Kacmar, K.M. (1991) 'Laboratory Research in Management: Misconceptions and Missed Opportunities', *Journal of Organizational Behavior*, 12, pp. 301–11.

Groves, R. and Kahn, R. (1980) *Comparing Telephone and Personal Interview Surveys*, New York: Academic Press.

Gummesson, E. (1991) *Qualitative Methods in Management Research*, Newbury Park, CA: Sage.

Gupta, V., Hanges, P.J. and Dorfman, P. (2002) 'Cultural Clusters: Methodology and Findings', *Journal of World Business*, 37, pp. 11–15.

Hakim, C. (1982) *Secondary Analysis in Social Research: A Guide to Data Sources and Methods with Examples*, London: George Allen and Unwin.

Hakim, C. (1992) *Research Design: Strategies and Choices in the Design of Social Research*, London: Routledge.

Hammersley, M. and Atkinson, P. (1995) *Ethnography: Principles in Practice*, London: Routledge.

Hammond, P.E. (ed.) (1964) *Sociologists at Work: Essays on the Craft of Social Research*, New York: Basic Books.

Hannah, L. and Ackrill, M. (2001) *Barclays*, Cambridge: Cambridge University Press.

Harman, E. and Montagnes, I. (eds) (1976) *The Thesis and the Book*, Toronto: Toronto University Press.

Harris, H. (2001) 'Content Analysis of Secondary Data: A Study of Courage in Managerial Decision Making', *Journal of Business Ethics*, 34, pp. 191–208.

Hart, C. (1998) *Doing a Literature Review: Releasing the Social Science Research Imagination*, London: Sage.

Hart, C. (2001) *Doing a Literature Search: A Comprehensive Guide for the Social Sciences*, London: Sage.

Hart, S.J. (1991) 'A First-Time User's Guide to the Collection and Analysis of Interview Data from Senior Managers', in N.C. Smith and P. Dainty (eds) *The Management Research Handbook*, London: Routledge, pp. 190–204.

Harvey, L. (1990) *Critical Social Research*, London: Unwin Hyman.

Harvey, M. and Evans, M. (2001) 'Decoding Competitive Propositions: A Semiotic Alternative to Traditional Advertising Research', *International Journal of Market Research*, 43, pp. 171–87.

Hassard, J. (1991) 'Multiple Paradigms in Organizational Analysis: A Case Study', *Organization Studies*, 12, pp. 275–99.

Healey, M.J. and Rawlinson, M.B. (1994) 'Interviewing Techniques in Business and Management Research', in V.J. Wass and P.E. Wells (eds) *Principles and Practice in Business and Management Research*, Aldershot, UK: Dartmouth, pp. 123–46.

Hedges, B. (1978) 'Sampling', in G. Hoinville, R. Jowell and associates (eds) *Survey Research Practice*, London: Heinemann, pp. 55–89.

Heller, F. (ed.) (1986) *The Use and Abuse of Social Science*, London: Sage.

Hellgren, B., Lowstedt, J., Puttonen, L., Tienari, J., Vaara, E. and Werr, A. (2002) 'How Issues Become (Re)constructed in the Media: Discursive Practices in the Astra–Zeneca Merger', *British Journal of Management*, 13, pp. 123–40.

Helmericks, S.G., Nelsen, R.L. and Unnithan, N.P. (1991) 'The Researcher, the Topic and the Literature: A Procedure for Systematizing Literature Searches', *Journal of Applied Behavioral Science*, 27, pp. 285–94.

Heracleous, L. and Barrett, M. (2001) 'Organizational Change as Discourse: Communicative Actions and Deep Structures in the Context of Information Technology Implementation', *Academy of Management Journal*, 44, pp. 755–78.

Hirsch, E.D. (1967) *Validity in Interpretation*, New Haven, CT: Yale University Press.

Hirschman, E.C. (1985) 'Scientific Style and the Conduct of Consumer Research', *Journal of Consumer Research*, 12, pp. 225–39.

Hochschild, A.R. (1983) *The Managed Heart: Commercialization of Human Feeling*, Berkeley, CA: University of California Press.

Hodgkinson, G.P. (ed.) (2001) 'Facing the Future: The Nature and Purpose of Management Research Re-assessed', *British Journal of Management*, 12, Special Issue.

Hodson, R. (2001) 'Disorganized, Unilateral and Participative Organizations: New Insights from the Ethnographic Literature', *Industrial Relations*, 40, pp. 204–30.

Hofstede, G. (1980a) *Culture's Consequences: International Differences in Work-Related Values*, Beverly Hills, CA: Sage.

Hofstede, G. (1980b) 'Motivation, Leadership and Organization: Do American Theories Apply Abroad?', *Organizational Dynamics*, Summer, pp. 42–63.

Hoinville, G., Jowell, R. and associates (1978) *Survey Research Practice*, London: Heinemann.

Holdaway, S. (1980) 'The Police Station', *Urban Life*, 9, pp. 79–100.

Holdaway, S. (1983) *Inside the British Police: A Force at Work*, Oxford: Blackwell.

Holsti, O.R. (1969) *Content Analysis for the Social Sciences and Humanities*, Reading, MA: Addison-Wesley.

Homan, R. (1991) *The Ethics of Social Research*, London: Longman.

Hossack, A. (1982) *Making a Summary*, London: Methuen.

Howard, K. and Sharp, J.A. (1983) *The Management of a Student Research Project*, Aldershot, UK: Gower.

Huff, A.S. (1999) *Writing for Scholarly Publication*, Thousand Oaks, CA: Sage.

Huff, A.S. (2000) 'Changes in Organizational Knowledge Production', *Academy of Management Review*, 25, pp. 288–93.

Huff, A.S. and Huff, J.O. (2001) 'Re-focusing the Business School Agenda', *British Journal of Management*, 12, Special Issue, pp. S49–S54.

Hult, M. and Lennung, S.-A. (1980) 'Towards a Definition of Action Research: A Note and Bibliography', *Journal of Management Studies*, 17, pp. 241–50.

Humphrey, C. and Scapens, R.W. (1996) 'Theories and Case Studies of Organizational Accounting Practices: Limitation or Liberation', *Accounting, Auditing and Accountability Journal*, 9 (4), pp. 86–106.

Hussey, J. and Hussey, R. (1997) *Business Research: A Practical Guide for Undergraduate and Postgraduate Students*, Basingstoke, UK: Macmillan.

Hyde, P. (2002) 'Organizational Dynamics of Mental Health Teams', unpublished PhD thesis, University of Manchester.

Hyde, P. and Thomas, A.B. (2002) 'Organizational Defences Revisited: Systems and Contexts', *Journal of Managerial Psychology*, 17, pp. 408–21.

International Military Tribunal (1949) *Trials of War Criminals before the Nuremberg Military Tribunals under Control Council Law No. 10*, vol. 2, Washington, DC: US Government Printing Office.

Irvine, J., Miles, I. and Evans, J. (1981) *Demystifying Social Statistics*, Cambridge: Pluto Press.

Jackall, R. (1988) *Moral Mazes: The World of Corporate Managers*, Oxford: Oxford University Press.

Jackson, N. and Carter, P. (2000) *Rethinking Organisational Behaviour*, Harlow, UK: Pearson.

Janesick, V.J. (1994) 'The Dance of Qualitative Research Design: Metaphor, Methodolatry, and Meaning', in N.K. Denzin and Y.S. Lincoln (eds) *Handbook of Qualitative Research*, Thousand Oaks, CA: Sage, pp. 209–19.

Jaques, E. (1951) *The Changing Culture of a Factory*, London: Tavistock.

Jeffcutt, P. and Thomas, A.B. (1991) 'Understanding Supervisory Relationships', in N.C. Smith and P. Dainty (eds) *The Management Research Handbook*, London: Routledge, pp. 237–44.

Jeremy, D.J. and Tweedale, G. (1994) *Dictionary of 20th Century Business Leaders*, London: Bowker Saur.

Jick, T.J. (1979) 'Mixing Qualitative and Quantitative Methods: Triangulation in Action', *Administrative Science Quarterly*, 24, pp. 602–11.

Jobber, D. (1991) 'Choosing a Survey Method in Management Research', in N.C. Smith and P. Dainty (eds) *The Management Research Handbook*, London: Routledge, pp. 175–80.

Joffe, M., Mackay, T. and Mitchell, J. (1986) *Buswork and Health: A Comparison of One Person Operators, Crew Drivers and Conductors*, Birmingham: TURC Publishers.

Jones, E. (2001) *The Business of Medicine: The Extraordinary History of Glaxo*, London: Profile Books.

Jung, J. (1971) *The Experimenter's Dilemma*, New York: Harper and Row.

Kanji, G.K. (1993) *100 Statistical Tests*, London: Sage.

Kanter, R.M. (1977) *Men and Women of the Corporation*, New York: Basic Books.

Kelemen, M. and Bansal, P. (2002) 'The Conventions of Management Research and Their Relevance to Management Practice', *British Journal of Management*, 13, pp. 97–108.

Keller, G. and Warrack, B. (2002) *Statistics for Management and Economics*, London: Thomson.

Kelly, M. (1998) 'Writing a Research Proposal', in C. Seale (ed.) *Researching Society and Culture*, London: Sage, pp. 111–22.

Kelman, H.C. (1965) 'Manipulation of Human Behaviour: An Ethical Dilemma for the Social Scientist', *Journal of Social Issues*, 21, pp. 31–46.

Kerlinger, F.N. (1964) *Foundations of Behavioral Research*, New York: Holt, Rinehart and Winston.

Kerlinger, F.N. and Lee, H.B. (2000) *Foundations of Behavioral Research*, Fort Worth, TX: Harcourt College Publishers.

Kervin, J.B. (1992) *Methods for Business Research*, New York: HarperCollins.

Kets de Vries, M. (1996) 'Leaders Who Make a Difference', *European Management Journal*, 14, pp. 486–93.

King, G., Keohane, R.O. and Verba, S. (1994) *Designing Social Inquiry: Scientific Inference in Qualitative Research*, Princeton, NJ: Princeton University Press.

Konrad, A.M. and Mangel, R. (2000) 'The Impact of Work–Life Programs on Firm Productivity', *Strategic Management Journal*, 21, pp. 1225–37.

Krippendorf, K. (1981) *Content Analysis: An Introduction to Its Methodology*, Beverly Hills, CA: Sage.

Kunda, G. (1992) *Engineering Culture: Control and Commitment in a High Tech Corporation*, Philadelphia, PA: Temple University Press.

Lam, S.S.K. and Schaubroeck, J. (2000) 'The Role of Locus of Control in Reactions to Being Promoted and to Being Passed Over: A Quasi Experiment', *Academy of Management Journal*, 43, pp. 66–79.

Lane, N. (2000) 'The Management Implications of Women's Employment Disadvantage in a Female-Dominated Profession: A Study of NHS Nursing', *Journal of Management Studies*, 37, pp. 705–31.

Lavrakas, P.J. (1995) *Telephone Survey Methods: Sampling, Selection and Supervision*, London: Sage.

Lawler, E. (ed.) (1985) *Doing Research That is Useful for Theory and Practice*, New York: Jossey-Bass.

Lazar, D. (1998) 'Selected Issues in the Philosophy of Social Science', in C. Seale (ed.) *Researching Society and Culture*, London: Sage, pp. 7–22.

LeCompte, M.D. and Schensul, J.J. (1999) *Designing and Conducting Ethnographic Research*, Walnut Creek, CA: AltaMira Press.

Lee, A. (1985) 'The Scientific Basis for Conducting Case Studies of Organizations', in Robinson, R.B. and Pearce, J.A. (eds) *Academy of Management Proceedings*, Boston, MA: Academy of Management, pp. 320–4.

Lee, A.S. (1989) 'Case Studies as Natural Experiments', *Human Relations*, 42, pp. 117–38.

Legge, K. (1988) 'Personnel Management in Recession and Recovery: A Comparative Analysis of What the Surveys Say', *Personnel Review*, 17 (2), pp. 2–72.

Lengnick-Hall, M.L. (1995) 'Sexual Harassment Research: A Methodological Critique', *Personnel Psychology*, 48, pp. 841–64.

Leong, S.W., Sheth, J.N. and Tan, C.T. (1993) 'An Empirical Study of the Scientific Styles of Marketing Academics', *European Journal of Marketing*, 28 (8/9), pp. 12–26.

Lewin, K. (1946) 'Action Research and Minority Problems', *Journal of Social Issues*, 2, pp. 34–46.

Lewins, A. (2001) 'Computer Assisted Qualitative Data Analysis', in N. Gilbert (ed.) *Researching Social Life*, London: Sage, pp. 302–23.

Lewis, G.J. and Harvey, B. (2001) 'Perceived Environmental Uncertainty: The Extension of Miller's Scale to the Natural Environment', *Journal of Management Studies*, 38, pp. 201–33.

Lieberson, S. and O'Connor, J.F. (1972) 'Leadership and Organizational Performance: A Study of Large Corporations', *American Sociological Review*, 37, pp. 117–30.

Lindzey, G. and Aronson, E. (eds) (1968) *The Handbook of Social Psychology*, Reading, MA: Addison Wesley.

Lindzey, G. and Aronson, E. (eds) (1985) *The Handbook of Social Psychology*, New York: Random House.

Linstead, S. (1997) 'The Social Anthropology of Management', *British Journal of Management*, 8, pp. 85–98.

Litwin, M.S. (1995) *How to Measure Survey Reliability and Validity*, Thousand Oaks, CA: Sage.

Locke, K. (2001) *Grounded Theory in Management Research*, London: Sage.

Locke, L.F., Spirduso, W.W. and Silverman, S.J. (1998) *Reading and Understanding Research*, London: Sage.

Locker, K.O., Reinsch, N.L., Dulek, R. and Flatley, M. (1994) 'What Makes an Article Publishable?', *Bulletin of the Association for Business Communication*, 57 (2), pp. 59–66.

Lupton, T. (1959) 'Social Factors Influencing Norms of Production in British Factories', unpublished PhD thesis, University of Manchester.

Lupton, T. (1963) *On the Shop Floor*, Oxford: Pergamon.

Lupton, T. (1984) 'The Functions and Organization of University Business Schools', in A. Kakabadse and S. Mukhi (eds) *The Future of Management Education*, Aldershot, UK: Gower, pp. 203–17.

Lupton, T. (1985a) 'Foreword', in D.A. Buchanan and A.A. Huczynski, *Organizational Behaviour: An Introductory Text*, Englewood Cliffs, NJ: Prentice Hall, pp. xi–xv.

Lupton, T. (1985b) 'Let the Data Speak', MBS Working Paper no. 100.

Lyles, M.A. (1990) 'A Research Agenda for Strategic Management in the 1990s', *Journal of Management Studies*, 27, pp. 363–75.

McCall, G.J. and Simmons, J.L. (eds) (1969) *Issues in Participant Observation: A Text and Reader*, Reading, MA: Addison-Wesley.

McCutcheon, D.M. and Meredith, J.R. (1993) 'Conducting Case Study Research in Operating Management', *Journal of Operations Management*, 11, pp. 239–56.

Macdonald, K. (2001) 'Using Documents', in N. Gilbert (ed.) *Researching Social Life*, London: Sage, pp. 194–210.

McEvoy, G.M. (1997) 'Organizational Change and Outdoor Management Education', *Human Resource Management*, 36, pp. 235–50.

McEvoy, G.M. and Cascio, W.F. (1987) 'Do Good or Poor Performers Leave? A Meta-analysis of the Relationship between Performance and Turnover', *Academy of Management Journal*, 30, pp. 744–62.

Macfarlane, B. (1997) 'In Search of an Identity: Lecturer Perceptions of the Business Studies First Degree', *Journal of Vocational Education and Training*, 49, pp. 5–20.

Maclure, R. and Bassey, M. (1991) 'Participatory Action Research in Togo: An Inquiry into Maize Storage Systems', in W.F. Whyte (ed.) *Participatory Action Research*, Newbury Park, CA: Sage, pp. 190–209.

Madge, J. (1963) 'Pioneers in Industrial Sociology', in *The Origins of Scientific Sociology*, London: Tavistock, pp. 162–209.

March, J.G., Sproull, L.S. and Tamuz, M. (1991) 'Learning from Samples of One or Fewer', *Organization Science*, 2, pp. 1–13.

Margetts, J. (1991) *Who's Who in Industry*, London: Fulcrum.

Mariampolski, H. (1999) 'The Power of Ethnography', *Journal of the Market Research Society*, 41, pp. 75–86.

Marsh, C. (1979) 'Opinion Polls: Social Science or Political Manoeuvre?', in J. Irvine, I. Miles and J. Evans (eds) *Demystifying Social Statistics*, London: Pluto Press, pp. 268–88.

Marshall, G. (ed.) (1998) *Oxford Dictionary of Sociology*, Oxford: Oxford University Press.

Marshall, R.S. and Boush, D.M. (2001) 'Dynamic Decision-Making: A Cross-cultural Comparison of U.S. and Peruvian Export Managers', *Journal of International Business Studies*, 32, pp. 873–93.

Martin, P.Y. and Turner, B.A. (1986) 'Grounded Theory and Organizational Research', *Journal of Applied Behavioral Science*, 22, pp. 141–57.

Matthews, V. (1993) 'What a Load of Old Rubbish', *Marketing Week*, 16 (32), p. 26.

May, T. (1997) *Social Research: Issues, Methods and Processes*, Buckingham, UK: Open University Press.

Mazza, C. and Alvarez, J.L. (2000) 'Haute Couture and Pret-a-Porter: The Popular Press and the Diffusion of Management Practices', *Organization Studies*, 21, pp. 567–88.

Merton, R.K. (1973) 'The Normative Structure of Science', in N.W. Storer (ed.) *Robert K. Merton. The Sociology of Science: Theoretical and Empirical Investigations*, Chicago: University of Chicago Press, pp. 267–78.

Messallam, A.A. (1998) 'The Organizational Ecology of Investment Firms in Europe', *Organization Studies*, 19, pp. 23–46.

Mestelman, S. (ed.) (1998) 'Laboratory Methods in Economics', *Managerial and Decision Economics*, 19 (4/5), Special Issue.

Miles, M.B. and Huberman, A.M. (1984) *Qualitative Data Analysis: A Sourcebook of New Methods*, Beverly Hills, CA: Sage.

Miles, M.B. and Huberman, A.M. (1994) *Qualitative Data Analysis*, Thousand Oaks, CA: Sage.

Milgram, S. (1963) 'Behavioral Study of Obedience', *Journal of Abnormal and Social Psychology*, 67, pp. 371–8.

Milgram, S. (1964) 'Issues in the Study of Obedience: A Reply to Baumrind', *American Psychologist*, 19, pp. 848–52.

Miller, A.G. (1986) *The Obedience Experiments: A Case Study of Controversy in Social Science*, Westport, CT: Praeger.

Miller, D.C. (1991) *Handbook of Research Design and Social Measurement*, Newbury Park, CA: Sage.

Mills, C.W. (1959) *The Sociological Imagination*, London: Oxford University Press.

Mintzberg, H. (1970) 'Structured Observation as a Method to Study Managerial Work', *Journal of Management Studies*, 7, pp. 87–104.

Mintzberg, H. (1971) 'Managerial Work: Analysis from Observation', *Management Science*, 18 (2), B97–B110.

Mintzberg, H. (1973) *The Nature of Managerial Work*, New York: Harper and Row.

Mirvis, P.H. and Seashore, S.E. (1979) 'Being Ethical in Organizational Research', *American Psychologist*, 34, pp. 766–80.

Mishler, E.G. (1986) *Research Interviewing: Context and Narrative*, London: Harvard University Press.

Mitchell, J.C. (1983) 'Case and Situation Analysis', *Sociological Review*, 31, pp. 187–211.

Mitchell, V.W. (1992) 'The Gravid Male: An Essay on Delivering a PhD', *Management Research News*, 15 (8), pp. 18–23.

Monder, R. (1996) 'Uncovering the Management Process: An Ethnographic Approach', *British Journal of Management*, 7, pp. 35–44.

Morgenstern, O. (1963) *On the Accuracy of Economic Observations*, Princeton, NJ: Princeton University Press.

Morris, C. (1993) *Quantitative Approaches in Business Studies*, London: Pitman.

Morrison, D.E. and Henkel, R.E. (eds) (1970a) *The Significance Test Controversy: A Reader*, London: Butterworths.

Morrison, D.E. and Henkel, R.E. (1970b) 'Significance Tests in Behavioral Research: Skeptical Conclusions and Beyond', in D.E. Morrison and R.E. Henkel (eds) *The Significance Test Controversy: A Reader*, London: Butterworths, pp. 305–11.

Morton-Williams, J. (1993) *Interviewer Approaches*, Aldershot, UK: Dartmouth.

Moser, C.A. (1967) *Survey Methods in Social Investigation*, London: Heinemann.

Moss, M.S. (2000) *Standard Life, 1825–2000: The Building of Europe's Largest Mutual Life Company*, Edinburgh: Mainstream.

Moxley, J.M. (ed.) (1992) *Writing and Publishing for Academic Authors*, Lanham, MD: University Press of America.

Mumford, E. (1995) *Effective Systems Design and Requirements Analysis: The ETHICS Approach*, London: Macmillan.

Mumford, M.D., Zaccaro, S.J., Johnson, J.F., Diana, M., Gilbert, J.A. and Threlfall, K.V. (2000) 'Patterns of Leader Characteristics: Implications for Performance and Development', *Leadership Quarterly*, 11, pp. 115–33.

Murtha, T.P., Lenway, S.A. and Bagozzi, R.P. (1998) 'Global Mind-Sets and Cognitive Shift in a Complex Multinational Corporation', *Strategic Management Journal*, 19, pp. 97–114.

Nandhakumar, J. (1997) 'Issues in Participant Observation: A Study of the Practice of Information Systems Development', in G. McKenzie, J. Powell and R. Usher (eds) *Understanding Social Research: Perspectives on Methodology and Practice*, London: Falmer Press, pp. 210–20.

Numagami, T. (1998) 'The Infeasibility of Invariant Laws in Management Studies: A Reflective Dialogue in Defence of Case Studies', *Organization Science*, 9, pp. 2–15.

Oppenheim, A.N. (1992, 2000) *Questionnaire Design, Interviewing and Attitude Measurement*, London: Continuum.

Orne, M.T. (1962) 'On the Social Psychology of the Psychological Experiment with Particular Reference to Demand Characteristics and Their Implications', *American Psychologist*, 17, pp. 776–83.

Osborne, J.D., Stubbart, C.I. and Ramprasad, A. (2001) 'Strategic Groups and Competitive Enactment: A Study of Dynamic Relationships between Mental Models and Performance', *Strategic Management Journal*, 22, pp. 435–54.

Otley, D.T. and Berry, A.J. (1994) 'Case Study Research in Management Accounting and Control', *Management Accounting Research*, 5, pp. 45–66.

Pahl, R.E. and Pahl, J. (1965) *Managers and Their Wives*, Harmondsworth, UK: Penguin.

Pahl, R.E. and Winkler, J.T. (1974) 'The Economic Elite: Theory and Practice', in P. Stanworth and A. Giddens (eds) *Elites and Power in British Society*, London: Cambridge University Press, pp. 102–22.

Pandit, N., Cook, G.A.S. and Swann, G.M.P. (2001) 'The Dynamics of Industrial Clustering in British Financial Services', *Service Industries Journal*, 21 (4), pp. 33–61.

Parasuraman, S. and Simmers, C.A. (2001) 'Type of Employment, Work-Family Conflict and Well-Being: A Comparative Study', *Journal of Organizational Behavior*, 22, pp. 551–68.

Partington, D. (2000) 'Building Grounded Theories of Management Action', *British Journal of Management*, 11, pp. 91–102.

Pasmore, W. and Friedlander, F. (1982) 'An Action Research Programme for Increasing Employee Involvement in Problem-Solving', *Administrative Science Quarterly*, 27, pp. 343–62.

Pearsall, J. (ed.) (1999) *Concise Oxford Dictionary*, Oxford: Oxford University Press.

Pepper, S.C. (1948) *World Hypotheses: A Study in Evidence*, Berkeley, CA: University of California Press.

Peters, M. and Robinson, V. (1984) 'The Origins and Status of Action Research', *Journal of Applied Behavioral Science*, 20, pp. 113–24.

Peterson, R.A. (1984) 'Asking the Age Question: A Research Note', *Public Opinion Quarterly*, 48, pp. 379–83.

Pettigrew, A. (1985) *The Awakening Grant: Continuity and Change in ICI*, Oxford: Blackwell.

Pettigrew, A. (1992) 'On Studying Managerial Elites', *Strategic Management Journal*, Special Issue, 13, pp. 163–82.

Phillips, D.L. (1973) *Abandoning Method*, San Francisco, CA: Jossey-Bass.

Phillips, E. and Pugh, D.S. (2000) *How to Get a PhD*, Buckingham, UK: Open University Press.

Pinder, C.C. (1977) 'Concerning the Application of Human Motivation Theories in Organizational Settings', *Academy of Management Review*, 2, pp. 384–97.

Podsakoff, P.M. and Organ, D.W. (1986) 'Self-Reports in Organizational Research: Problems and Prospects', *Journal of Management*, 12, pp. 531–44.

Polkinghorne, D. (1983) *Methodology for the Human Sciences: Systems of Inquiry*, Albany, NY: State University of New York Press.

Polkinghorne, D. (1988) *Narrative Knowing and the Human Sciences*, Albany, NY: State University of New York Press.

Potter, J. (1996) *Representing Reality: Discourse, Rhetoric and Social Construction*, London: Sage.

Prasad, A. and Mir, R. (2002) 'Digging Deep for Meaning: A Critical Hermeneutic Analysis of CEO Letters to Shareholders in the Oil Industry', *Journal of Business Communication*, 39, pp. 92–116.

Procter, M. (1996) 'Analyzing Other Researchers' Data', in N. Gilbert (ed.) *Researching Social Life*, London: Sage, pp. 255–86.

Propp, V.I. (1968) *The Morphology of the Folktale*, ed. L.A. Wagner, Austin, TX: University of Texas Press.

Pugh, D.S., Mansfield, R. and Warner, M. (1975) *Research in Organizational Behaviour: A British Survey*, London: Heinemann.

Punch, K.F. (1998) *Introduction to Social Research: Quantitative and Qualitative Approaches*, London: Sage.

Punnett, B.J. (1988) 'Designing Field Experiments for Management Research outside North America', *International Studies of Management and Organization*, 18, pp. 44–54.

Raelin, J. (1999) 'Preface to The Action Dimension in Management: Diverse Approaches to Research, Teaching, and Development', *Management Learning*, Special Issue, 30, pp. 115–25.

Randall, M.L., Cropanzano, R., Bormann, C.A. and Birjulin, A. (1999) 'Organizational Politics and Organizational Support as Predictors of Work Attitudes, Job Performance, and Organizational Citizenship Behavior', *Journal of Organizational Behavior*, 20, pp. 159–74.

Rapoport, R.N. (1970) 'Three Dilemmas in Action Research', *Human Relations*, 23, pp. 499–513.

Rathje, W. and Murphy, C. (2001) *Rubbish! The Archaeology of Garbage*, Tucson, AZ: University of Arizona Press.

Rathje, W.L., Hughes, W.W. and Jernigan, S.L. (1977) 'The Science of Garbage: Following the Consumer through His Garbage Can', in W. Locander (ed.) *Marketing Looks Outward*, Chicago: American Marketing Association, pp. 56–64.

Raymond, L., Bergeron, F. and Rivard, S. (1998) 'Determinants of Business Process Reengineering Success in Small and Large Enterprises: An Empirical Study in the Canadian Context', *Journal of Small Business Management*, 36, pp. 72–85.

Reason, P. and Bradbury, H. (eds) (2000) *Handbook of Action Research*, London: Sage.

Reinharz, S. (1992) *Feminist Methods in Social Research*, Oxford: Oxford University Press.

Remenyi, D., Williams, B., Money, A. and Swartz, E. (1998) *Doing Research in Business and Management: An Introduction to Process and Method*, London: Sage.

Richardson, L. (1994) 'Writing: A Method of Inquiry', in N.K. Denzin and Y.S. Lincoln (eds) *Handbook of Qualitative Research*, Thousand Oaks, CA: Sage, pp. 516–29.

Rickards, M. (2000) *The Encyclopedia of Ephemera*, London: British Library.

Rickman, H.P. (1990) 'Science and Hermeneutics', *Philosophy of the Social Sciences*, 20, pp. 295–316.

Roethlisberger, F.J. (1941) *Management and Morale*, Cambridge, MA: Harvard University Press.

Roethlisberger, F.J. and Dickson, W.J. (1939) *Management and the Worker: Technical vs. Social Organization in an Industrial Plant*, Cambridge, MA: Harvard University, Graduate School of Business Administration.

Rondinelli, D.A. and Berry, M.A. (2000) 'Environmental Citizenship in Multinational Corporations: Social Responsibility and Sustainable Development', *European Management Journal*, 18, pp. 70–84.

Rosen, M. (1985) 'Breakfast at Spiro's: Dramaturgy and Dominance', *Journal of Management*, 11 (2), pp. 31–48.

Rosen, M. (1991) 'Coming to Terms with the Field: Understanding and Doing Organizational Ethnography', *Journal of Management Studies*, 28, pp. 1–24.

Rosenthal, R. (1966) *Experimenter Effects in Behavioral Research*, New York: Appleton-Century-Crofts.

Royce, J.R. (1964) *The Encapsulated Man*, New York: Van Nostrand.

Russell, B.H. (2002) *Research Methods in Anthropology*, Walnut Creek, CA: AltaMira Press.

Ryan, B., Scapens, R.W. and Theobold, M. (2002) *Research Method and Methodology in Finance and Accounting*, London: Thomson.

Rynes, S.L., Bartunek, J.M. and Daft, R.L. (2001) 'Across the Great Divide: Knowledge Creation and Transfer between Practitioners and Academics', *Academy of Management Journal*, 44, pp. 340–55.

Salaman, G. and Thompson, K. (1978) 'Class Culture and the Persistence of an Elite: The Case of Army Officer Selection', *Sociological Review*, 26, pp. 283–304.

Salancik, G.R. and Meindl, J.R. (1984) 'Corporate Attributions as Illusions of Management Control', *Administrative Science Quarterly*, 29, pp. 238–54.

Salkind, N.J. (2000) *Statistics for People Who (Think They) Hate Statistics*, Thousand Oaks, CA: Sage.

Sambrook, S. (2001) 'HRD as an Emergent and Negotiated Evolution: An Ethnographic Case Study in the British National Health Service', *Human Resource Development Quarterly*, 12, pp. 169–93.

Sanday, P.R. (1979) 'The Ethnographic Paradigm(s)', *Administrative Science Quarterly*, 24, pp. 527–38.

Sanger, J. (1996) *The Compleat Observer? A Field Research Guide to Observation*, London: Falmer Press.

Saunders, M. and Lewis, P. (1997) 'Great Ideas and Blind Alleys? A Review of the Literature on Starting Research', *Management Learning*, 28, pp. 283–99.

Saunders, M., Lewis, P. and Thornhill, A. (1997) *Research Methods for Business Students*, London: Pitman.

Sawyer, H.G. (1961) 'The Meaning of Numbers', speech before the American Association of Advertising Agencies.

Sayer, A. (1992) *Method in Social Science: A Realist Approach*, London: Routledge.

Sayer, A. (2000) *Realism and Social Science*, London: Sage.

Scandura, T.A. and Williams, E.A. (2000) 'Research Methodology in Management: Current Practices, Trends, and Implications for Future Research', *Academy of Management Journal*, 43, pp. 1248–64.

Scapens, R.W. (1990) 'Researching Management Accounting Practice: The Role of the Case Study Methods', *British Accounting Review*, 22, pp. 259–81.

Scheurich, J.J. (1997) 'A Postmodernist Critique of Research Interviewing', in *Research Method in the Postmodern*, London: Falmer Press, pp. 61–79.

Scheurich, J.J. (1997) *Research Method in the Postmodern*, London: Falmer Press.

Schön, D. (1983) *The Reflective Practitioner*, London: Temple Smith.

Schonlau, M., Fricker, R.D. and Elliott, M.N. (2002) *Conducting Research Surveys via E-Mail and the Web*, Santa Monica, CA: RAND.

Schumacher, E.F. (1995) *A Guide for the Perplexed*, London: Vintage.

Schwandt, T.A. (1994) 'Constructivist, Interpretivist Approaches to Human Inquiry', in N.K. Denzin and Y.S. Lincoln (eds) *Handbook of Qualitative Research*, Thousand Oaks, CA: Sage, pp. 118–37.

Schwartzman, H.B. (1993) *Ethnography in Organizations*, Newbury Park, CA: Sage.

Scott, J. (1990) *A Matter of Record: Documentary Sources in Social Research*, Cambridge: Polity Press.

Seale, C. (ed.) (1998) *Researching Society and Culture*, London: Sage.

Seale, C. and Kelly, M. (1998) 'Coding and Analysing Data', in C. Seale (ed.) *Researching Society and Culture*, London: Sage, pp. 146–63.

Seely, J. (1998) *The Oxford Guide to Writing and Speaking*, Oxford: Oxford University Press.

Seers, A. and Woodruff, S. (1997) 'Temporal Pacing in Taskforces: Group Development or Deadline Pressure', *Journal of Management*, 23, pp. 169–87.

Sharpe, D.R. (1988) 'Shop Floor Practices under Changing Forms of Managerial Control: A Comparative Ethnographic Study', unpublished PhD thesis, University of Manchester.

Shipman, M. (1988, 1997) *The Limitations of Social Research*, London: Longman.

Silverman, D. (1993, 2001) *Interpreting Qualitative Data: Methods for Analysing Talk, Text and Interaction*, London: Sage.

Silverman, D. (2000) *Doing Qualitative Research: A Practical Handbook*, London: Sage.

Simonton, D.K. (1998) 'Political Leadership across the Life Span: Chronological versus Career Age in the British Monarchy', *Leadership Quarterly*, 9, pp. 309–20.

Slater, D. (1998) 'Analysing Cultural Objects: Content Analysis and Semiotics', in C. Seale (ed.) *Researching Society and Culture*, London: Sage, pp. 233–44.

Slater, S.F. and Olson, E.M. (2000) 'Strategy Type and Performance: The Influence of Sales Force Management', *Strategic Management Journal*, 21, pp. 813–29.

Slater, S.F. and Olson, E.M. (2001) 'Marketing's Contribution to the Implementation of Business Strategy: An Empirical Analysis', *Strategic Management Journal*, 22, pp. 1055–67.

Smircich, L. (1983) 'Organizations as Shared Meanings', in L.R. Pondy, G. Morgan and T.C. Dandridge (eds) *Organizational Symbolism*, Greenwich, CT: JAI Press, pp. 55–65.

Smith, N.C. (1991) 'The Case-Study: A Vital yet Misunderstood Research Method for Management', in N.C. Smith and P. Dainty (eds) *The Management Research Handbook*, London: Routledge, pp. 145–58.

Smith, N.C. and Dainty, P. (eds) (1991) *The Management Research Handbook*, London: Routledge.

Spinelli, E. (1989) *The Interpreted World: An Introduction to Phenomenological Psychology*, London: Sage.

Spradley, J.P. (1979) *The Ethnographic Interview*, New York: Holt, Rinehart and Winston.

Squire, P. (1988) 'Why the 1936 *Literary Digest* Poll Failed', *Public Opinion Quarterly*, 52, pp. 125–33.

Stake, R.E. (1994) 'Case Studies', in N.K. Denzin and Y.S. Lincoln (eds) *Handbook of Qualitative Research*, Thousand Oaks, CA: Sage, pp. 236–47.

Stake, R.E. (1995) *The Art of Case Study Research*, London: Sage.

Stanworth, P. and Giddens, A. (1974) 'An Economic Elite: A Demographic Profile of Company Chairmen', in P. Stanworth and A. Giddens (eds) *Elites and Power in British Society*, London: Cambridge University Press, pp. 81–101.

Stark, A. (ed.) *International Journal of Management Reviews*, Oxford: Blackwell.

Stevens, S.S. (1951) 'Mathematics, Measurement and Psychophysics', in S.S. Stevens (ed.) *Handbook of Experimental Psychology*, New York: Wiley, pp. 1–49.

Stewart, R. (1965) 'The Use of Diaries to Study Managers' Jobs', *Journal of Management Studies*, 2, pp. 228–35.

Stoecker, R. (1991) 'Evaluating and Rethinking the Case Study', *Sociological Review*, 39, pp. 88–112.

Strauss, A. and Corbin, J. (1990) *Basics of Qualitative Research: Grounded Theory Procedures and Techniques*, Newbury Park, CA: Sage.

Stringer, E.T. (1999) *Action Research: A Handbook for Practitioners*, London: Sage.

Strube, M. (1994) 'Experimentation as Reality', *Journal of Applied Behavioral Science*, 30, pp. 402–7.

Sudnow, D. (1968) 'Normal Crimes', in E. Rubington and M. Weinberg (eds) *Deviance: The Interactionist Perspective*, New York: Macmillan, pp. 158–69.

Susman, G.I. and Evered, R. (1978) 'An Assessment of the Scientific Merits of Action Research', *Administrative Science Quarterly*, 23, pp. 582–603.

Tajfel, H. and Fraser, C. (eds) (1978) *Introducing Social Psychology*, London: Penguin.

Tayeb, M. (1991) 'Inside Story: The Sufferings and Joys of Doctoral Research', *Organization Studies*, 12, pp. 301–4.

Tesch, R. (1990) *Qualitative Research: Analysis Types and Software Tools*, New York: Falmer.

Thietart, R.-A. (2001) *Doing Management Research: A Comprehensive Guide*, London: Sage.

Thomas, A.B. (1988) 'Does Leadership Make a Difference to Organizational Performance?', *Administrative Science Quarterly*, 33, pp. 388–400.

Thomas, A.B. (2001) 'Women at the Top in British Retailing: A Longitudinal Analysis',
Service Industries Journal, 21 (3), pp. 1–12.

Thomas, A.B. (2002) 'The Changing Structure of Inter-corporate Relations among Britain's
Largest Retail Firms, 1975–97', *Service Industries Journal*, 22 (4), pp. 22–40.

Thomas, A.B. (2003a) 'The Coming Crisis of Western Management Education', in
P. Jeffcutt (ed.) *The Foundations of Management Knowledge*, London: Routledge.

Thomas, A.B. (2003b) *Controversies in Management: Issues, Debates, Answers*, London:
Routledge.

Thomas, A.B. (2003c) 'Organizing the Past: A History and Its (De)Construction', in
S. Linstead (ed.) *Text/Work: Representing Organization and Organizing Representation*, London: Routledge.

Thomas, A.B. and Al-Maskati, H.H. (1997) 'Contextual Influences on Thinking in
Organizations: Tutor and Learner Orientations to Organizational Learning', *Journal of
Management Studies*, 34, pp. 851–70.

Thomas, A.B. and Partington, K. (1981) 'Wanted: Company Director', *The Director*,
March, pp. 34–5.

Ticehurst, G.W. and Ross-Smith, A. (1992) 'Communication Satisfaction, Commitment,
and Job Satisfaction in Australian Organizations', *Australian Journal of Communication*, 19, pp. 130–44.

Ticehurst, G.W. and Veal, A.J. (2000) *Business Research Methods: A Managerial
Approach*, Frenchs Forest, NSW: Pearson.

Tonkiss, F. (1998) 'The History of the Social Survey', in C. Seale (ed.) *Researching
Society and Culture*, London: Sage, pp. 58–71.

Tranfield, D. and Starkey, K. (1998) 'The Nature, Social Organization and Promotion
of Management Research: Towards Policy', *British Journal of Management*, 9,
pp. 341–53.

Tsoukas, H. (2000) 'What Is Management? An Outline of a Metatheory', in S. Ackroyd
and S. Fleetwood (eds) *Realist Perspectives on Management and Organisations*,
London: Routledge, pp. 26–43.

Turabian, K.L. (1996) *A Manual for Writers of Term Papers, Theses, and Dissertations*,
Chicago: University of Chicago Press.

Turner, B.A. (1971) *Exploring the Industrial Subculture*, London: Macmillan.

Turner, B.A. (1983) 'The Use of Grounded Theory for the Qualitative Analysis of
Organizational Behaviour', *Journal of Management Studies*, 20, pp. 333–48.

Tymchuk, A.J. (1982) 'Strategies for Resolving Value Dilemmas', *American Behavioral
Scientist*, 26, pp. 159–75.

Udwadia, F.E. (1986) 'Management Situations and the Engineering Mindset', *Techno-
logical Forecasting and Social Change*, 29, pp. 387–97.

Usher, P. (1997) 'Challenging the Power of Rationality', in G. McKenzie, J. Powell
and R. Usher (eds) *Understanding Social Research: Perspective on Methodology and
Practice*, London: Falmer Press, pp. 42–55.

Usher, R. (1997) 'Telling a Story about Research and Research as Story-Telling:
Postmodern Approaches to Social Research', in G. McKenzie, J. Powell and R. Usher
(eds) *Understanding Social Research: Perspectives on Methodology and Practice*,
London: Falmer Press, pp. 27–41.

Usunier, J.-C. (1998) *International and Cross-cultural Management Research*, London:
Sage.

Van de Ven, A.H. (1989) 'Nothing Is Quite So Practical as a Good Theory', *Academy of Management Review*, 14, pp. 486–9.

Van Maanen, J. (1979) 'The Fact of Fiction in Organizational Ethnography', *Administrative Science Quarterly*, 24, pp. 539–50.

Van Maanen, J. (1988) *Tales of the Field: On Writing Ethnography*, Chicago: University of Chicago Press.

Wallace, W. (1979) 'An Overview of Elements in the Scientific Process', in J. Bynner and K. Stribley (eds) *Social Research: Principles and Procedures*, Harlow, UK: Longman, pp. 4–10.

Wallis, R. (1977) 'The Moral Career of a Research Project', in C. Bell and H. Newby (eds) *Doing Sociological Research*, London: Allen and Unwin, pp. 149–67.

Walsh, D. (1998) 'Doing Ethnography', in C. Seale (ed.) *Researching Society and Culture*, London: Sage, pp. 217–32.

Warmington, A. (1980) 'Action Research: Its Methods and Its Implications', *Journal of Applied Systems Analysis*, 7, pp. 23–39.

Warren, R. and Tweedale, G. (2002) 'Business Ethics and Business History: Neglected Dimensions in Management Education', *British Journal of Management*, 13, pp. 209–19.

Warwick, D.P. (1975) 'Social Scientists Ought to Stop Lying', *Psychology Today*, February, pp. 38–40, 105–6.

Wass, V.J. and Wells, P.E. (eds) (1994) *Principles and Practice in Business and Management Research*, Aldershot, UK: Dartmouth.

Watson, T.J. (1994a) *In Search of Management: Culture, Chaos and Control in Managerial Work*, London: Routledge.

Watson, T.J. (1994b) 'Managing, Crafting and Researching: Words, Skill and Imagination in Shaping Management Research', *British Journal of Management*, Special Issue, 5, pp. 77–87.

Watson, T.J. (1994c) 'The Theorising Process in Management Research: Interdisciplinary Insights in an Ethnographic Study of Managerial Work', paper presented to the Annual Conference of the British Academy of Management, University of Lancaster.

Watson, T.J. (1995) 'Shaping the Story: Rhetoric, Persuasion and Creative Writing in Organisational Ethnography', *Studies in Cultures, Organizations and Societies*, 1, pp. 301–11.

Watson, T.J. (2001) *In Search of Management: Culture, Chaos and Control in Managerial Work*, London: Thomson.

Wayne, S. and Ferris, G.R. (1990) 'Influence Tactics, Affect and Exchange Quality in Supervisor–Subordinate Interactions: A Laboratory Experiment and Field Study', *Journal of Applied Psychology*, 75, pp. 461–8.

Webb, E. and Weick, K.E. (1979) 'Unobtrusive Measures in Organizational Theory: A Reminder', *Administrative Science Quarterly*, 24, pp. 650–9.

Webb, E.J., Campbell, D.T., Schwartz, R.D. and Sechrest, L. (1966) *Unobtrusive Measures: Non-reactive Research in the Social Sciences*, Chicago: Rand McNally.

Webb, E.J., Campbell, D.T., Schwartz, R.D. and Sechrest, L. (1999) *Unobtrusive Measures*, Thousand Oaks, CA: Sage.

Weber, R.P. (1990) *Basic Content Analysis*, Newbury Park, CA: Sage.

Weick, K.E. (1985) 'Systematic Observational Methods', in G. Lindzey and E. Aronson (eds) *The Handbook of Social Psychology*, vol. 1, *Theory and Methods*, New York: Random House, pp. 567–634.

Weitzman, E.A. and Miles, M.B. (1995) *Computer Programs for Qualitative Data Analysis*, Thousand Oaks: Sage.

Wells, G. (1981) *The Successful Author's Handbook*, London: Macmillan.

White, H. (1978) *Tropics of Discourse: Essays in Cultural Criticism*, Baltimore, MD: Johns Hopkins University Press.

Whyte, W.F. (ed.) (1991) *Participatory Action Research*, Newbury Park, CA: Sage.

Whyte, W.F., Greenwood, D.J. and Lazes, P. (1989) 'Saving Jobs in Industry: The Xerox Corporation', *American Behavioral Scientist*, 32, pp. 513–51.

Wolcott, F. (1975) 'Criteria for an Ethnographic Approach to Research in Schools', *Human Organizations*, 34, pp. 111–27.

Wood, D. (1978) 'Interviewing', in G. Hoinville, R. Jowell and associates, *Survey Research Practice*, London: Heinemann, pp. 90–104.

Yan, A. and Gray, B. (2001) 'Antecedents and Effects of Parent Control in International Joint Ventures', *Journal of Management Studies*, 38, pp. 393–416.

Yin, R.K. (1981) 'The Case Study Crisis: Some Answers', *Administrative Science Quarterly*, 26, pp. 58–65.

Yin, R.K. (1984, 1989, 1994) *Case Study Research: Design and Methods*, London: Sage.

Yin, R.K. (1993) *Applications of Case Study Research*, London: Sage.

Yule, G.U. (1944) *The Statistical Study of Literary Vocabulary*, Cambridge: Cambridge University Press.

Zikmund, W.G. (1994) *Business Research Methods*, Fort Worth, TX: Dryden Press.

Index